THE SHY PRINCESS

Queen Victoria with Princess Beatrice, 1880

THE SHY PRINCESS

*The Life of Her Royal Highness
Princess Beatrice, the youngest daughter
and constant companion of Queen Victoria*

DAVID DUFF

FREDERICK MULLER LIMITED

First published in Great Britain 1958 by Evans Brothers Limited

This reissue first published in Great Britain 1974 by
Frederick Muller Ltd., Edgware Road, London NW2 6LE

Printed and bound in Great Britain by
Redwood Burn Limited
Trowbridge & Esher
ISBN 0 584 10264 x

Contents

AUTHOR'S NOTE

I AM indebted to Her Majesty Queen Victoria Eugenia and to the Marquess of Carisbrooke for providing me with personal information regarding the life of Her Royal Highness Princess Beatrice; for reading the manuscript, and for the gift of their time; and for permission to reproduce pictures and photographs in their possession.

I am also indebted to Prince Wolfgang of Hesse for permission to use letters of Princess Beatrice and Queen Victoria to the Empress Frederick, and for allowing me to reproduce photographs and portraits at Friedrichshof.

ILLUSTRATIONS

Queen Victoria with Princess Beatrice, 1880 *frontispiece*

between pages 32–33

Queen Victoria and the Prince Consort, 1859

Princess Alice, Prince Alfred, the Princess Royal and Princess Helena as characters represented in the play of *Les Savoyards*

Princess Beatrice by Winterhalter, 1859

Princess Louise, Princess Beatrice and Queen Victoria, 1867

Princess Beatrice aged 5 years old

Princess Louise, 1863

between pages 64–65

Princess Beatrice, 1881

The Royal Family Tree

Princess Victoria of Hesse, Princess Elizabeth of Hesse and Princess Beatrice, 1880

between pages 96–97

Prince Henry of Battenberg, 1874

The Royal Family, 1861

Prince Louis Napoleon, 1879

Princess Beatrice, the Duchess of Connaught and the Grand Duke of Hesse at Balmoral, 1882

between pages 128–129

Princess Christian

The Princess of Battenberg

Prince Alexander of Hesse

Wedding-day photograph of Prince and Princess Henry of Battenberg

Princess Beatrice and Prince Henry with Prince Alexander, 1886

PROLOGUE

ON the 30th September 1864, Gladstone wrote from Balmoral to Catherine, his wife:

'No incident of note here during the last 24 hours except that the Princess Beatrice had a tooth out—a loose single one. But the Q., Prince Alfred, the valet, and somebody else all tried and failed; Dr. Jenner was called in: by this time (and no wonder) the child was excited, and there was a chase after her round the room: at last Dr. J caught her and secured her head under his arm. It was in doubt whether she was to receive the pound, which it seems is the usual fee to the patient in such cases.'

Except for such minor domestic happenings, the visit of the Chancellor of the Exchequer to Deeside proved peaceful. The Queen talked pleasantly of general matters and expressed the hope that the planets and stars were not inhabited. Gladstone's reply, 'Are you not a little jealous, Madam?', would perhaps have been better worded by Disraeli. The worst moment of his stay was when his trousers split ten minutes before he was due to join the Queen at dinner.

One bond, and there were few, between Queen and statesman, was a love of children. Gladstone had been a frequent visitor to the royal nurseries and his own children had played with the Princes and Princesses. Now his particular pet was Beatrice, the last born of Victoria and Albert. This was not only because she was the most amusing of the Royal children—'the flower of the flock', her mother called her—but Gladstone knew what a vital part 'Baby' had played, unknowingly, in the past seven years, years which had covered the decline in the Prince Consort's health, his death, and the deep haemorrhage of grief of his widow, which threatened to weaken her body and derange her reason.

It was to Beatrice that Prince Albert would turn in those last years of life when fits of gloom gripped his tired brain and body. It was Beatrice whose smile was to rally him in his last illness. And it was to Beatrice that the Queen ran on the evening of her husband's death, taking her to her own bed and wrapping her in the night clothes of the man whom she would always mourn.

Princess Beatrice belonged to what was known in the schoolroom as the 'Osborne set'. These were the children born after the building of the royal home by the shores of the Isle of Wight.

In a family of nine, where the eldest is engaged to be married before the youngest is born, there must of necessity be a dividing line between the age groups. The year 1850 may be taken as being on that line—half-time for a century—half-time for the marriage of Victoria and Albert—with four children in the schoolroom, three in the nursery, and two to follow.

Prince Albert was then twenty-nine, three months younger than his wife. In their ten years of marriage much had happened to age the pair beyond their years, and Albert more so than his wife. The Queen had produced seven healthy children, and, physically, she had stood the strain well. Violently in love with her husband, she was still of girlish appearance. In queenship she had been hurt by the knife of experience, and the wound of unpopularity had festered before it had healed, but she had learned always to have a mentor, a man near to ward off the worst of the blow. King Leopold, Lord Melbourne,

Baron Stockmar—and now, above all, Albert. There was ever to be a man there, until the twilight of her days. Then a daughter, her youngest, Beatrice, took the rôle. There was another man there, waiting, but to him she never called as she had to those others. He was her eldest son, the Prince of Wales.

Albert was both an enigma and a contradiction. Possessing an absorbent brain which could carry knowledge as clean blotting paper carries fine writing, he was clear-sighted for his time, but not outstandingly so. He could converse freely on subjects as far apart as the disposal of sewage and the unification of Germany; the racial problems of India and the provisioning of an army; the evils of gambling and the breeding of pigs.

Tears would come into his eyes over the sufferings of a puppy, yet at Balmoral he would have stags driven close past him, and shoot them down. He could (to many people's surprise) ride hard across Cottesmore country, but considered Ascot a bore. Had he been born into a more humble home in Coburg he might well have become a university professor, lived twice as long, indulged in walking tours in the Thuringian mountains, and built himself a reputation as a highbrow, a wit and a man of vision.

Throughout his married life he remained completely unattracted by other women. Unlike his father, he would not smile back into a pair of lovely eyes that smiled at him. His handshake was rarely more than a cold German touch. The prettiest of women simply had no temptation for him—in sharp contrast with other members of his own family, and the families of the Georges. Fortunate indeed that this was so. Signs of jealousy showed even if the Queen considered that a man was taking up more of her husband's time than she regarded as necessary. Yet here she had no real cause for alarm, for Albert was too firmly wedded to the Coburg way of thinking to strike up any close friendship in England.

There were also signs of jealousy over 'Vicky', whom Albert adored. Victoria, the Princess Royal—'Vicky' to the family, and also answering to 'Pussy'—was the eldest child of Victoria and Albert, having been born in November, 1840. Inheriting her father's intelligence and the martinet tendencies of her mother, she thrived under the doctrine of Stockmar that education should begin from the day of birth. At the age of three, she spoke English and French fluently. By 1850 preparations were already being made for her to play a leading rôle in the affairs of Europe. This she did, as the tragic Empress Frederick of Germany.

Albert Edward, Prince of Wales, was a year her junior. He was just 'Bertie'. A rebellious, loving little Celt, he developed an early aversion to books, which increased through the years. He did not take kindly to his father's ideas on the training of a future monarch. He adored his two eldest sisters, indulged in extravagant love affairs with middle-aged ladies, and was apt to attack boys of his own age who were brought in to play with him.

Alice[1]—dear, sweet 'Alee'—and Alfred[2]—'Affie'— followed at intervals of less than eighteen months. Age coupled them closely in the schoolroom. She was artistic and kind and modern in her thinking. He was an ordinary boy, destined for the Navy.

Helena,[3] the half-way child, was born in May, 1846, and was known as 'Lenchen'. She married a poor prince from Germany who, to Queen Victoria's dismay, smoked a pipe. Christian was his name, and his original intention in coming to England had been to marry the widow Victoria. Unduly optimistic on any count, he would certainly have been wiser to leave his pipe behind.

[1] Later Grand Duchess of Hesse.
[2] Later Duke of Edinburgh and Saxe-Coburg and Gotha.
[3] Later Princess Christian.

In 1850 Louise was only two. 'Loo-loo' they called her. She was destined to be the first Princess to marry, with the Sovereign's official sanction, outside the confines of a reigning house since Mary, youngest daughter of Henry VII, married the Duke of Suffolk in 1515. She was also to be the only childless child of Victoria and Albert. When Duchess of Argyll, she confided in a lady-in-waiting that she had had over 150 letters of advice on the subject, but that none of them was any good.

Also upstairs was a three-month-old boy who had just been named Arthur, and had the Duke of Wellington as godfather. Arthur of Connaught was the Queen's favourite son, as her last-born child was to be her affirmed favourite daughter.

Around the royal children was a bodyguard of attendants, forming a hedge through which the Princes and Princesses could take only peeps of the world beyond. At the sole gate in the hedge their father stood on permanent duty.

Above the seven nurses came Lady Lyttelton, the royal governess, and Lady Caroline Barrington, who succeeded her. English, German and drawing were taught by individual governesses. Hair was looked after by Monsieur Nestor and clothes by Miss Skerret.

These, and a number of others, surrounded their charges as the household moved laboriously from Osborne to Buckingham Palace, London to Windsor, Windsor to Balmoral, and from Scotland back to the Isle of Wight again. Only excursions on the royal yacht varied the scene.

Moving day was a nightmare for the 'bodyguard'. Lady Lyttelton called it 'the grand jour d'emballage', but on the return from Balmoral she had to admit that nursery packing troubles were somewhat thrown into the shade by the problem which faced the wardrobe woman of finding space in which to stow the antlers of stags shot by Prince

Albert. And those train journeys! On one return to Windsor a nurserymaid was taken ill; the maids of honour and the main luggage went astray at a junction; night clothes and playthings followed on the next train—and the royal children '. . . taken with tearing spirits, and a rage for crawling, climbing, poking into corners, upsetting everything, and after a little while being tired, cross and squally for hours'.

Sometimes Lady Lyttelton wondered if so much travelling was good for her charges, but wherever they moved the royal tribe maintained its splendid isolation. If a few Eton boys were asked over to Windsor to spend part of the afternoon with 'Bertie', Prince Albert always stayed with them to see that the conversation followed the right lines.

There were a number of reasons why the royal children were not allowed to mix freely with other children. Firstly, their father was not on terms of familiarity and understanding with the parents of the sort of boys and girls who might be expected to be asked round to play. He did not understand the English gentry, and therefore concluded that his children would not understand theirs. He feared, above all, that the loose habits and tastes of the fathers might come out in their sons. In addition, there was still a score to settle. The Tories had been against his marriage and even spread the rumour that he was a Papist.

Another reason for the seclusion in which the Princes and Princesses were kept was that neither their father nor their mother had, as children, experienced normal family life, with happy parents and brothers and sisters to romp with and to knock sense into them. Victoria's father, the Duke of Kent, had died when she was two, and she was his only child. The marriage of Albert's parents had also broken up when he was five, and he and his brother were left in their father's care.

Yet Queen Victoria and Prince Albert were loving

parents. If the mother sometimes lost touch and patience with the elder ones when they reached the schoolroom and their 'teens', her peculiar position, her youth, and her all-devouring wish to have full possession of Prince Albert, were responsible.

She wrote to her friend, Princess Augusta of Prussia, in 1856:

> '... I find no especial pleasure or compensation in the company of the elder children. You will remember that I told you this at Osborne. Usually they go out with me in the afternoon (Vicky mostly, and the others also sometimes), or occasionally in the mornings when I drive or walk or ride, accompanied by my lady-in-waiting, and only very occasionally do I find the rather intimate intercourse with them either agreeable or easy.'

As their uncle Ernest[1] witnessed, the girls were brighter at their lessons than the boys. This must have been a contributory cause for the stubbornness of 'Bertie' in his fight against education. It is on the mistakes made over the training of this Prince that the royal parents are too often judged. The reasons why these mistakes were made are both easy to discern and to understand.

The most telling reason was the ever-present fear in the parents that the failings of their ancestors might be passed on to their children. Hence the nursery garden was hoed constantly to ensure that no seeds of extravagance, sloth or other evils should take root among the young plants of study, thrift and discipline.

This was Baron Stockmar's[2] theme song, and he sang it long and loud. It was the Queen's 'wicked uncles'—already exaggerated characters—who were constantly held up as the danger. Danger there was from heredity, but it was not entirely restricted to uncles. The parents of both Queen Victoria and Prince Albert had had their romantic

[1] Brother of Prince Albert.   [2] Prince Albert's adviser.

and marital problems, and evinced tastes and weaknesses which now had to be guarded against.[1]

So, in the evenings at Buckingham Palace and Windsor in the 1840's, the young Royal couple devised a standard of behaviour, learning and discipline which would exclude their family from the legacies of the past.

The child who came closest to this standard was their youngest, Princess Beatrice. For twenty-five years she was to be the 'other right hand' of Queen Victoria. In the words of her daughter, Her Majesty Queen Victoria Eugenia of Spain: 'She (Princess Beatrice) had to be in perpetual attendance on her formidable mother. Her devotion and submission were complete, and on account of her shyness, few people realized that my mother was extraordinarily cultured, wrote in French and German as well as English and played the piano extraordinarily well, and was able to read the most difficult music as if it were a book. . . .'

[1] See Appendix A, 'The Parentage of Queen Victoria and Prince Albert'.

1
'Baby'

AFTER 1850 the tempo of child-bearing slowed. The family excitement of 1851 was the Great Exhibition in the Crystal Palace, and this was Prince Albert's child. Despite the forecasts of the high Tories, who were opposed to the ideas of the Queen's husband, the Exhibition was an overwhelming success. The following year John Campden Neild[1] died, and in his will left half a million pounds to Queen Victoria. Her money troubles were over, and the bogey of her father's debts forgotten, but she had been taught to be thrifty, and thrifty she remained. In this she was encouraged by Albert who, when he won prizes in cattle shows, invariably pocketed the money and ignored all criticism for so doing.

It was not until April 1853 that the eighth child was born. He was named Leopold, after 'Uncle' in Belgium. He suffered from the bleeding disease, which travels from generation to generation through the female line. He was not allowed to play with his elder brother, Arthur, in case boyish pranks and enthusiasm led to disastrous results. Leopold inherited the intelligence of his father, without his forcefulness.

[1] John Campden Neild was somewhat of an eccentric. During the last thirty years of his life he spent little, concentrating on the increase of the fortune which he had inherited from his father. Unmarried and without relations, he left all his wealth to Queen Victoria. The Queen provided for his servants, gave an annuity to a woman who had once prevented him from committing suicide, rebuilt the chancel of a church in Buckinghamshire where Neild had property, and arranged for a window to be placed there as a memorial.

2

Meanwhile, 'Vicky', the Princess Royal, was growing up fast, and it was with her future that the Queen and Prince Albert were mainly concerned in the period prior to the birth of their youngest child.

Plans for the marriage of the Princess Royal had been made tentatively before she was ten. It was the Queen's friend, Princess Augusta of Prussia, who first proposed that she should marry her son, Prince Frederick William, but it was Leopold of Belgium who, behind the scenes, was drawing the Coburg net tighter around Europe.

In September 1855 Frederick William visited Balmoral and immediately captivated the young Princess. 'Vicky' went red as a beetroot when her father caught her stealing glances at the visitor. The young couple were so insistent on spending their time together that the Queen, who thought it her duty to chaperone, was hard pressed to find time to attend to her manifold duties.

After only a week of his stay on Deeside, a very determined Prince Frederick approached the Queen and Prince Albert and announced that he would like a decision on whether he could marry 'Vicky', and desired it before he returned home. The royal parents, while agreeing in general, expressed the view that, as she was so young, it might be better if he waited a little time, at least until his next visit. But on the 29th Prince Frederick William handed a sprig of white heather to 'Vicky' and proposed to her as they rode down Glen Girnoch.

Frederick William was then twenty-four, his bride ten years younger. Allowing for her forwardness, she was still too young to receive a proposal of marriage, but the planners would have their way, and Prince Frederick William was, fortunately for them, very persistent. Albert finally stipulated that the wedding should not take place until after the Princess's seventeenth birthday and her confirmation, and that the cngagement should, meantime, remain a secret. Of course, it leaked out.

It was finally decided that the formal engagement should be announced in the spring of 1857, and timed to coincide with the birth of the last child of Queen Victoria and Prince Albert.

Four years had passed since such an occasion, and it had been generally considered in the country that the Palace nurseries would henceforth be empty. The Queen was rising thirty-eight, and four boys were enough to safeguard the succession to the Throne, to care for Coburg and cover duties at home; and four girls sufficient to provide the necessary unions with the Continent and company for their parents.

Now a ninth child was on its way.

King Leopold had warned the Queen, early in her married life, against having too numerous a family, but this was one piece of Uncle's advice which had been strictly ignored. She had adopted the apostolic approach.

There were other reasons why the family should not be increased. Firstly, the country was already bearing a financial burden for eight Princes and Princesses, as a section of the Press was never tired of pointing out. Secondly, with war in the Crimea and unrest in India, the work facing the Queen and Prince was more than sufficient to fill their days. Albert was always at his desk at seven each morning, working by the light of his green shaded lamp, and his health was showing signs of failing. A weakling as a child, his hair was now thinning on top, his body had become flabby, his skin pale. It would have seemed a time to ease back on responsibilities, rather than to increase them.

It was Victoria who had the ardour, and she was determined to hold her husband, all of him, by every means open to her. A baby was the one human creature with whom he could relax completely—a safety valve for the emotions, neither criticising nor answering back, allowing him to forget that he was a foreigner in the land, allowing him to do simple things with good excuse, allowing him to laugh.

But the doctors now firmly warned the Queen and Prince that this child should be their last.

Princess Beatrice was born on the 14th April 1857 at a quarter to two p.m. Sixteen days later died her great-aunt Mary, Duchess of Gloucester, last surviving child of King George III. Thus overlapped the paths of two women whose joint span of life covered two centuries less a score of years. Men who fought at Culloden were alive at that span's beginning, and men were fighting in jet aircraft at its close.

Londoners knew that the event was at hand when they saw an empty royal carriage leave the Palace stables and head south towards Vauxhall Bridge. Later they saw it return with Mrs. Lilly, the nurse, whose presence was symbolic at royal births.

The accomplishment of the event was signalled by the posting of a bulletin at Buckingham Palace and the firing of guns at the Tower and in the Park.

Throughout the afternoon members of 'the nobility and gentry' called at the Palace to pay their respects. The passing of a century has made little alteration in the names of those who call on such occasions—the Duke and Duchess of Marlborough, Mrs. Gerald Wellesley, Lieutenant-General Cavendish, the Countess of Malmesbury, the Earl and Countess of Airlie, and Lady Henry Churchill. And of course the Gladstones, the Palmerstons, and Lady Lyttelton.

Meantime, the Archbishop of Canterbury was busy composing a special prayer, arranging to have sufficient copies printed, and these circulated to all churches throughout the country, for inclusion in Divine Service the following Sunday, the first after Easter.

Slowly, the news spread throughout the world. In

far-away Nebraska, U.S.A., there is today a town called Beatrice. It was founded in 1857.

On the day after the birth Prince Albert sat beside his wife's bedside and wrote, on her behalf, a letter to Princess Augusta of Prussia:

'Mother and baby are doing well. Baby practises her scales like a good *prima-donna* before a performance, and has a good voice! Victoria counts the hours and minutes like a prisoner. The children want to know what their sister is to be called, and dispute which names will sound best, and Vicky says with a sad sigh, "The little sister will never have known me in the house."'

In May the engagement of Princess Victoria to Prince Frederick William was officially announced, and the Princess was voted by Parliament an annuity of £8,000 and a dowry of £40,000. Her father commented that, though this sum was not large, at least it made her independent.

One of the first joint duties of the engaged couple was to stand as sponsors to the new baby at her baptism on 16th June in the Private Chapel of Buckingham Palace. She screamed when the Archbishop held her at the Font, but thereafter relapsed into silence. The names chosen were BEATRICE MARY VICTORIA FEODORE. Great-aunt Mary was dead, but her name was to live on.

A luncheon followed in the new Ball Room. George, now Duke of Cambridge, was there. Forgotten and ploughed into time were the wild oats of his youth. His actress wife, Louisa FitzGeorge, was living happily and quietly in a house in Queen Street, Mayfair, and an ever-widening circle of interesting folk were being attracted to her drawing-room. But she was not at the baptism. Prominent among those present was the Archduke Maximilian, later Emperor of Mexico, who was executed by the Republicans at Queretaro.

Eight days after the christening, the Princess Royal

caught fire. She was sealing an envelope when the wide sleeve of her muslin dress touched the candle and the flame ran up her arm, inflicting a very nasty burn.

On the following day the title of Prince Consort was conferred upon Albert. No longer did the Queen have to appear before the British people with her *foreign* husband. A more practical advantage was that of identification of signature, as there were already three 'Prince A's' among his sons.

Throughout that summer foreign royalties and nobilities poured into London to take part in the festivities arranged for the forthcoming wedding of Prince Frederick William and the Princess Royal. All had to visit the nursery and admire the Queen's youngest child. She was known in the family as 'Baby' and, because of her position at the tail, the name was to adhere to her for many a year.

In July the royal family moved to Osborne, and thus 'Baby' began her connection with the island that was to mean so much to her. Among those who crowded into her nursery was the Empress Eugénie, a woman who was so greatly to influence her life, and that of her daughter.

The Queen was thrilled with her new treasure and eager to show off her beautiful baby to her relations and friends. In August, Princess Augusta of Prussia sent her a picture of a young grandson and it was only natural that the proud mother should take the opportunity of sending in return a photograph of Beatrice, 'a darling little baby, so fat, with a skin like satin, great blue eyes and the tiniest little mouth you can imagine; and besides she is so lively and good-tempered.'

A few months later 'Vicky' was married in the Chapel Royal, St. James's. So many tears were shed, even by sailor Alfred, that it must be wondered why the Queen allowed her daughter, whom she still treated as a schoolgirl, to be married two months after her seventeenth birthday and thereafter to be exiled to a none too friendly or pleasant land.

One of the few members of the family who did not cry was Beatrice, which may have been one of the reasons why the bride spent all the spare time that she had in her last days in England, playing in the nursery with her youngest sister.

Alone in the Palace, after the wedding, the Queen relapsed into floods of tears, and not even the presence of 'Baby' could console her, for, as she wrote to Vicky: 'Dear little Beatrice makes us so melancholy as I always think of you being so fond of her'.

The Queen's almost daily letters to Berlin were full of snippets about the youngest in the family. When it was cold at Osborne 'Baby' was put into leggings and, her mother said: '. . . looks like a foreign baby'. 'Today Beatrice paid Grandmamma a visit and looked charming in a blue satin bonnet and little black cloak with ermine. . . .' 'Beatrice is now sitting in your little old chair, tapping on the table where her eight brothers and sisters played before her. She is a great darling. . . .'

The Princess's first birthday was made into a great occasion. Grandmamma Kent came to breakfast, and the table was decorated with a giant 'B' in flowers, surrounded by candles. Gifts were piled high. Vicky sent a woolly lamb and a rose set in stones. The former was preferred.

The Queen wrote to her eldest daughter:

'Your thoughts will be much with us today and your really lovely little sister, who has a new cap which is very pretty, and looks like an old picture. . . . She is a great beauty, and you will also think much of this day last year when I was so ill, though without any danger; to me certainly today is more pleasantly spent!'

As the months passed Prince Albert felt the loss of his eldest daughter still more deeply. He had lost a confidante, a willing pupil, a daughter who was part of the Coburg he loved. He laughed less often, his eyes were dull, and he devoted himself more and more to the work that piled up on his desk.

The Queen noticed this, and did her best to counteract it. In the evenings at Osborne she would take him by the hand and lead him through the gardens to listen to the nightingales which reminded him of Coburg. Only for the minute could he be cheered, but the Queen noticed that he truly relaxed only when he was playing with Beatrice.

'Baby' adored her father from the first. As soon as she could crawl she would follow him around, and he would often leave his work and go to the nursery to play with her before she went to sleep. Sometimes he would pick her up and carry her to his organ where she bounced on his knee while he played the tunes he loved. Significantly, the Queen's main birthday present to her husband on his thirty-ninth birthday was a life-size painting of Beatrice by Horsley.

Because the Queen realised this love which her husband held for their youngest child, because she saw how the lines of worry left his face when he watched her at play, and because she was their last-born, Princess Beatrice was allowed more leniency and freedom from discipline than her brothers and sisters had enjoyed. The child of mature parents, she developed fast. At two it was said of her that she could 'jabber so fast and plain, is full of wit and fun and graceful as a fairy, meddles with everything, makes her remarks on all—quite exquisite'.

She was most interested in Moses. When Vicky sent her parents a chrome-lithograph on which a lovely child was depicted, the Queen said it was just like Beatrice. The latter, however, insisted it was Moses. And Moses it remained.

She soon realised the strength of her position, and took full advantage of it. She cheeked the Queen and the Prince

Consort to an extent that must have mightily amused the Prince of Wales. One morning she remarked: 'I was very naughty last night. I would not speak to Papa, but it doesn't signify much!'

The Queen tried to control her diet. 'Baby mustn't have that. It's not good for baby.' Upon which Beatrice helped herself, remarking, 'But she likes it, my dear.'

Early she showed a leaning towards the poetic, composing a limerick which began, 'There was an old lady called Gusta . . .'. The target of this shaft, Lady Augusta Bruce, lady-in-waiting to the Duchess of Kent, called to see her at a time when she was recovering from measles, and was greeted with the remark, 'You'd better not touch me. I have still a little Weazles and you might take it.'

Princess Frederick William, after a visit to London, commented that she looked like a little fairy, and her brothers idolised and spoilt her. She was as much painted, photographed and sketched as a leading actress. The Duchess of Kent had a picture of her in a black velvet frock. Major Elphinstone, Governor to Prince Arthur, was presented with a portrait of her at Christmas, 1859. Earlier she was photographed on her mother's knee, and next year alone, standing, rather perilously it seems, upon a chair. She was painted by both Winterhalter and Lauchert.

For Christmas, 1858, the Prince Consort gave his wife a marble statue of Princess Beatrice in a nautilus shell; he also gave her a 'colossal full-length statue in bronze of a Nude.'

Another influence which had a relaxing effect in the royal nurseries in the last years of the 1850's was that of the Queen's mother, the Duchess of Kent. She was an old woman now, and the teeth of ambition had long been pulled. Hers had been a hard life, and a lonely one. She had fought, and scraped, and schemed to gain her ends; but now, in the evening, all was peaceful, and she had softened as the sun went down. She not only spoilt 'Baby', but was also the champion of the younger children when they incurred their parents' displeasure.

The daily life of Princess Beatrice and her brothers and sisters of the 'Osborne set' was spartan in its simplicity. Jane Jones, nurse to Prince Arthur, summed it up: 'The royal children were kept very plain indeed; it was quite poor living, only a bit of roast meat and perhaps a plain pudding.'

When Madame de Bunsen saw the meals served in the royal schoolroom she expressed the opinion that they would not be considered good enough by the wife of a successful businessman.

The Princesses were taught to be careful and tidy with their clothes. Kid gloves, after being worn, had to be blown into so that the fingers should not lose their shape. Bonnet ribbons had to be neatly rolled so that they would appear uncreased on their next appearance. Ribbons from the Queen's discarded hats were ironed out and used to tie round the sleeves of her daughters' dresses.

The influence of Baron Stockmar was to be seen in the upbringing of the girls as well as the boys. It was he who urged that the Princesses should early be taught to be efficient housemaids, cooks, seamstresses and embroiderers.

'Baby' learned to cook at Osborne where special facilities existed. In 1854 the Swiss Cottage, brought in sections from Switzerland, had been erected in the grounds. In its small kitchen, fitted with miniature ranges, the Princesses were taught domestic science the easy, happy way.

They had their own gardens and were encouraged to cook their own produce. Sometimes the Queen and Prince Consort would dine at the Cottage, so that they might see for themselves what progress their daughters were making. Sometimes the girls would bake for sick folk in the neighbourhood, but their most regular order was 'for export'.

Each week they cooked a batch of pies and cakes to send to their eldest sister. This was taken by Queen's Messenger to Potsdam, together with his more conventional packages.

The children had a natural history museum of their own, and on their walks were instructed by their father to collect any items that might be of geological or botanical interest. Through the years, and by the efforts of so many children, a great number of curiosities were deposited there.[1]

Those last years of the 1850's were happy ones for the royal children who lived with their parents. Alice, the fawn, wild and beautiful, deeply sentimental, was old enough to act mother to Beatrice when the Queen was called away by her duties. Helena, approaching her teens, was the strong, silent type, not above punching a brother on the nose if he offended. The girls, generally proving the more intelligent, were never believers in giving precedence to Princes. Louise was rather shy and retiring but already showed signs of the artistic gifts which she was later to develop. Arthur, his mother's favourite boy, was happy with his soldiers. Leopold, temperamental and none too strong, was the most clever of the boys at his lessons. And 'Baby' simply went her own sweet way, caring nothing for anybody.

The individualism of Arthur and 'Baby' appealed most to the Queen. It was a characteristic that she appreciated, as she showed so markedly in her later friendships. When Arthur was at an age when he had just mastered handwriting, he borrowed threepence from sister Alice. She heard no more of it until a letter arrived for her addressed simply, 'Princess Alice, Windsor Castle'. Inside were three pennies and this note: 'My Dear Princess Alice, Here's the threepence, Yours affectionately, Arthur.'

Alfred had a strong taste for amusement and mischief. On discovering that a certain gentleman who attended

[1] In 1915 the entire collection was rearranged and classified.

Court padded his calves he crept up behind him and decorated the bulges with a gaily painted selection of flags secured to pins.

Punishment for Princesses who committed breaches of etiquette or gave way to temper consisted of solitary confinement in their bedrooms. This led the boys to make attempts to succour the captive Princess in her Tower. They would creep along in the shadows of the oil-lit corridors, bearing morsels of food or bulletins of the goings on in the world outside. But the guards grew wise, and hands were apt to come out of the darkness and grip gallant Princes by the hair.

The Queen herself had little time for the psychological approach. She was driving one day with 'Bertie' and Alfred through crowded streets. The former, sitting before her in the carriage, was holding his hat most correctly and had just the right smile on his face, but Alfred, beside her, kept his hat on and was sulkily surveying the multitude. As the Queen bowed and smiled affably to left and right, nobody would have guessed that she had one eye on her sons. Suddenly, in a flash, without ceasing her bowing or her smiling, she wiped Alfred's hat off with one hand and fetched him a resounding clout on the side of the face with the other.

There is no record of punishments for 'Baby'. Firstly, one feels that she was too clever for that and, secondly, by the time she reached schoolroom age, death's earthquake had shattered Queen Victoria's life and the black-edged period had begun. But, spoilt as she may have been, Princess Beatrice was brought up in the same atmosphere of simplicity as her elder brothers and sisters. At Balmoral, her room was sparely furnished and she slept in a little iron bedstead. In one corner sat a plain china doll with twisted legs of sawdust.

Before she was three and a half years old, Princess Beatrice was already the very proud aunt of a nephew and a niece. Her nephew was Prince Frederick William Victor Albert, later the Kaiser, and her niece was Princess Charlotte, the Kaiser's sister.

Being an aunt not only raised her status, but gave her a wonderful excuse to avoid doing those things which she did not wish to do. She would reply briskly: 'I have no time—I must write letters to my niece.'

Poor Princess Frederick William had had a very bad time during the birth of her first child. It was a premature delivery, and one of her doctors did not arrive until after the event. His urgent summons had, by error, been put into a posting box instead of hurried round by hand.

Not until two days after the birth of the boy, called William, was it discovered that the left shoulder socket had been badly injured and the muscles bruised. No doctor would attempt the readjustment, and so the arm hung, weak, paralysed. The parents did all they could to cure the fault, even strapping the right arm to his side so that he would be encouraged to use his left, but the arm remained withered, and led to an inferiority complex which is said by many to have influenced the trend of later events.

The nature of the man was in him at his birth. Before he was five, before the extent of his handicap can have been realised, he told Her Majesty the Queen of England, her children and her entourage, to their faces, that they were a 'pug-nosed' lot. He was to be the cause of much trouble, and much sorrow, to his Aunt Beatrice, and in the end the weapons of his army would kill her much-loved son.

The Queen was constant in her requests that 'Vicky' should visit England. This her daughter was only too happy to do—provided that 'Fritz' could come with her. So deeply was she in love with him that as yet, in her hypnotic state, she hardly felt the needles of Prussia. She paid a short visit, alone, to her parents in the spring of 1859 to give them first-hand news of their grandchild, and to tell them the truth about his arm.

Her family greeted her with the full flood of affection that had been built up by the absence of over a year. Within minutes of her arrival Princess Frederick ran to the nursery to greet Beatrice, upon whom she reported: '. . . anything as sweet, apart from our own little one, I really have never seen'.

Queen Victoria held the belief, throughout most of her life, that marriages arranged by her were, *ipso facto*, destined to be happy. In many cases they were—but not always. A story is told of the days after the marriages of her two eldest daughters to German princes, when she first began to see the disadvantages of such alliances. Seeking a husband for one of her younger daughters she asked a young nobleman, whom she considered eligible, to stay at Balmoral. On his first evening at the Castle a member of the household tactfully hinted at the plans for his future. It proved a considerable shock to the guest, who took prompt action. Next morning he rode over to a nearby house, where his sister's best friend was staying. He had not met her before, but immediately asked her to marry him; and she accepted. Back at Balmoral he was able to reveal, equally tactfully, that he was engaged. He was not asked again.

Prince Albert's desire to find a bride for his eldest son was not connected with match-making for match-making's sake, but because he honestly thought that an early marriage was essential if 'Bertie' were to develop into a man suitable for monarchy. Already the boy had shown a distressing taste for tobacco, and the only books he seemed to enjoy were those to be bought at railway stations. And, just round the next corner of the years, lurked the greatest danger of all—'girls'.

In the evenings at Osborne, close study was being made of the royal families of Europe, and the names of seven princesses who might prove suitable were listed. They were then numbered according to preference. The planners faced one supreme difficulty: they knew that 'Bertie', most awkwardly, would insist on a pretty bride. And that narrowed the list somewhat.

Meantime, Princess Beatrice was seeing less and less of her brothers and sisters. The Prince of Wales, unaware of the plans being hatched for his future, was despatched on trips to Canada, America, Germany and Italy, and began his lonely sojourns at the universities. Prince Alfred, to his father's delight, passed his naval examinations with flying colours, and went off to the Mediterranean to join his ship. And Prince Arthur was handed over to the care of a Governor, Major Elphinstone. The latter was quick to win the confidence and trust of the Queen. He was also a great favourite with the younger Princesses, particularly Louise and Beatrice, and when he accidentally let out the date of his birthday they all brought him presents.

Fixed holidays were unknown in the royal schoolroom, but great occasions were made of festive dates like birthdays. When their parents moved on a year, regular fêtes were staged. When all their presents had been laid out on a table and duly admired, the children 'recited their poems and played their pieces of music and exhibited their works of art and science all extremely good'.

Christmas was the highlight of the year. On Christmas Eve, 1859, Elphinstone was called upstairs to see the array of presents and describes the scene: 'All the young ones were in ecstasies. The effect was very fine. The centre room with tables all round and several Christmas trees contained the presents of the Royal family. The Queen's corner was to the right, the Prince's beyond. The number of presents each had was tremendous, more than they can appreciate. The little Princess Louise said it was " *Vraiment un peu trop extravagant* ".'

Snow was one of the few excuses allowed for closing lesson books. The Prince Consort, in particular, liked snow because it reminded him of the mountains where he had left his heart. In the great freeze of '59–60, when a deep fall lay sparkling under a brilliant sun, the Prince of Wales and members of the household began building a snowman in the garden at Osborne. The Prince Consort came out to join them, soon followed by the Queen. Then Beatrice and her brothers and sisters were released, shrieking with delight, their dogs, 'Deckel' and 'Boy', adding to the noise. The snowman was given a carrot for a nose and crowned with a hideous round hat. This had once belonged to Alfred who left it behind when he joined the Navy. Relegated to the 'dressing-up' box, it was known as the 'Cylinder'.

By dint of much stamping and shuffling a slide was made, and there was a sledge for little people like Beatrice, with motive power provided by her father.

In his diary for this year Major Elphinstone made special note of the fondness of the Prince Consort for his youngest daughter.

'The Prince entered the room, and as I was on the point of leaving he called me back to arrange about Prince Arthur's taking longer lessons in writing in which he is very backward. Then he commenced to play with the little Princess Beatrice; took her on his knee and I was much struck with the affectionate manner in which he played with the child . . . .'

In the summer a meeting took place which made it seem likely that a second of 'Baby's' sisters would shortly be lost to Germany. Prince Louis of Hesse was in the royal party for Ascot week. To the Prince Consort, horse-

Queen Victoria and the Prince Consort at Osborne, July 1859

Above: Princess Alice, Prince Alfred, the Princess Royal and Princess Helena, as characters represented in the play of *Les Savoyards,* 1854 (*from the album of the Empress Frederick at Friedrichshof*).

Left: Princess Beatrice by Winterhalter, 1859 (*from the print at Friedrichshof*)

Above: Princess Louise, Princess Beatrice and Queen Victoria. On the box, John Brown and driver. Birmingham, 1867

Right: Princess Beatrice aged 5 years old in 1862. (*From the painting by Lauchert, by permission of Her Majesty Queen Victoria Eugenia*)

Princess Louise, March 1863

racing was ever one of the more dreary and tedious ways of passing an afternoon, and this meeting was even more trying than usual, as it teemed with rain most of the time. But Alice did not notice the rain as she sat and walked beside Louis of Hesse. This romance did not follow the usual rules of the marriage game, and took the Queen somewhat by surprise. She had no intention of losing Alice for quite a while yet, and wrote to Uncle Leopold informing him that she would delay the match as long as she reasonably could. Louis, however, was as persistent as Frederick William had been, and he was back again in November.

In September the Queen and her husband had seen their grandson for the first time. Prince William was now over eighteen months old and the long wait before he was introduced to his grandparents was none of Albert's choosing. He had made constant suggestions to his eldest daughter that the Queen and he should see the child and was irritated by a series of evasive replies.

In his letters to Berlin he made frequent references to the antics and lovableness of his own 'Baby' and, when Charlotte was born, suggested that Aunt Beatrice be made the model for the upbringing of the new princess. There came a stage when a meeting could be staved off no longer. William's withered arm grew no better and the grandparents must judge for themselves. The rendezvous was to be Coburg, in September.

The Prince Consort looked forward to the trip, to seeing the new generation, to basking in the autumn light of the mountains and in the smiles of old friends. Yet from the moment that Albert the Good set out to meet the boy who was to be Kaiser, it was as if a curse had been put upon him.

On the way to Coburg, the royal party received news that the Prince's step-mother, the Dowager Duchess of Coburg, was very ill. She died before the journey was

3

completed, and a bevy of relations in deepest mourning met the Queen and her Consort at the station.

Prince William was led in by his English nurse and made a suitable impression, the arm apparently escaping notice. But otherwise the disasters continued.

Albert was nearly killed in a carriage accident when the horses took fright and galloped into a closed level-crossing gate. One horse was killed, and the coachman severely injured. The Prince was so bruised and shaken that Stockmar, who saw him soon afterwards, cried, 'God have mercy on us! If anything serious should happen to him he will die!'

The finger of death seemed to be on Coburg. The people Albert had known as a boy were dead, or aged, or had lost the clarity of the boyhood picture that had remained so vivid in his exile.

Duke Ernest saw his brother dab his face with a hand-kerchief and thought at first that he was tending to the scratches which he had received in the carriage accident. Then he saw that Albert was crying. He told Duke Ernest that he would never see Coburg again.

In December the Prince Consort was taken ill. The doctors described it as 'a touch of English cholera', and he struggled to his feet again.

In January the King of Prussia died and 'Vicky' became Crown Princess. Then, in March, the Duchess of Kent died. Beatrice lost a champion in her grandmother, a guardian who had cared for her while her parents were away, a story-teller whose only attempt at discipline was to say, in a shrill German accent, 'Baby must not be notty'.

The Duchess was seventy-five, and the Queen must have been aware that her mother's life was drawing to a close. Relations between the two had not always been happy, yet the Queen allowed the death to overwhelm her. But it cannot have been grief alone which caused her to collapse so completely. There was another factor to be

considered—the omnipotence of death. Death to Victoria
was like the wave to Canute. Only death and Bismarck
would not obey her bidding—and she outlasted Bismarck.
In defiance of death she loosed a flood of propaganda to
counteract the ravages of time and built memorials to
last beyond her vision of the years.

Finally, the doctors intervened, and advised that the
Queen be spared any effort or strain. She could no longer
bear loud talk or laughter, and her children saw little of
her. She had a relapse on Beatrice's birthday in April,
because the Duchess had so idolised 'Baby' and was not
alive to share what should have been a happy day.

The Queen's condition imposed more duties on her
husband who had also been appointed sole executor in the
Duchess's will. Her Comptroller had himself died only a
few days before, and the Consort was left with the task of
sifting the terms of the will, with its multiple bequests,
and also the Duchess's papers, reaching back to her first
marriage. There was much here that no other eyes but his
could see, papers connected with the Duke of Kent's
debts and details of Julie de St. Laurent and her children.[1]

He was finding it difficult to sleep. Small ills, such as
toothache and colds, became magnified, and were hard to
shake off. His nerves were jagged and increasingly he
dreaded the thought of speech-making.

The period of mourning for their grandmother also
hung heavily upon the children, but the pall began to lift
in May, and there came the exciting day when Mr. Mayall,
the photographer, arrived at the Palace. His previous
photographs had proved in such great demand both from
members of the Royal Family and the public that the
negatives were quite worn out. They were all photographed singly and in groups, with and without go-carts,
and Beatrice managed to be in most of the pictures.

The Prince of Wales was the cause of the next burden

[1] See Appendix A.

on the Consort. 'Bertie' was annoying his Mama, whose nerves were still frayed from the loss of her mother. She was beginning to take an active aversion to her eldest son. She did not like the way he sat at meals, or the way he dressed, or his taste in books, and she wrote to him, at Cambridge, expressing her views.

A more serious problem than table manners was 'Bertie's' marriage. Crown Princess Frederick William had not been idle in the matter of the list of likely brides which had been prepared at Osborne. The candidates had been summoned to a dinner for inspection, but were all found wanting, with the exception of Princess Alexandra, daughter of Prince Christian of Schleswig-Holstein—Sonderburg—Glucksburg, next heir to the throne of Denmark.

After the usual overtures and enquiries, the matter was speedily settled. 'Bertie' knew nothing as yet about the girl with whom he would spend his life and share his throne, but Germany soon found out, and took strong exception. For one hundred and fifty years it had been the privilege of Germany to take the pick of Britain's princes and princesses for matrimonial purposes. Now the prize of marrying the eldest son of Queen Victoria was to be awarded to Denmark, whom Prussia was already planning to attack over the question of Schleswig-Holstein.

Nothing could stop the planners. Stage-managed by Crown Princess Frederick, a meeting was arranged for 'Bertie' and Alix. They were brought together in the Cathedral at Spires, in front of an altar, and there left alone while 'Vicky' went off with the Bishop to admire the frescoes. The couple exchanged photographs and shook hands twice. Though struck with the beauty of the girl before the altar, the Prince was not fooled by his sister, whose romantic experience was limited to receiving a sprig of white heather in Scotland.

Prince Albert's last happy days were spent that autumn at Balmoral. With the Queen, he and the elder children travelled there via Ireland, where the Prince of Wales was being baptised in regimental duties. Louise, Leopold and Beatrice journeyed up direct, and there was a family reunion on 4th September, followed by a round of picnics, expeditions, shooting parties and sketching sessions.

Towards the end of October came the last Highland ramble that Queen Victoria would ever take with her beloved husband. Sixteen miles they walked together, beneath a blue sky and racing white clouds. As far as the eye could see the mountains stood out clear and beautiful, more blue than grey, and the long shadows were reaching across the valleys before Victoria and Albert rode home for the last time.

On the Sunday before the Royal Family left for the south they attended morning service in Crathie church, where the Reverend Stewart stamped up to the pulpit and gave as the text for his sermon: '*Prepare to meet thy God, O Israel.*'

Back at Windsor, Albert lay sleepless through the nights, his brain racked by yet another problem. Two figures floated before his eyes—those of 'Bertie', and a young lady at Cambridge.

Late in November he went to Cambridge to settle matters once and for all with his son. It was a long day and he returned, relieved, but very weak and tired. By the beginning of December he was a dying man.

He had once told his wife that he did not cling to life, but had a terror of fever. Now he said that, if it came upon him, he would die. And it was, in fact, upon him, though he was told that he was suffering from rheumatism and influenza.

Four times during the nineteenth century, the royal doctors faced a fire of criticism over their treatment of patients—when Princess Charlotte died—when Kaiser

William was born—when Prince Albert died—and when the Emperor Frederick died.

In Prince Albert's case it was primarily Palmerston who was worried over the treatment and who urged that other opinions should be taken, while Lord Clarendon commented that those looking after the Prince were 'not fit to attend a sick cat'.

The seriousness of her husband's illness was not, however, appreciated by the Queen for some time. She thought that he needed something to cheer him up, and came to the conclusion that the one person who could best do that was his much loved youngest daughter.

So the Queen took Beatrice to see her father on the evening of 5th December. He kissed her, and she recited some French verses which she had just learned. The Prince laughed for the first time for days. The Queen told her to recite them again, which she did, delighted to have such an appreciative audience. Then, for some time, he held the child's hand, while she stood staring at him, wondering why he looked so strange. It was the last time that she saw her father. Her visit rallied him, but only for a while.

Beatrice was spared the agony that was the lot of the elder children. Arthur, called to his dying father, returned with a face so white that his Governor was shocked. Louise and Helena were also judged old enough to meet death. Alice read to him, played to him, and tended tirelessly, always with a smiling mask of composure, until the strain proved too much and she rushed to her own room and waited there until the mask was ready again.

On 14th December, shortly after midnight, the great bell of St. Paul's tolled over a silent city. Only then did Queen Victoria tear herself from her dead husband's side and run to the nursery where her 'Baby' slept. Taking Beatrice from the cot, she hurried to her own bed and there lay sleepless, clasping to her a child, wrapped in the night clothes of a man who would wear them no more.

2
Girlhood

W HEN, quite suddenly, there was no one left in the world to call her 'Victoria', the Queen's grief was so deep, so sincere and so alarming in its intensity that her senior ministers, her relations and her household were, for a few days, gravely concerned for her health and reason. Dr. Jenner, who wished to see the pent-up emotion escape down a waterfall of tears, prescribed the presence of Princess Beatrice—as often as possible.

The cure worked. Within a week, the Queen wrote to Uncle Leopold:

> 'If I *must live* on (and I will do nothing to make me worse than I am), it is henceforth for our poor fatherless children—for my unhappy country, which has lost *all* in losing him—and in *only* doing what I know and *feel* he would wish, for he *is* near me—his spirit will guide and inspire me!'

Princess Alice moved immediately from the sickroom of her father to her mother's bedroom. She slept there, and tended the Queen throughout the day. The strain on her was such that it was rumoured she was to break off her engagement with Prince Louis.

Angel as Alice was, she could not play the rôle now given to Beatrice. When her children left the nursery Victoria allowed queenship to take precedence over motherhood. There was always a tinge of restraint, but with four-year-old Beatrice the mother could forget the queen.

'Baby' was brought down to her mother as soon as she woke in the morning, and, seeing the new mourning headwear for the first time, the child referred to it as 'the sad cap'.

On 19th December the Queen and her younger children moved to Osborne. She was in no state to attend the Prince Consort's funeral, at which the Prince of Wales was the chief mourner. On that day, at the Queen's request, no guns fired their salute from Portsmouth across the narrow water.

Much as her relations and members of the household suffered from the Queen's prolonged grief, it was upon those Princes and Princesses still at home that the heaviest burden fell. Nine months before, when the Duchess of Kent died, they had learned something of what death meant—black clothes, subdued voices, seeing little of their mother, and, when they did, not knowing whether she would be unusually affectionate or unaccountably irritable. She was still grieving over the Duchess when the Consort's last illness began.

What had been but a mist of sadness now became a dark, unbroken fog of gloom, in which the children fumbled blindly for the things of fun which should go with childhood days. Those responsible for their care and education had received instructions that they were to talk often to their charges of their 'adored Papa and broken-hearted Mama'. The Queen laid down that HIS wishes, HIS plans, HIS views were henceforth to be their law. Every letter that the Queen now wrote to her children contained some reminiscence about their father, and these letters always ended, 'your unhappy Mama'.[1]

Sometimes, when she saw her eldest son, a shudder seemed to run through the Queen. Excellently as he had

[1] Florence Nightingale was later to say of her grief: 'She always reminded me of the woman in the Greek Chorus,.with her hands clasped above her head, wailing out her inexpressible despair.'

borne himself at his father's death and in the days that followed, she could not free herself of the belief that his behaviour had contributed towards her husband's death. A wise course was taken when, in February, 'Bertie' left for a prolonged tour of Egypt and the Holy Land.

Crown Princess Frederick had been too ill to travel from Germany to be present at her father's death-bed and funeral, and this may have been fortunate. The loss was sufficient, without exacerbation, and she was apt to side with her brother about the Cambridge affair.

With no relations to turn to but Uncle Leopold (who was apt to take advantage of the situation) and brother-in-law Ernest (who was taking after his father), it was but natural that the Queen should begin to rely more on the members of her household and her servants. This was the cue for John Brown, the Queen's 'particular gillie', to begin his upward climb.

On 1st May the Royal Family arrived at Balmoral for a short visit. It was too soon. Along every path, every track, on every hill, the Queen saw the ghost of Albert. She took her meals in her room and only two children were allowed with her at a time. Then back went the caravanserai to Windsor, where everything of Albert's was just as he had left it.

It was time to make ready for the wedding of Princess Alice to Prince Louis, arranged to take place at Osborne on 1st July. It was to prove an ordeal for everyone connected with it, with the possible exception of Princess Beatrice, who was to be a bridesmaid. For her there was the thrill of a new frock and the excitement of rehearsing her duties.

The Queen produced for the occasion much of the routine which had been used at her own wedding, and began the day by giving Alice the prayer-book which the Duchess of Kent had bestowed on her in 1840. The result of thus stirring her memories produced an even more prodigious display of grief than usual. After breakfast, to escape the gloom, George of Cambridge took Ernest of Coburg out into the garden to enjoy a cigar.

The altar had been set up in the dining-room beneath a picture of Albert dominating a family group. The Queen, seated throughout and peeping out from behind the shelter of 'Bertie', commented that bridesmaid Beatrice made a touching sight, but it was Victoria herself who dominated the scene, and no bride ever made softer music with a second fiddle.

In August the Queen gathered her diminishing brood around her and journeyed back to Scotland, there to supervise the erection of the first of the numerous Albert memorials. On the 21st she set out in her pony-chair, with Brown at the pony's head, for the summit of Craig Lowrigan, where a cairn was to be built. Four of her children rode behind. 'Sweet Baby (Beatrice) we found at the top. The view was so fine, the day so bright, and the heather so beautifully pink—but no pleasures, no joy! All dead!'

Meantime, negotiations had been proceeding for the marriage of the Prince of Wales to Princess Alexandra, and from Balmoral the Royal family travelled to Belgium, to stay with Uncle Leopold at Laeken and meet the Princess's family, who were assembled there.

This was an occasion of great excitement for Beatrice. Not only was she to go abroad for the first time, but she would see a new sister.

On the morning of 3rd September, in the drawing-room at Laeken, Mrs. 'Wally' Paget[1] introduced Princess Alexandra and her father, mother and sister to Queen Victoria. The Queen was favourably impressed with 'Alix', going so far as to call her lovely, but the feeling in

[1] Countess Walburga Hohenthal (lady-in-waiting to Princess Frederick William) who had recently married a member of the British diplomatic service, Mr. (later Sir) Augustus Paget.

the room was tense. The Queen made an awe-inspiring picture, that stern and sad-faced woman inspecting a girl before she turned the tide of her life into the channel ordained by Albert. King Leopold took the excuse of luncheon to lead the party away, the Queen lunching alone with 'Baby' Beatrice.

The marriage question settled, the Queen left with her children for Rheinhardtsbrunn, a castle in Thuringia, and the Prince of Wales was ordered to Laeken to make his proposal.

The Crown Princess and her children were at Rheinhardtsbrunn. There Beatrice first saw her nephew, William, who was riding on a donkey and, for some reason, holding a parasol over his head. Niece Charlotte, William's sister, was in her pram, and Aunt Beatrice was thus able to be fittingly condescending.

The next stop was Coburg, where Beatrice and her sisters were shown all the views that their father had loved, and taken on the walks that he had followed.

The Princess's nurse took her to the market where Beatrice bought a present for her mother—which thrilled the Queen immensely.

There was Stockmar to be seen, and tears to be shed over old photographs and relics. Then the King of Prussia arrived to spend a day with the visitors, and fortunately he kept the conversation away from politics.

Alexandra of Denmark had one more examination to take before she could pass out as the Princess of Wales. This consisted of a ten-day course at Osborne in November—her sole instructress being, of course, the Queen. 'Bertie's' presence not being required, he was sent off on a trip to the Mediterranean with his elder sister and her husband.

It was a grim experience for 'Alix', being summoned from her room, and then ordered back to it. It was a grim order that she received—to leave her family and her patriotism behind in Denmark, but a pleasant side of the visit was that she was able to get to know, and become firm friends with, her future sisters-in-law.

The Queen wished the wedding to be on the anniversary of her own, 10th February, but this danger was averted on the grounds that there would be too little time to prepare for the celebrations. It was fixed for 10th March. The public wanted the wedding to be in London, but the Queen, appalled at the thought of facing the cheering crowds, insisted on Windsor.

Her people were already becoming somewhat impatient with their Queen's complete retirement into the black. They paid their money, and they wanted a show—and a holiday —in exchange. As Sir Winston Churchill's father said, 'What larks', when, on the wedding day, he and other boys from Eton charged the police so that they could get a closer look at the bride. It was larks that the people wanted now, gilt on their ginger snaps and gin with their jellied eels.

Robbed of their chance of cheering the bride, Londoners decided to make the most of Princess Alexandra's drive through their streets as she made her way to Windsor, and the Corporation spent £40,000 on decorations, illuminations and triumphal arches. Windsor too was bedecked. Beatrice and the young children staying at the Castle were driven round the town to admire these decorations. 'Baby' returned much shocked, because she 'never thought there were *stays* in shops!'

On the morning of the wedding day the Queen first visited 'Alix' in her bedroom, finding her in her dressing-gown, and, quite understandably, very emotional. She afterwards inspected her three daughters, Helena, Louise and 'sweet Baby', all dressed alike in lilac and white. She then moved off to the Royal Closet of St. George's Chapel, from which vantage point she could keep an eagle eye on every detail of the ceremony.

Sitting, as she thought, in the shade, the Queen did not

realise that her grief had become more than private. Once again, as at Princess Alice's wedding, she dominated the scene, and the lonely figure brought tears even to the eyes of Palmerston.

To the Queen, it seemed that Beatrice, Albert's darling baby, stole the day. She wrote, fondly: 'I could not take my eyes off precious little baby, with her golden hair and large nosegay, and smiled at her as she made a beautiful curtsey.'

The service was uneventful, except for the behaviour of William of Prussia who, as a matter of course, had to draw attention to himself. Dressed in Highland costume, he was placed for safety between his uncles, Arthur and Leopold. As Lady Augusta Bruce wrote,

> 'He set his small uncles at defiance and managed to get the cairngorm out of the head of his dirk and to pitch it on the other side of the Choir for the sake of excitement! . . . I saw Prince Leopold take him by the shoulders. Afterwards I heard that in answer to the Queen's inquiry if he had been good, the answer was, "Oh, no, he was biting us all the time".'

After the ceremony was over, and the register had been signed, there was a family luncheon for thirty-eight relations—but the Queen again lunched alone with Beatrice.

The Queen took 'Baby' down with her to see the couple off on their honeymoon, 'Alix, looking lovely in a white silk dress, lace shawl, and white bonnet with orange flowers'. As the carriage bore them away at the start of half a century of married life, the Prince and Princess of Wales 'looked up lovingly' at the picture of Her Majesty Queen Victoria and her youngest child framed in an upstairs window of Windsor Castle.

Already, so soon after the death of the Prince Consort,

a change was showing in the behaviour and character of Princess Beatrice. When her father was alive she had been encouraged in her precociousness. He had treasured her pert remarks, and laughed away her naughtiness. She had been his antidote to depression. Now, the child was being put to a very different usage. Her mother was fashioning her into a walking-stick upon which she could lean.

In her widowhood the Queen was determined to receive considerable moral support from her daughters. In this direction, Crown Princess Frederick was ruled out. She was herself destined to be an Emperor's wife, and in any event was fast reaching a state where she was taking little notice of what her mother told her.

Princess Alice, who had proved her worth in a supporting rôle, was the one whom the Queen, somewhat selfishly, wished to retain. But Prince Louis had a life of his own to lead in Hesse and, though the young couple spent as much of their early married life as they could spare in England, Princess Alice even agreeing to remain at Windsor for the birth of her first child, they had no intention of being tied to Queen Victoria's apron strings.

Princess Louise was not too well adapted to this rôle. Shy, reserved, and with one foot in a secret world, her first interest was in art. Too supple a bough to whittle into a walking-stick. . .

The Queen finally announced to Uncle Leopold that, unless Alice lived constantly with her, plans must be made for Princess Helena to marry, in a year or two, some sensible Prince who understood quite plainly, from the start, that her home was to be his home.

Though the Queen planned to keep Helena and husband, yet unchosen, beside her, she had seen that young birds have a habit of flying away when they find a mate. She now decided, come what may, that Beatrice should be her main insurance against loneliness. 'Baby' had the right characteristics: she was young enough to be schooled in the part; she had been Albert's darling; and many years must pass before a husband need even be contemplated.

When, after the marriage of the Prince of Wales, Mr. Frith went to Windsor to complete his famous picture of the wedding scene, Princess Beatrice used to watch him at his work. One day, as she skipped around bombarding him with questions, he asked her whether she would have liked to have been a bridesmaid. She answered: 'No, I don't like weddings. I don't like weddings at *all*! I shall never be married. I shall stay with mother!' Already she understood her destiny.

Compared with that of her elder brothers and sisters, Beatrice's childhood was lonely. In the 1840's additions to the nursery came at intervals of eighteen months or so, and there was always someone to play with. By 1863 'Bertie', 'Vicky', Alice and Alfred were grown-up people and only to be seen on visits. Arthur was living with his Governor at Greenwich, though the Queen still watched every detail of her favourite son's welfare. Helena was seventeen and Louise fifteen, too old to share the interests of a child of six, so that left only nine-year-old Leopold, whom tutors kept busy most of the day. Anyway, one had to be very careful how one played with him, owing to his dangerous disease.

One interest common to the children of differing ages was acting. In 1863 they staged a scene from Racine's *Athalie*, and the Queen, by a drawing which she made, has kept the moment alive. Princess Beatrice is kneeling, her thick, golden hair covering her shoulders, and with her hands clasped before her.

Because of the death of Prince Albert, because of the gaps in the ages between the children and because she so loved her youngest daughter, Queen Victoria personally undertook a considerable part of the upbringing and education of Princess Beatrice. The schoolroom was close to her own sitting-room and, no matter how great the pressure of State affairs, she always found time to bath 'Baby' Beatrice herself.

The Princess's particular nurse was Mrs. Thurstone, who was in the Royal service from 1845–1865. Mrs. Thurstone had a difficult part to play in the gloom of the early 1860's, and Queen Mary's mother has left a charming picture of the nurse taking her charge out from the Castle, away from the tears, for an airing the day after the Prince Consort died. The Princess loved her nurse dearly and, on her retirement, it was arranged that Mrs. Thurstone should be provided with a little house near Kensington Palace, where Princess Beatrice visited her whenever she was in London.

The theme of the educational programme which the Queen laid down for Princess Beatrice was—hard work. She had studied hard herself as a child, and had grown to believe that work was a builder of moral character. Now she insisted on a stern curriculum for the daughter in whom she saw so much of herself.

A standard was set which had to be attained by the time Princess Beatrice was seventeen. By then she must be able to read, write and speak both German and French fluently. A background of Latin was to be absorbed. She must be well acquainted with European history, this being a subject in which the Queen was keenly interested. Grammar and pronunciation had also to be perfected.

The art of letter writing was to be mastered, both as regards form of address and etiquette; language must be simple, without waste of words. She must be able to read aloud, both clearly and with feeling. She must excel at the demanded attributes of a young lady of fashion—singing and playing the piano. The organ and composition were to be added if promise were shown in this direction. A sound knowledge of drawing was to be instilled, with emphasis on design, and sketching to be encouraged as a recreation.

From the viewpoint of domestic science she was to be taught to cook and master the economics of housekeeping; to mend and care for her own clothes; and to manage her own little garden.

Walks with her governess were to be taken as an opportunity to teach her of biology and entomology, and to familiarise her with flora and fauna.

As for exercise, riding was a first priority, and later driving. Swimming was to be practised at Osborne in the summer, and figure skating, when conditions were favourable, in the winter. Ballroom dancing was to be carefully taught.

There were to be no fixed holidays, as children know them today, only fête days, birthdays and family anniversaries, and occasions when she travelled with her mother.

It was a hard programme, and a difficult target to set before a little girl, but how wisely that programme was contrived was to be seen in later years.

Governesses were chosen by the Queen with great care and after strict enquiry. Prince Beatrice passed into the care of Fraülein Bauer, a serious and well-meaning person not noted for her good looks, and the more light-hearted Madame Norele. These two looked after the teaching of the German and French languages, and general education.

The famous Mr. Corbould, nicknamed 'Cobby', who had been a favourite with her elder brothers and sisters, taught her to draw. He found her very good at design, at which she was later to excel, but not possessing the artistic gifts of her sister Louise, although she was seldom happier than when spending a sketching afternoon with her mother or her teacher.

Princess Beatrice's music master was none other than Mr. (later Sir) Charles Hallé, the eminent pianist who, after establishing a reputation for himself in Paris, had

4

settled in England in 1848. To the Queen's delight Hallé reported that his pupil had inherited her father's gifts. She had a good ear and made quick progress with sight-reading.

The story is told that Hallé, wishing to demonstrate her daughter's talent in this direction, suggested that a duet should be played before the Queen. Master and pupil carefully practised the music that had been chosen for Princess Beatrice's first 'concert'. When the day came the Queen arrived at the music room and regally seated herself, while 'Baby' took her place on the stool, screwed up to the limit.

To her horror, when the child looked at the music which Hallé placed before her, she found that it was not the piece she had practised but one she had never seen before. She rebelled, but Hallé, taking his place beside her, urged her to try. He began to play, she picked it up, and by the time the recital was over the Queen was confirmed in her opinion that she had another musician in the family.

Princess Beatrice's mezzo-soprano voice was developed by two great favourites of the Queen, Miss Jessie Ferrari and Signor Tosti. Miss Ferrari, the talented daughter of a very clever father, was for many years a frequent visitor to Windsor, accompanying the Queen and Princess Beatrice in singing and in duets at the piano. Signor Tosti, who took British nationality and was knighted in 1908, was appointed singing-master to the Royal Family.

Another teacher who helped to develop Princess Beatrice's love of music was Mrs. Anderson, who had been the Queen's own music mistress. Known as 'Andy' in the Royal Family, her husband was Master of the Queen's private band and helped in the selection and build-up of the new organ installed in St. George's Hall at Windsor. Taking after her father, Princess Beatrice soon showed great promise at the organ. In later years she was often to play on Sundays in the Service-room at Balmoral.

To Queen Victoria the importance of music in education was paramount. Her daughters and the ladies of her household were expected to be able to sing or play on demand, and every worthwhile piece of music published was sent to her. It was a somewhat terrifying ordeal to perform before the Queen. On one occasion the young sister of a lady-in-waiting, who was reputed to have a promising voice, was called upon to sing before the Queen and Princess. The girl sang an operatic air, but left out the 'shake' at the close.

'Does not your sister shake?' asked the Queen.

'Oh! yes, ma'am', was the reply. 'She is shaking all over.'

Princess Beatrice was taught to ride in the great riding school at Windsor. Her favourite pony was also named Beatrice, and she was soon competent enough to ride out alone with her mother over the tracks and hills around Balmoral.

The Queen gave personal supervision to letter writing and reading aloud. She made the rule that, whenever she was called away on State business or on visits on which she could not take her daughter, Princess Beatrice should write to her every day. These letters were to be in the form of a diary, without wasted words, describing the events of the day. Reactions had to be given to lessons learned and any items of interest noted on walks or drives. Thus was the Queen able to keep in touch with her daughter's every move and also, on her return, to discuss with her the merits, or otherwise, of the letters.

When it is also considered that every teacher had to make a daily progress report on the Princess, it can be seen how little was left to chance in 'Baby's' upbringing.

Queen Victoria was very fond of being read to and, in the evenings, when they were so often alone together, she patiently imparted the art to Princess Beatrice, who learned to speak clearly and with the correct expression.

She was able to broaden her mind from the numerous volumes of travel and memoirs which the Queen favoured.

Keenly interested herself in acting and dancing, the Queen encouraged Beatrice. Acting was used as a means of practising both German and French, and also assisted poise. Robbed of the chance of taking part in the children's dances that had been a feature of the Christmas season before her father's death, Princess Beatrice had now to be content with individual instruction, but this covered the whole field of dancing as then practised. She was thrilled to be able to demonstrate the new steps but there was a touch of sadness in the sight of the little girl coming in alone, in her dancing frock, to pirouette before the mourning Queen.

Religious instruction was also cared for by the Queen, who had very definite views on the subject. When unable to take her daughter to church, she would go through the Collect and psalms for the day with her, and Princess Beatrice would read out the lesson. Sunday was not made a day for seclusion and moping, but one on which the emphasis was put on being and doing good. The Queen had personally drafted a memorandum on a Princess's religious training, in which she said:

'I am *quite* clear that she should be taught to have great reverence for God and for religion, and that she should have the feeling of devotion and love which our Heavenly Father encourages His earthly children to have for Him, and not one of fear and trembling.'

The Queen was a stickler for good manners, and any little nephew who came to visit Princess Beatrice had to be very careful to doff his hat the moment he entered the Palace. Never, for a minute, during her childhood days was Princess Beatrice allowed to be alone with a boy—not even a brother. Her mother always insisted on politeness to servants, although some of her children and grandchildren sometimes fell short of the standard which she demanded. On occasion, the Princess Royal had been sent to her room, to solitary confinement, for offending, and later the boy who was to be George V was turned over and smacked in public by the Queen for making a remark which she did not consider fitting.

From babyhood Princess Beatrice was taught to love animals. She had her own dogs, and early gave her heart to birds, doves and canaries being her favourites. When driving once near Balmoral with her mother, they were told that a fawn was lying at the bottom of a disused gravel pit. The Queen told the gillies to rescue it. When it was brought up, the Queen and Princess took it into the carriage with them and, with it lying across their knees, they returned to the Castle. They called it 'Victoria' and it lived at Balmoral for some ten years.

Some of 'Baby's' happiest times were spent in the kitchen of the Swiss Cottage at Osborne. She soon became an accomplished cook and a tribute to her prowess was the naming of a cake after her. In *The Pastrycook and Confectioner's Guide*, published in the 1880's, the recipe for 'Princess Beatrice Cakes'[1] appears between those for Lemon Cheese and Simnel Cakes.

'Baby' now stood in the somewhat strange status of aunt to most of the children who came to stay at Osborne, Windsor, Buckingham Palace and Balmoral. She had twenty-one nephews and nieces when she was fifteen. By the time she herself was married she had been an aunt thirty-five times, and a great-aunt five.

[1] 'Take $1\frac{1}{2}$ lbs. of butter, 2 lbs. of castor sugar, the yolk of 20 eggs and the whites of 10 eggs, $1\frac{3}{4}$ lbs. of flour, and the grated rind of 4 oranges; cream the butter and sugar together, add the yolks and the grated rind of the oranges, have the whites of the eggs well beaten. Then add the flour and stir all gently together; put into hoops nicely papered, and bake in a moderate oven; ice them over when cold, and pipe them with icing coloured with a little carmine.'

'Vicky's' children were arriving as regularly as had those of her mother. They dearly loved to visit England, where they found their grandmother less awesome than their paternal grandparents. Egged on by elder brother William, who told them what fun it was to tease uncles and aunts and who himself was not above throwing an aunt's muff out of the window when he drove with her in a carriage, the younger children got into all kinds of mischief.

Young Waldemar[1] was one of the chief culprits. He arrived on a visit to Buckingham Palace complete with a baby crocodile, by the name of Bob. This the imp let loose in the Queen's room whilst she was busy at her papers. Her Majesty, suddenly spotting a crocodile by her feet, let out a shriek of terror. Servants rushed in and the hunt was on, but Bob's jaws were already powerful, and no one dared to pick up the reptile. Waldemar, roaring with laughter, had his fill of fun before he consented to re-box Bob.

The Prussian children were in Scotland for the Queen's autumn visit of 1863. The Crown Prince and Princess were staying with the Prince and Princess of Wales at nearby Abergeldie, whilst Princess Alice and Prince Louis, with their baby daughter Victoria, were at Balmoral. To Beatrice, there was a child more interesting than any of her nephews and nieces—Alice's little Malay boy, 'Willem', who had been presented to the Princess in Darmstadt and was being trained in serving duties.

This boy created an absolute sensation on Deeside. One woman said she would have certainly fallen down with the shock of seeing him, but for the fact that the Queen was there. She added that nothing would induce her to wash his clothes *as the black would come off*!

As the years passed, the Queen leaned more and more upon her youngest daughter, taking her with her on all

[1] The Crown Prince's fourth son.

public occasions, not only for moral support but because she knew that the golden-haired child would distract some of the attention from herself. Princess Beatrice became increasingly serious and shy. There had been no signs of either seriousness or shyness in babyhood days— indeed, the contrary—but now that she was permanently under the black umbrella of her mother's grief, she spent too much of her time with grown-ups, and, although the Queen was in retirement from great occasions, attending such harrowing ceremonies as the unveiling of memorials to Prince Albert imposed a heavy strain upon the child.

She missed the humanising and broadening experiences of Arthur who, living with his Governor at Greenwich, was even able to ride incognito on a roundabout at the Crystal Palace and play football with the servants.

From the time of the Prince Consort's death to that of the Queen, some forty years later, Princess Beatrice was never away from her mother's side for more than a few weeks. In childhood a parting was rarely for more than some days. If the Queen went to Germany, Louise might be left behind in the care of Lady Barrington—but not Beatrice.

When most girls of her age would have hardly put away their dolls, she had to assume the duties of caring for, and sheltering, her mother. On one occasion the Crown Princess's daughter, Victoria, a favourite with the Queen, was allowed, as a special treat, to sleep with her grand-mother in her saloon-carriage on the journey north to Balmoral. Before departure Princess Victoria was most carefully briefed by her Aunt Beatrice on exactly how to behave, what to do and what not to do. One of the instruc-tions was to lie perfectly still. So still did little Princess Victoria lie that, in the morning, the Queen patted her head and said: 'You never moved all night, dear child.'

In August 1865 Princess Beatrice went with her mother to Coburg for the unveiling of the statue which had been erected there to Albert. For the first time since their father's death, all nine children were together. As the veil slipped from the statue each stepped forward to place flowers at the feet.

While in Germany, Princess Beatrice met a young man whom she was later to know very well. His name was Christian, and the Queen had bidden him to Coburg so that she might inspect him and see if he would make a suitable husband for Helena (the Prince thought that she was looking for a husband for herself). He passed the test. As was usual in such cases, Helena did not as yet know what was afoot.

Christian was a sensible and solid man, and had all the virtues for which the Queen was looking, yet the match was to create great controversy throughout Europe, not because of Christian's character, but because of his background. He was Prince of Schleswig-Holstein-Sonder-burg-Augustenberg.

For some two years Beatrice had noticed that, whenever her married brother and her married sisters came to stay at the same time, and the words 'Schleswig-Holstein' were spoken, strong feelings were aroused. So fierce did these disputes become that the Queen ordered her children never to mention 'Schleswig-Holstein' in her presence.

Sandwiched between Denmark and Germany, the Duchies of Schleswig-Holstein were claimed by Princess Alexandra's father, now King of Denmark; by the King of Prussia, and Bismarck; and by Duke Frederick, Christian's elder brother, who was backed by the smaller German states hostile to Prussia. Bismarck used the occasion as a preliminary bout on his road to becoming European champion. He won easily, without revealing his strength to his future opponents. But Queen Victoria's action in engaging her daughter to the brother of the man whom he had deposed was a slap in the face for Bismarck, and he did not like it.

That autumn was a bad time for the Queen who was worried about the upsets in Germany that were dividing her children's loyalties. The Prince of Wales was being lured again by sparkling eyes, the race crowd's roar, and other temptations which his father had tried so hard to smother. King Leopold and Palmerston died. Most worrying of all, the public was demanding, with noisy voice, that the Queen should throw off her mourning and that the pageant of royalty should be restored.

Monarchy was losing its grip, and Republicanism was growing. Senior Ministers warned the Queen, but she could not bring herself to make the change, or see that it was necessary. Each evening, in the bedroom, Albert's night-clothes were laid out on the bed and water poured into the basin so that a ghost might wash his hands. Seeing the danger, Alice and Louise did all they could to lighten the atmosphere, but their mother would not listen to them. Instead she clung to Beatrice who was too young to proffer advice. These were sad days indeed for a girl of only nine.

At last the pressure on Queen Victoria to emerge from her retirement became so strong that she had no alternative but to yield. The occasion was the opening of Parliament on 6th February 1866. The motive behind the emergence from the convent of her grief was to ensure that Parliament made satisfactory pecuniary provision for Princess Helena on her marriage, and Prince Alfred on his coming-of-age.

The Queen took steps, however, both in the arrangements and in her demeanour, to ensure that this first public appearance since her husband died should not be made a festive occasion. It might have been a great and uplifting day to her younger children, to whom it was a baptism in regal duties, instead of the tear-stained apology for pomp that it turned out to be.

The Queen wore an ordinary evening frock. The gilded

state coach was not used, and there were no flourishes of trumpets. The Lord Chancellor read the speech. 'Not a nerve in her face moved as he read. But her nostrils quivered and widened. Tears gathered on the fringe of the drooping eyelids. A few rolled down the cheeks. But the lids were not raised a hair's breadth.'

The speech over, the Prince of Wales helped the Queen into her carriage, and back she went to Osborne with her daughters.

Princess Helena and Prince Christian were married in July at Windsor, Princess Beatrice walking in the royal procession to the Chapel with her brother Arthur. In attendance on her were Lady Caroline Barrington (now referred to as 'The Lady Superintendent') and Lady Augusta Stanley who, as Lady Bruce and her grand-mother's lady-in-waiting, had been the target of 'Baby's' cheekiness when Prince Albert was alive.

Once again, Queen Victoria was to find that a marriage planned by herself was not to turn out exactly as she would have wished. Although Prince and Princess Christian lived at Frogmore, so near to Windsor, she was soon to discover that she had in fact lost her 'Lenchen', the daughter who had been such a support. Prince Christian was made a Ranger of Windsor Park and proved a most dutiful son-in-law, but the relations of a man and a woman take precedence over those of mother and daughter, and the coming of children exaggerates the case.

So, left at home, were Louise who, at eighteen, was showing her passport as she passed the frontier between reserve and Bohemia—and 'Baby' Beatrice, who had begun her apprenticeship so young that no human calling could seduce her from the task that she had to do.

In order fully to appreciate the development of the character of Princess Beatrice one must understand the enigma who bore her, and who branded 'Victoria Regina' on her 'Baby's' back. It is between the ages of forty-five and sixty-five that Queen Victoria is most hard to appraise and this period covered her daughter's formative years.

During the Queen's married life the influence of Prince Albert had been omnipresent, and natural instincts of love and motherhood had triumphed in part over the inner workings of her mind. For the first five years or so of her widowhood her grief was expected, respected and partly understood, and she was left alone with it.

In the afternoon of her life and in her loneliness, she became an even greater contradiction than her husband had been. Easy as it may be to classify 'Victorian', it is impossible to type 'Victoria'. Her leanings tied her to no race. No stratum of society could claim her—she bestowed her friendship on the individual, whether ingrained Etonian or one porridge-fed in a croft. She was religious, but accepted only what she wished. For example, she did not believe in the Devil, which forced one preacher, on being apprised, to remark, 'the puir, wee body'. Death was an inconvenience as well as a sorrow and, as Sir Henry Ponsonby recalled, he was expecting to be told to send a sharp letter to the Almighty about it.

She was a prodigious worker and yet would not under-take one of her most important tasks, that of showing her-self to the people. She had an almost childlike approach to politics but could on occasion produce a solution that would have done credit to a senior statesman. She had outstanding physical courage yet would fret over a minor complaint. She had a most efficient household, yet would herself supervise every detail from the list of those who dined at the various sittings to those who rode her many ponies.

She had complete confidence in herself in everything she did, yet felt like fainting when carrying out the routine procedure of opening Parliament. She kept herself within herself, yet begged for friendship and affection.

She was prepared to change a decision but not to be proved wrong. That was where Gladstone made his mistake. If he caught the Queen out, he would labour the point, and expound on it, until he was silenced with the cold utterance, 'That will be enough'.

She was a stickler for a fixed code of behaviour, yet anything but a prude. She expected married guests at the Palace to share a double bed, but would not let her Ladies walk out with her Gentlemen unchaperoned. A frivolous but harmless remark made at the dinner table might result in the Queen freezing into one of her terrifying silences, yet when a guest, unaccustomed to the routine, made a jest of a definitely sexual nature, and those unfortunate enough to be present gripped their chairs and waited for the bomb to go off, Queen Victoria burst into roars of laughter.

She was unaccountable and entirely unpredictable. She was apt to lose her temper, and was formidable when she did. A Cabinet Minister discovered that when he went down to Osborne to explain certain details of the Irish Home Rule Bill. During the interview a gentleman-in-waiting, a friend of the Minister, waited outside in the ante-room. Suddenly the door opened and out ran the Minister. Ignoring his friend, he hurried across the ante-room and disappeared.

Some time later the two met, and explanations followed in due course. The Minister said:

'The Queen stood in front of me. "Go back to those who sent you," she said, "and tell them that if this Bill passes Parliament, I abdicate!" That little woman seemed about six feet high. I was *awed*. I could say nothing. I felt afraid. "Go," cried the Queen, pointing to the door. I was so overcome that I obeyed her instantly, forgetting, in my confusion and fear, to kiss Her Majesty's hand or take leave.'

Her family soon learned to make themselves scarce at such moments. A member of the Household once encountered, in the garden of one of the royal homes, a little group of Royalties trotting purposefully along a path. On enquiring the reason for the exercise, he was given a backward nod and the two whispered words—THE QUEEN. The little group trotted on to disappear from view behind a potting shed.

Queen Victoria loved her children, but she loved them because they were her children rather than as individuals. She wanted no rivals. She was impatient when sons-in-law usurped part of the mantle of Prince Albert, and it was noticeable that she never saw very much of her daughters-in-law. She demanded support, but was apt to snub those children who gave it to her.

In the Queen's eyes it was Princess Beatrice and Prince Arthur who could do no wrong. Princess Alice knew that, and on a 'sad anniversary' in 1865, wrote to her mother: 'May the Almighty give you strength and courage to bear it! I am sure the dear sisters and brothers who are at home will try to cheer you with their different loving ways—above all—little Beatrice, the youngest of us all.'

Yet Princess Alice, who devoted so much of her short life to sympathising with her mother, was not above criticism. Perhaps she was too gentle, and her husband too poor. The Queen had a hearty respect for both a downright, strong character and a solid bank roll. Princess Helena also married a poor man. She lost some of her intimacy with her mother after marriage, and was apt to receive rebukes, as when she stayed at Buckingham Palace without first asking permission.

Princess Louise was too 'arty'. Prince Leopold, with his physical handicap, was almost bullied, every item of his comings and goings being subject to detailed order.

For no child, or for that matter minister, would the Queen alter the routine of her days. She travelled

backwards and forwards to Balmoral and Osborne to a set
plan. Once, when she was about to start on her afternoon
drive, she was told that Prince Arthur, after a prolonged
absence from home, was on his way to visit her, but even
for him she would not wait. Off she drove, though a wait
for a few minutes would have brought reunion with her
son.

Being the youngest, Princess Beatrice had certain
advantages. She had soon found that she could take
liberties, undreamed of by her elder brothers and sisters,
and escape scot-free. Early she rebelled against being
confined in the schoolroom of an evening, and after supper
would come downstairs to join the grown-ups at dinner.
And a welcome diversion she proved to the guests when
the Queen was in 'one of her moods'.

At the age of ten she reached a point when she was
sometimes even allowed out without her governess.
Princess Louise then took charge and, after the first
experiment, the Queen commented, 'sweet Beatrice was
very happy and very good'.

In the matter of drawing Beatrice was fortunate in
having Louise as companion. In an age when all young
ladies sketched or painted as part of their social accomplishments, Louise went far beyond the amateur standard. Clever as she was with her brush, she was even more
gifted with mallet and chisel, as the statue of her mother in
Kensington Gardens bears witness. There was some resis-
tance at home, where it was considered that sculpture was
a less suitable hobby for a princess than sketching, but it
was pointed out to the Queen that Princess Frederick
William had taken it up after her marriage, and that the
Consort had approved and expressed the view that 'as an
art it is even more attractive than painting'. That was
enough for the Queen, and she was very proud when her
daughter's work was exhibited in the Royal Academy
before she was twenty.

There were no Continental holidays in 1866 and 1867, Germany being in the turmoils of war. Bismarck knew that if he was to become champion, and win the title of Empire for Prussia, Austria and the Hapsburgs must first be humbled, and all the other little states which sided with them. In seven weeks Prussia overran Hanover, subdued Hesse and the other small states, and defeated the Austrians decisively at Sadowa.

The war was a terrible ordeal for Queen Victoria. Fighting on the one side was her son-in-law, Crown Prince Frederick William. Ranged on the other were another son-in-law, Prince Louis of Hesse[1]; her cousin, the blind King of Hanover; and her brother-in-law, Duke Ernest of Saxe-Coburg-Gotha.

To Princess Beatrice the war was notable because the Hesse children came to stay until the danger was over, and her mother spent much time collecting linen and other comforts to send to the wounded.

While Bismarck rested for a while between pounces, there was a most enjoyable holiday in Switzerland in 1868, the Queen travelling under the title of Countess of Kent. There was a stop in Paris, where the party stayed at the Embassy and the Empress Eugénie paid them a visit. Then on to Lucerne, where the Villa Wallace, overlooking the lake, had been taken for their use. It was so small that there was not an inch of space in which to accommodate Prince Arthur when, with his Governor, he called to see his mother and sisters.

This was one of the few occasion since her husband's death when the Queen allowed herself to relax and forget her grief. With her children, and mounted on her pony, Sultan, she climbed the 5,000-foot high Righi, and noted with much pride that her Highland attendants could match the Swiss hillmen. She visited a Roman Catholic church during a service and, though favourably

[1] Succeeded as Grand Duke in 1877.

impressed, announced that there was no danger of her forsaking the Protestant faith. She took Princess Beatrice for a trip to the further end of the lake to see Tell's Chapel—a visit which resulted in an ardent discussion at dinner as to whether William Tell ever in fact existed.

The great joke of the holiday was at the expense of Fraülein Bauer, Beatrice's German governess. Dr. Jenner, physician-in-attendance, took her for an expedition up the Righi and that evening at dinner revealed that the other tourists and the guides had thought them to be married. On the descent they were put *tête-á-tête* in the same aerial chair.

Fraülein Bauer was not a beauty, and when details were asked of the chair ride, everyone, including the Queen, was convulsed. Ponsonby reported: 'I have never seen her laugh so much.'

Great excitement was caused in England during this visit by the report appearing in a French newspaper that the Fenians[1] were planning to assassinate the Queen and her children while at Lucerne. A man had been arrested outside the Swiss hotel by two English police agents, and it was believed that he had not come alone. Two days later, a London newspaper reported that a madman called William Wood had tried to enter the apartments occupied by the Queen, had been arrested, found insane and handed over to the British Legation. No connection was found with Fenianism.

Thus, without harm, Princess Beatrice first learned the meaning of the word 'assassin', a word which she was later to learn to dread. Though the affair was officially ended, there remained contradictions and inconsistencies. A young man had in fact been arrested. He was neither Fenian nor madman, and his name *was* Wood. It may be noted that Wood was the name taken by the family of the

---

[1] An Irish political organisation having for its object the overthow of English rule in Ireland.

Princess Beatrice, 1881 (*from the album of the Empress Frederick at Friedrichshof*)

Louis II G.D. of m. Wilhelmine of Baden
Hesse-Darmstadt

Louis III

Alexander (3)
of Hesse
m.
Julia of
Battenberg

see below

Marie (4)
m.
Alexander II

Charles (2)
m.
Elizabeth
of Prussia

Henry   William   Louis IV m. Alice (3)
of Hesse

Beatrice (9)
m.
Henry of
Battenberg

Louise
m.
D. of
Argyll

Alfred (4)
D. of
Edinburgh
m.
Marie of
Russia

Leo
L

He
Wa

Francis (5)
Joseph
m.
Anna of
Monte-
negro

Alexander (3)
of
Bulgaria
m.
Johanna
Loisinger

Henry (4)
m.
Beatrice

Louis (2) m. Victoria
of
Batten-
berg
Marquess
of
Milford
Haven

Irene (3)
m.
Henry
of
Prussia

Elizabeth (2)
m.
G.D. Serge

Alix (5)
m.
Nicholas
II

Ernest Louis (4) m.
G.D. of Hesse (div)
m.
(2)
Eleanore

Victoria   3
m.   others
(2)
G. D.
Vladimirovitch
(Cyril) of Russia

Marie
m.
Ferdinand
of
Rumania

A
of

Marie (1)
m.
Gustav of
Erbach-
Schonberg

George
Marquess
of Milford
Haven
m.
Nadeja
d. of
Michael
of Russia

Louise
m.
Gustav VI
of Sweden

Alice
m.
Andrew
of Greece

Louis m. Edwina
Earl   Ashley
Mountbatten
of Burma

Arthur

Tatiana

David
Marquess
of
Milford
Haven

Patricia
m.
John,
Lord
Brabourne

Pamela

Norton   Michael

Alexander
Marquess of
Carisbrooke
m.
Lady Irene
Denison

Leopold   Maurice

Ena
m.
Alfonso XIII
of Spain

George
m.
Marion
Stein

Lady Iris
Mountbatten

Alfonso   Jaime   Beatriz   Maria
Christina

Juan   Gonzalez

David   James   Robe

In some ca

THE RUSSIAN ROYAL FAMILY
Marie of Hesse m. Alexander II

Marie
m.
Alfred,
D. of
Edinburgh

Alexander III
m.
Marie
(Dagmar)
of Denmark

Serge
m.
Elizabeth
of Hesse

Paul
m.
Alexandra

4 others

Nicholas II
m.
Alix of Hesse

5 others

5 children
assassinated
1918

m. ALBERT OF SAXE-COBURG-GOTHA

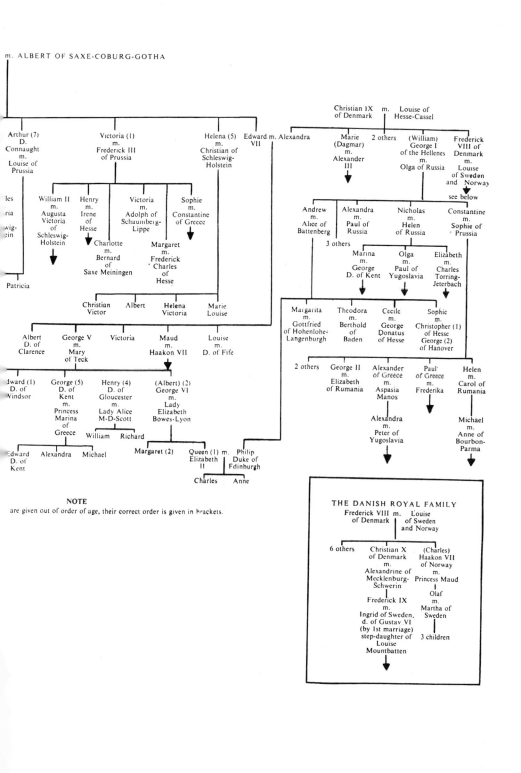

Christian IX m. Louise of
of Denmark Hesse-Cassel

Arthur (7)
D. Connaught
m. Louise of Prussia

Victoria (1)
m. Frederick III of Prussia

Helena (5)
m. Christian of Schleswig-Holstein

Edward m. Alexandra
VII

Marie (Dagmar)
m. Alexander III

2 others

(William) George I of the Hellenes
m. Olga of Russia

Frederick VIII of Denmark
m. Louise of Sweden and Norway
see below

William II
m. Augusta Victoria of Schleswig-Holstein

Henry
m. Irene of Hesse

Victoria
m. Adolph of Schaumberg-Lippe

Sophie
m. Constantine of Greece

Andrew
m. Alice of Battenberg
3 others

Alexandra
m. Paul of Russia

Nicholas
m. Helen of Russia

Constantine
m. Sophie of Prussia

Charlotte
m. Bernard of Saxe Meiningen

Margaret
m. Frederick Charles of Hesse

Marina
m. George D. of Kent

Olga
m. Paul of Yugoslavia

Elizabeth
m. Charles Torring-Jeterbach

Christian Victor   Albert   Helena Victoria   Marie Louise

Margarita
m. Gottfried of Hohenlohe-Langenburgh

Theodora
m. Berthold of Baden

Cecile
m. George Donatus of Hesse

Sophie
m. Christopher (1) of Hesse George (2) of Hanover

Albert D. of Clarence

George V
m. Mary of Teck

Victoria

Maud
m. Haakon VII

Louise
D. of Fife

2 others

George II
m. Elizabeth of Rumania

Alexander of Greece
m. Aspasia Manos

Paul of Greece
m. Frederika

Helen
m. Carol of Rumania

Edward (1) D. of Windsor

George (5) D. of Kent
m. Princess Marina of Greece

Henry (4) D. of Gloucester
m. Lady Alice M-D-Scott

(Albert) (2) George VI
m. Lady Elizabeth Bowes-Lyon

Alexandra
m. Peter of Yugoslavia

Michael
m. Anne of Bourbon-Parma

Patricia

Edward D. of Kent   Alexandra   Michael

William   Richard

Margaret (2)

Queen (1) m. Philip Elizabeth II Duke of Edinburgh

Charles   Anne

THE DANISH ROYAL FAMILY

Frederick VIII m. Louise
of Denmark of Sweden and Norway

6 others

Christian X of Denmark
m. Alexandrine of Mecklenburg-Schwerin

Frederick IX
m. Ingrid of Sweden, d. of Gustav VI (by 1st marriage) step-daughter of Louise Mountbatten

(Charles) Haakon VII of Norway
m. Princess Maud

Olaf
m. Martha of Sweden

3 children

Bassano

Princess Victoria of Hesse (mother of Earl Mountbatten) with Princess Elizabeth (Ella) of Hesse (centre) and their aunt, Princess Beatrice, 1880

eldest son of the Duke of Kent, the Queen's father, by Julie de St. Laurent. And the Duke first met Julie in Switzerland.

That winter of 1868 was hard and there was plenty of skating to be enjoyed at Osborne. The Queen liked to see her daughters figure-skating and, so that she could learn the art, Princess Beatrice had a cork bung placed between her skates to steady her. She revolved helplessly while members of the Household teased her.

The favourite sport on the ice was hockey, of a rough-and-tumble variety, in which all joined whether they were adept or not, but the Queen did not approve of the resultant *mêlée*, so care had to be exercised. When the silhouette of her outrider appeared on the sky line, the game had to be stopped immediately, and all sticks hidden on the bank. As her carriage approached, the Queen would see the party studiously practising figure-skating. After she had stopped awhile, admired and criticised, she would drive off. No sooner was she out of sight than sticks were retrieved, and the game was on again.

There were, of course, casualties, of whom Sir Theodore Martin was one. He had been entrusted with the writing of the Life of the Prince Consort and, as he was visiting Osborne, he was lured on to the ice. He fell, badly injured a leg, and was put to bed, complete with splints. Thrilled to have a wounded man in the house, Beatrice paid him many visits. The Queen herself brought him two extra large pillows, an incident which he never forgot, for there were few men who had enjoyed the distinction of having been tucked up by Queen Victoria.

In the Royal homes two subjects held the attention in the years 1868 to 1871. The first was the marriage of Princess Louise, and the second, the Franco-Prussian war. Both affected Princess Beatrice closely. The marriage

5

of her sister was to leave her alone with her mother, and start her on her thirty-year career as the Queen's other right hand; the collapse of the Second Empire was to bring her into close touch with a young man of whom she was to become very fond and with whom her name was to be coupled.

In 1868 Princess Louise was twenty. Her three sisters had all been married by the time they had reached this milestone—'Vicky' being the mother of two children—which made Louise look quite an old maid. The fate of this lovely Princess had become the subject of wide speculation. Would the Queen follow the plan that she had adopted in the case of the Princess Royal and Princess Alice, and thus expose her youngest daughters, Louise and Beatrice, to the tragedies unavoidable in the train of European squabbles? Would she choose some minor royalty, as she had done in the case of Helena, and keep him out at grass, and out of trouble, at home? Or would she break with tradition and allow Louise and Beatrice to marry into noble British families? When it became known that Princess Louise had bestowed her pliable affections on a young clergyman whom she had met at Windsor and subsequently requested that she be allowed to enter an Anglican sisterhood, public interest became even more intense.

In 1868 it was strongly rumoured that she was to marry the Crown Prince of Denmark, and a Danish newspaper came out with the statement that the engagement had actually taken place. With vivid memories of what had happened five years before in Schleswig-Holstein, and the quarrels that had broken out between the Prince and Princess of Wales on the one hand, and the Crown Prince and Princess on the other, with the Hesses joining in, the Princess could hardly be expected to relish that union— unless she was deeply in love, which she was not.

The next candidate was a friend of 'Bertie's'—Prince

William of Orange. Fortunately, in this case, preliminary enquiries by the Queen revealed that this Prince had a detailed acquaintance with the boulevards of Paris, and, as anything to do with Paris savoured of Beelzebub to the Queen, the matter was quickly dropped.

A suggestion now emanated from Germany that a certain member of the Prussian royal family was admirably suited. Princess Louise staged an immediate rebellion, and her mother agreed with her. She had had enough of Prussia, but to the Broad Church Queen there still loomed the danger of the Anglican sisterhood, and she decided that a British candidate must be produced—and quickly.

The Queen delved into the constitutional and legal problems connected with the marriage of a Princess to a commoner and decided that there were no difficulties which could not be overcome. She then carried out the wise move of recruiting her eldest son on to her side. Having written to the Crown Princess and told her that in no circumstances would she or Louise hear of the Prussian marriage, she informed the Prince of Wales of the step she had taken.

While 'Bertie' might well have supported the claims of the candidates of Denmark and Orange, he was dead set against the Prussian alliance. In addition he must have been pleased to join an issue on his mother's side for a change—especially at her invitation. He agreed that holding together was most important but raised certain objections to his sister marrying a commoner.

It is easily understandable why the Queen, in her search for a husband for Princess Louise, should have first turned to Scotland. Prince Albert had been happiest there, and so was she. The climate suited her; she liked the character of the people; and she could drive amongst them without fuss. She loved the hills, the woods and the lochs, and the tracks which wound among them. She found infinite peace in spending the afternoon sketching with Louise, while Beatrice played happily around with Jane Churchill. She found exhilaration in riding out on 'Sultan', with Beatrice beside her on her own pony, 'Beatrice'. She enjoyed being an ordinary mother, and taking Beatrice out for drives without a governess. She found it fun to take tea by a loch side, to drive home in the twilight, to have dinner with 'good dog' Sharp at her feet, a drop of whisky in her claret, and Beatrice prattling by her chair before she went to bed. And she liked to re-visit the houses at which she had stayed with Albert, such as Inveraray, which they had visited in 1847. They had both been very attracted at the time by their host's baby son. He would be twenty-four now. . . .

In that autumn of 1869 there was a most enjoyable holiday awaiting Princess Beatrice in Scotland. She and her mother and sister went for a ten-day stay to a house called Invertrossachs, overlooking Loch Vennachar, to the west of Callander. With them went their dogs, their ponies and their carriages.

From this centre they made trips into the surrounding countryside, and the Queen wrote: 'This solitude, the romance and wild loveliness of everything here, the absence of hotels and beggars, the independent simple people, who all speak Gaelic here, all make beloved *Scotland* the proudest, finest country in the world.'

Sunday was wet, so the Queen and her two daughters held a service of their own, and Beatrice read the Collect. All three planted trees to commemorate their visit to Invertrossachs, before taking the train back to Balmoral.

Before leaving Deeside the Queen, whose mind was set on finding a husband for Princess Louise, had a talk with Dr. Norman Macleod about the suitability of a certain young man. So it happened that among the guests at Balmoral the following autumn was the Marquis of Lorne, twenty-five-year-old heir to the Duke of Argyll.

On the afternoon of the 3rd October 1870 two carriages left the grounds. The first, containing the Queen, Princess Beatrice and Mrs. Ponsonby, headed for Pannanich Wells, two miles from Ballater. The second took Princess Louise and Lord Lorne, Lady Ely and Lord Hatherley, to the lodge at Glassalt Shiel.

As the Queen let Beatrice taste the water, impregnated with iron, from the well, and showed her the old inn where Brown had once been a servant, her thoughts were concerned with what was happening on the other expedition. It had been arranged that the two chaperones should allow the young couple to walk alone to the Dhu Loch.

The Queen and Beatrice arrived back at seven, but there was still no sign of the others. It was dark when at length Louise ran into the Castle, breathless, to tell her mother and sister that she was engaged.

Meanwhile, Bismarck was active again. Paris had enjoyed a false spring that year. Cavalry trotting in the sunshine . . . uniforms of sky-blue, scarlet and green . . . clanking swords and flashing breast-plates . . . coquetry and cocksureness on the boulevards . . . the last of the great days.

By November the mob ruled the capital, the Emperor was a prisoner of war in Germany, his Empress a fugitive in England, and the cavalry, shut up at Metz, had eaten their horses—and surrendered.

Queen Victoria deeply worried at first over the fate of her daughters, 'Vicky' and Alice, if the French hordes swept through Germany, had quickly to change her thoughts, and ponder on the fate of the Empress Eugénie when Bismarck reached Paris, or the people turned against Napoleon.

On 5th September the mob moved on to the Tuileries, and the Empress Eugénie had not even a nightdress with her as she was smuggled out of a side door. Posing as the wife of the Emperor's American dentist, who accompanied her, she was rushed in relays of carriages to Deauville. There the owner of a British yacht was persuaded to carry the last Empress of the French to England. At Hastings she was reunited with her son, the Prince Imperial.

On 30th November the Queen and Princess Beatrice left Windsor for Chislehurst in Kent, where the Empress was staying at Camden Place. She and the Prince Imperial were waiting at the door to greet them, and Beatrice presented the Empress with a nosegay from Louise.

Five days later Beatrice met the Empress and her son again when they came to Windsor. While the children took the Prince Imperial on a conducted tour of the Castle, the Queen and Empress drove to the Mausoleum to see 'the dear reclining statue' of Albert, which was always lit up in the afternoon.

The ghost of Albert was for once not present when Princess Louise was married, on a glorious spring day, at Windsor. The Queen gave her daughter away, and looked happier before the public gaze than she had for ten long years. In compliment to the bridegroom, Prince Leopold wore the kilt. Next to him walked Princess Beatrice, 'in high spirits, wearing a pink satin dress, her light hair hanging freely behind'. A shower of old shoes and a new broom were thrown after the honeymoon carriage as it moved away.

Princess Beatrice was now on her own.

3

'Benjamina'

IN August of 1871 Princess Beatrice began her real apprenticeship as secretary and companion. The Queen was ill—more seriously so than her ministers and the public realised. The constant carping over her financial hoarding, the demands that she should appear more often in public, the shootings and the fires in Paris, had all taken their toll of her nerves. She developed an abscess under her arm and rheumatic gout at the same time. Ten years of grief and grieving had taken her from robust youth to the evening of age.

The doctors at Balmoral, Jenner and Marshall, wanted another opinion and, after some persuasion, the Queen agreed that Lister should be summoned from Edinburgh. Arriving at Balmoral, the famous surgeon advised an immediate operation for lancing the abscess, and this was performed by local anaesthetic and with the aid of very little chloroform, which the Queen did not like.

The illness lasted for two months, and all her children journeyed to Deeside to comfort her, but it was to Beatrice, unencumbered by an in-law, that the Queen turned for her main support, and to her she dictated her Journal whilst her right arm was *hors de combat*.

In December, at Sandringham, the Prince of Wales contracted typhoid. This was the second shock that her sons had given her that year. In the summer Prince Arthur had fallen out of a window at Buckingham Palace and landed on the helmet of a very surprised policeman on duty below. The Prince escaped with severe concussion, but the Queen worried about what *might* have happened.

The news of the Prince's illness reached her at Balmoral the first morning on which she felt well enough to get up and take breakfast with Princess Beatrice and her other children. The fever grew worse and a fortnight later, on 8th December, an urgent message called the Queen to Sandringham. The next day Beatrice and Leopold were sent for, and the Duke of Cambridge also arrived.

Deep, hard crusted snow lay over the fields of Norfolk. Early went the light, and as the night froze into silence, so a dread fear seized Queen Victoria that, on the 14th December 1871 (the tenth terrible anniversary of the death of her husband), her eldest son, the heir to the Throne, would die. The illness was following much the same lines—Princess Alice was there, administering, as she had done ten years before. There was, sometimes, the same wild look in her son's eyes that she so well remembered.

On the 11th the Queen was told by Sir William Jenner, that the Prince of Wales might 'go off' at any moment, and she hurried to his room in her dressing-gown. Her children—except 'Baby'—joined her. 'Bertie' fought on. The final crisis came on the 13th, the eve of the dreaded day. Alice in tears, said 'There can be no hope'. The Queen hardly left her son's room. Then, as she held his hand, he turned towards her and demanded, wildly, 'Who are you?' He stared at her for a time before whispering 'It's Mama. It is so kind of you to come'. Next morning the crisis was over, and by the afternoon the Queen was able to go out for a quiet drive with Princess Beatrice.

The Queen said: 'Had *my* Prince had the same treatment as the Prince of Wales, he might not have died.' She forgot, perhaps, that Albert might have lacked the same will to live.

After much discussion Princess Beatrice and her three brothers were sent away, as Sandringham was feeling the strain of so many visitors. The Duke of Cambridge was not making things easier by waging total war on smells and drains, and declaring certain bedrooms uninhabitable. Princess Louise was ejected from hers. He continually traced pipes and opened manholes. Finally, a man arrived to investigate the smell, which turned out to be a gas leak.

The illness, and seemingly miraculous recovery of the Prince of Wales, had a profound effect on public opinion —so much so that Republicanism died instead. To some it brought vividly home the tragedy of the Queen, watching by the bedside of her raving son, waiting for him to die on that tenth anniversary. To others, the appeal lay in the story that the Prince, after the final crisis, had demanded a glass of beer, and thereafter fallen into a refreshing sleep.

Forgotten, for a time, were the stories of his debts, his gambling, his romances—even becoming embarrassingly involved in the Mordaunt divorce. There was no audience now for those who criticised the Queen's hoarding— though there was an increasing, and enthusiastic, demand that she show herself more to her people.

This she did on 27th February, when she drove to St. Paul's for the Thanksgiving Service for the recovery of the Prince of Wales. She described it as a day never to be forgotten. It was certainly unforgettable to Princess Beatrice, who drove in the carriage with her mother and brother.

The Emperor Napoleon and Empress Eugénie, re-united in exile, had been invited to the Palace to see the start of the procession, and the Empress was greeted by Princess Beatrice, looking very pretty in a mauve dress trimmed with swansdown. Seven open carriages led the procession, in one of them the Princes Alfred, Arthur and Leopold, and a small boy called George, who was destined to be King for over a quarter of a century.

The Queen had a Sovereign's escort, her six-horse State landau following the quaint old vehicle of the

Speaker. The Princess of Wales sat beside the Queen, and opposite the Prince of Wales, lame and looking somewhat weak, and Princess Beatrice, with 'Eddie', the Prince's eldest son, between them.

The reception by the enormous crowds was overpowering and unbounded. At Temple Bar the gates were shut against the Queen, and then opened, this being the last occasion on which the traditional ceremony was carried out, as six years later the Bar was removed to Theobalds Park, Hertfordshire. There it has stood ever since, its site in Fleet Street being marked by the memorial which keeps alive the day on which the Queen and Prince of Wales drove to St. Paul's.

Back at the Palace the Queen took Princess Beatrice out on to the balcony, and for the first time the fourteen-year-old girl looked out over a sea of faces, saw the ripple of waving hands and heard the roar as the waves of cheering broke out in the Mall.

Two days later Arthur O'Connor, an eighteen-year-old Irish boy, pointed a pistol point blank at the Queen as she dismounted from her carriage at Buckingham Palace. In a second Brown had jumped on him, holding him to the ground until the police came. The pistol later proved to be unloaded, but that detracted little from the initial shock to the Queen.

Twenty-four hours later the Queen and Princess Beatrice drove in that same carriage to Paddington *en route* for Windsor. As Princess Alexandra said to her mother-in-law, 'It is no pleasure being a Queen'.

In the summer of 1873 the Shah of Persia decided that he would tour the capitals of Europe, an announcement which caused widespread excitement, for he was a person of considerable import to the Foreign Office. In Berlin he drove round on sight-seeing trips with a large basket of strawberries on his knee, ceaselessly sucking the fruit and throwing the stalks on to the road. The Crown

Princess's younger children were horrified when the rumour reached them that members of his retinue were killing sheep in the royal apartments. They hastened to warn their contemporaries in London.

In London, he stayed for a fortnight at Buckingham Palace and, though he paid three visits to the Queen at Windsor, the responsibility for entertaining him rested largely on the Prince of Wales. The Shah was a somewhat unusual visitor. He crossed his hands across his breast as a salute, and at a review of troops he rode a horse with a tail dyed pink, while one of his followers preferred magenta. Another fell off and showered the grass with diamonds. The Shah asked his host if, when he came to the throne, he would be in a position to cut off the Duke of Sutherland's head. He also expressed surprise that the eyebrows of English girls did not meet across the bridges of their noses, a growth which found great favour in his own country.

Princess Beatrice was now sixteen, and when the Shah came to Windsor to receive the Order of the Garter, she took her place as one of the Queen's grown-up daughters. They were all in a state of great excitement, not knowing what the day would produce. It started badly, as the order for troops to line the way to the Castle had gone astray, and no troops appeared. In the last few frantic minutes a skeleton show of Guards was put together.

Princess Beatrice sat by the window with her mother, to watch the Shah arrive. To their horror they saw that his retinue filled eleven carriages.

Three Princesses supported their mother as she received the Shah. The Queen described the following moments:

'Then I asked him to sit down, which we did on two chairs in the middle of the room (very absurd it must have looked, and I felt very shy), my daughters sitting on the sofa.'

At lunch Princess Beatrice sat next to Prince Abdul who was intrigued and delighted with the pipers circling the table during the meal.

A few days after the Shah had gone on his way, the Queen and Princess Beatrice were enjoying quiet after-noon tea in the garden at Osborne, in a shady spot near the pines and the ilex trees, when a telegram arrived. It was from Prince Alfred, who said: 'Marie[1] and I were engaged this morning. Cannot say how happy I am. Hope your blessings rests on us.'

The peace of the summer afternoon was shattered. The Queen knew of the friendship but had not dreamed that it would progress with such rapidity, and as yet she had not seen Marie. After another cup of tea a telegram arrived from the Emperor and Empress of Russia con-firming the news.

The wedding took place in January 1874, at St. Peters-burg, the first marriage of a brother or sister that Princess Beatrice could not attend, but she was partly compensated by the festivities at Osborne to mark the day, with lighted warships putting on a firework display. That evening, at the Queen's dinner party, she wore for the first time the Victoria and Albert Order which her mother had bestowed upon her.

Beatrice, Arthur and Leopold were now the only un-married children of the Queen—and the hunt was already in full cry after a bride for Arthur. The Queen was most anxious that her favourite son should find a wife whom he loved and who was at the same time suitable. He was created Duke of Connaught and sent off on frequent trips round Europe with his Governor, the latter clinging firmly to a worn copy of the *Almanach de Gotha*.

At all halts Colonel Elphinstone found instructions waiting for him from the Queen. Arthur had better look lively or all the best Princesses might get snapped up.

[1] Grand Duchess Marie, the Tsar's only daughter.

The help of the Crown Princess and Princess Alice was recruited and, although they put forward a number of names, none was found suitable. Either they had looks without virtue, or virtue without looks; character without attraction, or deportment without brains.

The Queen was to have a long wait before the next of her children was to marry.

By 1874 the marriages which had already taken place had provided Princess Beatrice with a formidable array of nephews and nieces. The Waleses had five children— 'Eddy', aged ten—'Georgie', nine—Louise, seven— Victoria, six—and Maud, five. Another son had been born in 1871, but he lived only twenty-four hours. He was christened Alexander on the day of his birth, and was buried at Sandringham.

The Crown Prince and Princess of Germany had also completed their family, this now being made up of four girls and three boys, ranging from William in his sixteenth year to baby 'Mossy' in her second.

The Hesses had five girls and two boys, the eldest being Victoria, at eleven, and the youngest May, still in her cot. Princess Alice's fourth daughter, born in 1872 and destined to be Tsarina of Russia, she named Alix (because the Germans could not pronounce 'Alice') Helena Louise Beatrice, after herself and her sisters. Alice also had her tragedy. Early on a May morning in 1873 her children came into her room. As she lay in bed, she watched Alix playing with her brothers, 'Ernie' and 'Fritty'. They leaned out of different windows, calling to one another. Three-year-old 'Fritty' fell, landing on the paved courtyard below. He never recovered consciousness. The boy had inherited the bleeding disease and his mother had cosseted him since birth. Her grief approached that of Queen Victoria for Prince Albert, but she lacked the stamina and the tough streak which ran through her mother.

The Christians had two boys, Christian Victor and Albert, and two girls, Helena Victoria and Louise. The last named, and youngest, was Princess Marie Louise, who died in 1956, a few weeks after the publication of her reminiscences.

Princess Beatrice was the favourite aunt of the Queen's grandchildren. To them she was more like an elder sister and still young enough to take part in their games. A particular friend was the boy who was destined to succeed his father as George V; his first entry in his diary, begun in the 1870's, was that he had played croquet that afternoon with Aunt Beatrice. But the life she was leading was changing her into a very shy princess. The Queen's dislike of making public appearances, or meeting, on terms savouring in any way of familiarity, those outside her circle of advisers and household, communicated itself to her daughter. Princess Beatrice was playing an important supporting rôle to her mother, but at the same time she was being sheltered from contact with the outside world. The book of life was being translated to her in parts, as her mother thought fit, and the Queen's translation was not always in accordance with the generally accepted version.

She was early taught by the Queen to avoid assiduously anything which appeared to be connected with publicity. All intrusions into privacy were unforgivable. An incident in 1873 confirmed the Princess in the same opinion. She had gone with her mother to stay at Inverlochy Castle, a quiet visit with meals taken together and piano duets in the evenings. One afternoon they drove from Ballachulish up the Glencoe Pass, resting at its head to eat a picnic lunch and sketch the mountains.

'Here, in this complete solitude', wrote the Queen, 'we were spied upon by impudently inquisitive reporters, who followed us everywhere; but one in particular . . . lay down and watched with a telescope and dodged me and Beatrice and Jane Churchill, who were walking about. . . .'

Brown strode down and told the man that the Queen would like him to move away. The reporter refused, saying that he had as much right to be there as the Queen. He called up his companions, and for a moment it looked as if Brown would have to fight them all. But those who had remained in the background wanted no trouble, and took their bellicose friend away.

It was in the seclusion, the peace, the silence of those holidays in the Highlands, in the years when she was alone with her mother, that integral parts of the character of Princess Beatrice were formed. She learned equanimity from the people; she had time to read and study, she had time to draw and play the piano; she saw how the Queen carried out her duties, and she learned how not to be lonely, though not mixing freely with other girls of her own age.

In January 1874, when she was sixteen, Benjamin Disraeli became Prime Minister for the second time, and a shaft of sunlight relieved the somewhat dull routine life of herself and her mother. The brilliant Jew, whom Prince Albert had considered somewhat flamboyant and over-dressed, was an old man now, and lonely without his wife. He had a genuine affection for the Queen and her daughter, and appeared much flattered when he saw that Princess Beatrice was wearing the bee-shaped brooch which he had presented to her. It was given to his chosen women as a badge of friendship.

Dinner was a gayer affair when he was at Osborne or Balmoral. In those heavy silences, broken only by the clatter of plates, silences which had been so frequent since the Consort died, Disraeli would sit unspeaking for a time, smiling to himself and letting his eyes roam the table. Then he would throw at Princess Beatrice some provocative remark that was a challenge to her wit. She would take it up, and the Queen always joined in. Or he would compliment the shy girl beside him on some item of her appearance—her hair or her shoes. He was the first man to say such things.

Disraeli was very good for her, yet she was never at ease with him, as she suspected that he was making fun of her mother, and to her that was a cardinal sin. In truth this strange man had the capacity to love, and laugh at, a woman at the same time.

The Queen, who knew more about her Prime Minister than many guessed, saw him as a mixture of comic actor and brilliant statesman, an invalid and a true friend, a courtier and a tired old man. She did everything to ease his journeys to her, and cared for his health, and she allowed him to sit in her presence. For he treated her as a woman instead of a public department.

After he had become Lord Beaconsfield, the Queen and Beatrice visited him at Hughenden, where they both planted trees to commemorate their visit. They wandered with him round the Italian garden that he had himself designed, and admired his pictures, treasures and photographs. It was a day which both were to remember.

So, also, was the 18th of August, 1875, when three lives were lost in a collision between the royal yacht *Alberta* and the schooner *Mistletoe*. The Queen, Princess Beatrice and Prince Leopold had left Osborne at half-past five, bound for Balmoral. The sun was shining and the sea calm as they embarked on the *Alberta* at Trinity Pier and moved off towards the mainland, followed by the *Victoria and Albert*. As they neared Stokes Bay, Princess Beatrice touched her mother's arm and said: 'Mama, there is a yacht coming against us.'

The Queen swung round, to see tall masts and wide sails almost above her. The next moment there was a terrific crash, the sound of rending wood, screams and shouts, and the *Alberta* heeled over and shook violently.

Ponsonby ran to see that the Queen and Princess were safe and unharmed. Being amidships at the time, they were. Their first anxiety was for those in the bows, for there the Household had a habit of gathering during the trip across the Solent. Then, to their great relief, Leopold appeared, with the news that there were no casualties on the *Alberta*.

Within two minutes of the collision the schooner sank. As she disappeared, the Queen hurried forward, shouting, 'Take everyone on board'.

By the time the Queen and Princess Beatrice reached the rail, the *Mistletoe* had gone, and only a few spars and deck-chairs floated on the water. One of the *Alberta*'s crew was swimming around with a life-belt and the pitiful figure of a man, with face black and still, was being hauled on board. The Master of the schooner also died despite strenuous attempts at artificial respiration, and the *Alberta* did not leave the spot until a long but vain search was made for a woman who had been aboard the *Mistletoe*.

It was on her eighteenth birthday in 1875 that 'Baby' became 'Benjamina'. Ever since Prince Albert had first fondled her on his knee, she had been known in the family as 'Baby'. The quick development of 'Vicky' compared with that of Beatrice was largely accounted for by the seventeen-year gap between them, but Beatrice was now a Princess of marriageable age, and being referred to as 'Baby' was not quite fitting. Suddenly, somewhat to everyone's surprise, she had become a woman.

She had brought more happiness to the Queen than any of her other children. There had been no tantrums, no waywardness, no leanings towards bohemianism, no extravagances in religion, no yearnings to free women

6

from the shackles of the age, and, above all, no longing to wander off with a foreign prince.

Rumours began to flash around that Princess Beatrice would shortly become engaged. It was popularly believed that another Scottish nobleman would join the Royal Family. This was strengthened by the news that the Queen and her daughter were to stay with the Duke and Duchess of Argyll at Inveraray in September.

What better opportunity and setting could there be for the inspection and introduction of a likely suitor? The Queen had used such a plan before. The Duke and Duchess knew all the right type of young men, and could ask them to their seat without suspicion being aroused; and, after all, the marriage of Princess Louise and Lord Lorne had turned out to be a great success.

To the more knowing, many difficulties were visible. It was obvious that the Princess had become almost indispensable to the Queen. There could be no replacement now. She had found the daughter whom she wished to have by her side, and had no intention of losing her. Fortunately for her, Beatrice was adhering to her early professed decision that she would stay with 'Mama'. Therefore, if a young man were to propose, he would have to realise clearly that, on his marriage, his home would be the Queen's home and that his wife would continue to play the part that she was now playing in support of her mother. Such conditions ruled out eligible suitors who were set on making their own careers, who wished to live in their family homes and run their estates, or whose interests might take them much abroad.

The rumour-mongers found little, after all, to discuss in the visit to Inveraray. Princess Beatrice hardly left her mother's side and, although there was quite a large house party, the Queen took many of her meals alone with Beatrice and Louise, with John Brown waiting on them. On the occasions when she lunched with a few chosen guests, she invariably went upstairs soon afterwards, and took Princess Beatrice with her. Most mornings and after-noons she walked or drove out with her daughters, and the sketch books went with them.

The big event of that stay was the ball given by the Duke for his tenants. This was held in a pavilion which had been put up for the celebrations at the time of the wedding of Princess Louise. Between seven and eight hundred people were there, but, to the Queen's disgust, the band which came from Glasgow could not play reels. Princess Beatrice danced with one of the Duke's foresters and partnered Mr. John Campbell in a reel, to the music of the pipes.

At the end of a week the Queen and her 'Benjamina' returned to Balmoral, where their interest was fully taken up by the illness and death of John Brown's father. There was no sign of any romance.

The gossips switched their line, and began discussing the rather startling suggestion of an alliance with the Prince Imperial of France.

Queen Victoria had ever a warm corner in her heart for the losing side and the under-dog. In the face of human tragedy she could forget the past and overlook infringements of her strict code of behaviour. She had welcomed the Empress Eugénie at the start of her exile, taking Princess Beatrice with her to Chislehurst. Now, when Napoleon III reached Camden Place from his prison in Germany, she lost no time in visiting him.

Swept from her memory were the bitter criticisms that her husband had levelled at the Emperor in 1861; for-gotten the scares roused by France's rearmament. Forgot-ten, also, her pro-Prussian sympathy before the outbreak of war, and her fears for the safety of Alice and 'Vicky', and their families. Also overlooked was the Emperor's *affaire* with the Comtesse Louise de Mercy-Argenteau, who had visited him in his captivity at Wilhelmshöhe.

She saw only a tragic ruler who had lost his country, a little man suffering from an incurable disease from which he was shortly to die, a man whose charming courtesy had captivated her in 1855, and whose spell remained potent. So it was that she asked him to Buckingham Palace on the day of thanksgiving for the recovery of the Prince of Wales.

Louis Napoleon, the Prince Imperial, was the only son of Napoleon III and Eugénie. He had been born in 1856, and was just over a year older than Princess Beatrice. He had met a number of the British Royal Family in the years before the Franco-Prussian War. In 1865, Prince Arthur visited the Tuileries and was met by the Prince Imperial, who introduced him to the Emperor and Empress. The young French Prince was described by Colonel Elphinstone, Arthur's Governor, as: '. . . pale, delicate face, intelligent and sweet, very shy, evidently too much by himself'. Two years later, another visit was paid, and comment made on the Prince Imperial's nice approach and perfect manners. In 1868 the Queen and Princess Beatrice made a short stop in Paris on their way to Switzerland.

The fall of France and the fate of his father and mother had a deep effect on Louis Napoleon. He studied hard at Chislehurst, and, after a short period at King's College, London, became a cadet at the Royal Military Academy, Woolwich, to the Emperor's great delight. All the hopes of Napoleon and Eugénie were now centred on their son.

Despite a recuperating holiday in the Isle of Wight in the later summer of 1872, Napoleon's days were running out, and by January he was dead.

The Queen was waiting at Windsor for the bulletins of his progress and, when the final message arrived, she rushed off a letter to Eugénie, sending it by hand to

Chislehurst. She also telegraphed the news to Empress Augusta and Crown Princess Frederick, and was much pleased when she received kind replies from the two wives of Napoleon's enemies. She passed them on to the Prince Imperial.

It was the Queen's first wish that the Prince of Wales should attend the Emperor's funeral, but his open and strongly asserted backing of the French cause throughout the war meant that his presence might be interpreted by Prussia as provocative. There was danger, too, of an Imperialist demonstration. The British Royal Family each sent their representatives, and it was left to the Queen to show the depth of her feelings. She provided the magnificent sarcophagus in which the Emperor's body was to lie, and she and Princess Beatrice went to Camden Place to watch the start of the Emperor's funeral procession.

A month later, on a foggy, raw morning in February, the Queen and Princess Beatrice went to Chislehurst and there, in the Roman Catholic Chapel of St. Mary, they knelt before the coffin of Napoleon III and placed wreaths on the black velvet pall. They drove on to Camden Place, where the Prince Imperial was waiting to greet them at the door. While Empress Eugénie poured out her sorrow to Queen Victoria in the privacy of her boudoir, Louis Napoleon talked with Beatrice.

It is readily understandable that the ex-Empress should cherish the hope that her son would one day marry Princess Beatrice. Highly emotional, she had lost her country, her husband, her possessions, and been close to death—all within three years. In her travail she had been helped, comforted and supported by the Queen and her youngest daughter. She was never to forget. Left alone with her son, he became the whole essence of her being, and her dearest wish was that he should marry the quiet, understanding girl who was always at the Queen's side.

Louis Napoleon was growing into a studious and popular young man, and a most dutiful son. Underneath, the fire of ambition had begun to burn, but he had kept it well in check. He was making a favourable impression with the right people, notably the Duke of Cambridge, the Commander-in-Chief. Already acquainted with Prince Arthur, he soon came on more intimate terms with Prince Leopold, the two being near in age.

The politicians were content that the Prince Imperial should enjoy the friendship of the Royal Family and the favour of military leaders, as long as he kept well clear of any Bonapartist activities. While there was a chance of a Napoleon returning to rule France, even the mention of Louis Napoleon marrying Princess Beatrice was political dynamite. It would be an impossible situation—the Queen's eldest daughter married to the probable Emperor of Germany, and her youngest daughter playing a similar rôle in France.

Meanwhile, Princess Beatrice had developed a most effective method of scotching all talk about her matrimonial future. She did not allow any mention of engagements to be made in her hearing, as General Ponsonby learned, to his cost. He was sitting next to the Princess at dinner, and, in the course of conversation, mentioned that someone well known to those at the table was shortly to be married. Silence fell, so thick with disapproval that one could almost feel it. Later, he received a message that the question of marriage must never be mentioned again in Princess Beatrice's presence.

Not for her the rose-red flush of 'Vicky', the sentimental glances of Alice, or Louise's threat of entering a sisterhood. The shy Princess had her own way of stopping rumours, and this suited her mother.

The affection that the Queen and Princess Beatrice held for the Empress Eugénie and her son was never hidden, but rumour waited in vain for signs of an engagement. The Prince continued his quiet, uneventful life, well-behaved and giving no cause for alarm—until he produced the bombshell that he was determined to go to South Africa, where the Zulu War had broken out.

He laid his plans carefully. Before speaking to his mother, he obtained permission from the Duke of Cambridge to go out with the troops in the capacity of spectator and observer, attached to the staff of Lord Chelmsford. The Queen bid him to come and see her before he left. So it was that Princess Beatrice saw Louis Napoleon for the last time. Three months later, on 1st June 1879, his body, mutilated and unrecognisable, pierced by eighteen *assegais*, lay alone by the banks of the Ityatosi River.

At twenty minutes to eleven, on the evening of the 19th June, the Queen was writing in her room at Balmoral when Beatrice, in a state of deep upset, ran in with a telegram in her hand, crying, 'Oh! the Prince Imperial is killed!'

Her mother put her hands to her head and cried out, 'No, no! it cannot, cannot be true! It can't be!' Beatrice collapsed into sobs and handed over the telegram which gave preliminary details of the tragedy. Dawn was breaking over Deeside before they went to bed.

The Queen decided to end her visit immediately and return to Windsor. The next day, after a melancholy lunch taken with Beatrice in the Prince Consort's room, they drove to the station, crossing the new bridge over the Tay.[1] At every station they bought newspapers to see if there were more details of the Prince's death.

On her return to Windsor the Queen travelled to Camden Place to try to console the Empress. And on the 11th July the body of the Prince Imperial arrived at Woolwich, and was met by the Prince of Wales.

[1] In December of that year the bridge collapsed, carrying with it a train and its passengers.

The Queen and Princess Beatrice were at Camden Place for the funeral, which took place the following day. On arrival they knelt before the coffin in the Chapelle Ardente, placed their wreaths upon it, and prayed. Then, from a secluded spot, they watched the funeral procession form up.

Of the eight pall bearers, four were sons of the Queen. The coffin, draped in the flags of Britain and France, was placed on a gun carriage. The Prince Imperial's horse, 'caparisoned in black and gold', was led to its position behind the coffin. The band began its soft music and the procession wound its way across the Common towards the church.

The Queen went back into the house to see the Empress Eugénie. She and Princess Beatrice were shown into a room so dark that they could not see where she sat. The Empress asked faintly if Beatrice was there, and kissed her.

A suggestion was made, and backed by the Queen, that a statue of the Prince Imperial should be placed in Westminster Abbey. A Memorial Committee was formed, on which the Prince of Wales and Prince Leopold sat. The plan led to much controversy, and at length a compromise was reached with the decision that a recumbent statue should be erected in St. George's Chapel, Windsor.

In the autumn, the Empress visited Scotland, staying at Abergeldie. In quiet drives with the Queen and her daughter she recovered to a certain measure from the shock of her son's death, and even laughed at the sight of her French maids trying on kilts which they had borrowed. But she could never forget, and next spring set sail for Zululand. Throughout the night of the first anniversary of the Prince Imperial's death she sat in lonely vigil at the spot by the Ityatosi River where the *assegais* had struck him down. She knelt long by a marble cross which had already been set up there by Queen Victoria.

Travelling eight hundred miles, over rough country in a four-horse carriage, to pay that tribute, she wrote: 'I am left alone, the sole remnant of a shipwreck; which proves how vain are the grandeurs of this world. . . . I cannot even die; and God, in his infinite mercy, will give me a hundred years of life. . . .' It was an almost accurate prophecy, for she was in her ninety-fifth year when she died.

She was not to be alone. Always she would have the friendship and support of the quiet girl who had had such a deep affection for her son. She was to be godmother to Princess Beatrice's daughter, and to see that godchild become Queen of Spain.

On 13th April 1878 Queen Victoria danced a waltz— her first for eighteen years. She was celebrating. Tomorrow, 'Benjamina' would be twenty-one, and Arthur was in love. She was happy, because her two favourite children were with her at Osborne. The Marine Band played during dinner, and afterwards there was an impromptu dance in the drawing-room, members of the Household joining in. Prince Arthur, an excellent waltzer, partnered his mother who, rather to her surprise, found that she could do it as well as ever.

Next morning, at eight o'clock, the band played birthday music beneath Princess Beatrice's window. Smiling, she came out to acknowledge the tribute.

That day the Queen wrote in her Journal:

'. . . And how many prayers and thanks went up to our Heavenly Father for this darling child, whose birth was such a joy to us, and who is my blessing and comfort, whom God will, I know, keep near me and preserve! I could but feel my heart full, in thinking the little Baby (whom) my darling one loved so much, to whom he almost gave his last smile, had grown up to girlhood and to be of age, and *he* (should) never have been there, to guide and protect her!'

With Princess Beatrice's birthday, all of Queen Victoria's nine children had reached adulthood. To the public she was better known than any other of her brothers and sisters, particularly those who spent much of their time abroad. She had had a boat named after her, and a wing of the London Hospital. She was always with her mother at the opening of Parliament, a duty which the Queen willingly undertook while Disraeli was Prime Minister. The old ceremonial was back, the Princesses sitting on the Woolsack, facing the Throne, a procedure which was to continue throughout Queen Victoria's reign.[1]

Prince Arthur was sharing the limelight with Princess Beatrice at this time because of his engagement to Princess Louise Marguerite of Prussia. The Duke of Connaught was twenty-eight, and his mother's efforts to find him a bride had relaxed somewhat. His request for permission to marry was a surprise to her, and not altogether a pleasant one, for she did not like Prussians. But reports of Louise were good, and the Crown Princess wrote that she could not think of a sister-in-law whom she would like better, and she was sure that the two would make each other supremely happy.

Prince Arthur had accompanied the Prince of Wales to Berlin in February for a double wedding. The Crown Princess's daughter, Charlotte, was marrying Prince Bernard of Saxe-Meiningen, and the eldest daughter of Prince Frederick Charles of Prussia was marrying the heir to the Grand Duke of Oldenburg. Princess Charlotte was thus the first of Queen Victoria's grandchildren to marry.

In all the excitement of the two weddings Prince Arthur had become firm friends with Prince Charles Frederick's

[1] It was changed for the first Parliament of Edward VII, the royal ladies taking their places on each side of the Cloth of State.

youngest daughter, Louise, without anyone, even his sister, noticing. Thereafter he spent as much time as he could in Berlin, the pleasure of being near Louise outweighing the discomforts of a Prussian life.

The engagement period was long, as Princess Alice, Grand Duchess of Hesse, died on 14th December 1878, and the marriage had to be postponed.

Sad beyond the measure of words was the death of 'dear, sweet' Alice. She was only thirty-five. The kiss of a child suffering from diphtheria ended her life. And she died on the anniversary of the day on which she had seen her father die, and also that of the turning-point in the near fatal illness of the Prince of Wales.

The death of Princess Alice posed an immediate problem, the future of her children. Since 'Fritty' and Baby May were dead, these numbered five. Victoria was aged sixteen, Elizabeth (Ella) fifteen, Irene thirteen, Ernest (Ernie) eleven, and Alix (Alicky) seven.

The Queen had never taken the claims of the Grand Duchy of Hesse very seriously. She had endeavoured to make Louis and Alice live with her in England after their marriage, pooh-poohing the need for their presence in Darmstadt, and pointing out that they had not even a suitable house there. Somewhat annoyed by her failure in this direction, she had next suggested that her grandchild, Victoria, should live with her, and it had needed tact on the part of Princess Alice to evade the demand. She pointed out that her mother had now so many grandchildren that they could take turn and turn about in visiting her. Thus, she need never be without one.

The Queen therefore saw the problem of the upbringing of Alice's children as one belonging peculiarly to her, though in fact it was the concern of the Grand Duke.

One of the solutions which the Queen thought up, and

which soon became common talk in Darmstadt, was that Beatrice should become the step-mother of Princess Alice's children. Such a course would entail pecuniary sacrifice on the part of the Queen, but this she was prepared to suffer to achieve her aim.

Princess Beatrice was now approaching her twenty-second birthday. She was sensible, even-tempered, and of an age when she should be married. She was accustomed to dealing with children, being an aunt to so many. Previous marriage plans had gone astray, but here was an ideal chance to marry a prince well known to them, of pleasant disposition, though not over-strong in character. It went as a matter of course that, should a marriage take place, Princess Beatrice and the children would spend much of their time with her.

There was only one obstacle to the plan which the Queen had in mind (excepting the feelings of the couple involved) and that was the illegality of such a marriage. The sister of a dead wife could not marry the latter's husband.

To the Queen this rule seemed absurd, and she was backed by the Prince of Wales. Prince Albert had believed that it was quite in order for such marriages to take place, and that was enough for her. The point was settled, and anyone who went against her was plainly doing so out of spite or sheer stupidity.

The matter came up again very shortly after the death of Princess Alice. On 7th May 1879 the Queen wrote in her Journal.

'Saw Lord Beaconsfield at 1. Talked of the loss of the Bill, permitting the marriage with a sister-in-law, in favour of which Bertie presented a petition, and which we are most anxious should pass. It has passed the Commons but is thrown out in the Lords, the Bishops being so much against it. Lord Beaconsfield is in favour of it, but the whole Cabinet against it!! Incredible!...'[1]

With the Prince Imperial dead, and union with Louis of Hesse forbidden by law, Princess Beatrice continued her even way by the side of her mother.

Great excitement, meanwhile, prevailed over the forthcoming Connaught wedding, now arranged for 13th March 1879. The Duke had no foreboding about the date, saying cheerfully that any day that one married Louise of Prussia could not fail to be lucky.

This was to be a splendid occasion, with no touch of gloom to dim the gilt, but the Court was somewhat out of touch with really splendid occasions, and a number of queries arose, particularly as to the dress of the ladies. Lady Churchill wanted to know if the ladies should wear trains. If so, and she were to hold up Princess Beatrice's train, who would hold up hers?

There were twenty-six Royalties at the dinner that the Queen gave at Windsor on the eve of the wedding. She noticed that Arthur looked tired and worried and gave instruction that he 'must be looked after and *dosed* for he is yellow and green'.

It was a brilliant day, and everyone was happy as Arthur of Connaught was married to his 'Louischen'. As they drove away at the start of their honeymoon the young man who was to become George V threw an old slipper at the carriage. It was cleverly caught by the Duke, who tossed it back with the remark that he hoped his nephew could bat better than he bowled.

A few days later the Queen and Princess Beatrice left for a month's holiday in Italy, staying at Baveno, on Lake

[1] It was not until 1896 that the Bill was passed, being sponsored by the Prince of Wales. Even then the Archbishop of Canterbury was of the opinion that it would never have become law had not the Prince of Wales rounded up a number of peers who rarely attended the House on other occasions.

Maggiore, where they were visited by King Humbert and Queen Margherita. It was the first time that either the Queen or her daughter had entered the country, and they were both entranced by the scenery.

Soon after their return to England a telegram arrived announcing that the Crown Princess's daughter, Charlotte, had had a baby. That made Queen Victoria a great-grandmother at sixty, and Princess Beatrice a great-aunt at twenty-two.

Princess Beatrice now set about the task of designing a Birthday Book, the first of three books with which she was to be associated. This volume consisted of a framed page for each day of the year, and an index sufficiently large to cope with the natal anniversaries of an army corps of friends. Each month was introduced by a poem, encircled by a wreath of foliage and flowers typical of the season.[1]

On 1st March of that year Lord Beaconsfield dined at Windsor for the last time with the Queen and Princess Beatrice. Later in the month he was taken seriously ill, and realised that he was dying. From Osborne and Windsor came frequent letters and supplies of spring flowers, but the old statesman was no longer able to receive royal visitors. He died on 19th April and the Queen sent a wreath of primroses to his funeral.

The Queen and Princess Beatrice drove from Windsor to Hughenden on 30th April. They went into the vault where the coffin lay and the Queen placed upon it a wreath of white camellias. Later they had tea in his library, and once again they seemed to hear his eager, impassioned voice.

Years of war followed, with British forces engaged both in the Transvaal and Egypt, and the Queen sadly missed the advice of her old friend. There were many reviews,

[1] The book, published in 1881, had a large sale, and the proceeds were sent to the Belgrave Hospital for Children.

inspections and parades to be attended by Princess Beatrice, and some personal anxiety, as the Duke of Connaught was in command of the Guards Brigade in Egypt.

On the afternoon of 2nd March 1882, Roderick Maclean fired a revolver at the Queen and Princess Beatrice as they drove from Windsor station to the Castle. The Queen thought the explosion was the noise of an engine on the line, but Princess Beatrice saw it all. She saw Maclean take aim and fire, and she never said a word.

There were six rounds in the revolver, and a photographer wrenched it from Maclean's hand before the second could be fired. Then the Eton boys rushed up, the two leaders, armed with umbrellas, beating Maclean to the ground. Police officers rescued him from further damage.

On arrival at the Castle the Queen and Princess Beatrice quietly had tea together, whilst telegrams were despatched to members of the family to say that they were safe. The Prince of Wales, at the theatre that night, passed on the news to an audience who received it with wild applause.

The Queen, seated at her desk at Windsor, was entering in her Journal a description of the day. She wrote: 'Nothing can exceed dearest Beatrice's courage and calmness, for she saw the whole thing. . . .'

The following day, mother and daughter walked together to the Mausoleum, and there, kneeling by the Prince Consort's tomb, thanked God for their escape.

It was discovered that Maclean had previously spent periods in lunatic asylums, and it was ordered that he should be detained at the Crown's discretion.

Before the hubbub had died down, the Queen and Princess Beatrice left for a holiday on the Riviera, staying at Mentone, in a villa overlooking the sea. It was the first of a series of journeys that became a ritual.

It was a wonderful holiday for both mother and

daughter. They were able to roam the garden in privacy, and there were endless views to sketch.

The Fleet was visiting the ports of southern France at the time and Princess Beatrice was received with full naval honours on board the *Inflexible*. She also 'borrowed' a gunboat to take her shopping in Nice.

The shopping expeditions, the drives into the hills behind, the flowers, the sunshine, the sea below, the gaiety and the welcome, all combined to help Princess Beatrice to fall in love with this coast, part of the homeland of the Prince Imperial. Before she returned to England she had passed her twenty-fifth birthday, and a military band played in her honour. France was never to forget Prince Beatrice's birthday.

The autumn visit to Balmoral that year had had its moments of worry for the Queen and Princess Beatrice, for the Duke of Connaught was fighting in Egypt, and both dreaded the arrival of a telegram such as had come four years before, telling them of the death of the Prince Imperial.

Just before lunch on 12th September, Brown brought another telegram to Queen Victoria. 'A great victory; Duke safe and well.' The battle of Tel-el-Kebir was won.

She hurried to Princess Beatrice's room, where the Duchess of Connaught was sitting with her sister-in-law. Thereafter Balmoral went gay. In the afternoon, the Duke and Duchess of Albany[1] arrived for their first visit together to Deeside and the Queen and Princess Beatrice drove to Ballater station to meet them. The four drove back to the Castle and were met by all the members of the Household, the servants and the tenants of three estates. A table bearing whisky and glasses had been laid out, and toasts were drunk to the Duke of Connaught, his Duchess,

[1] The marriage of Prince Leopold, Duke of Albany to Princess Helen of Waldeck–Pyrmont had taken place on 27th April, 1882.

Prince Henry of Battenburg, October 1874 (*from the album of the Empress Frederick at Friedrichshof*)

The Royal Family, 1861. *Left to right—back row:* Princess Helen
Princess Alice. *Front row:* the Princess Royal, Prin

e Prince of Wales, the Prince Consort, Queen Victoria, Prince Alfred,
:opold, Princess Beatrice, Princess Louise, Prince Arthur

Left: Prince Louis Napoleon (Prince Imperial), 1879

Below: Princess Beatrice, the Duchess of Connaught and the Grand Duke of Hesse at Balmoral, 1882

his baby daughter, and the troops in Egypt, Brown being the chief proposer.

A bonfire was lit on the top of Craig Gowan, and after dinner Princess Beatrice and the Duchess of Connaught led a party of jubilant tenants and servants up to the top of the hill where the fire blazed, pipers climbing with them.

The Queen, with Prince Leopold and his wife, Princess Helen, sat by the window of Princess Beatrice's room, watching the distant figures silhouetted against the flames, listening to the cheering and the faint music of the pipes. John Brown stayed with her, as of course he always did.

But in 1883 he died, and there was another hole in the heart of the Queen, and a very familiar presence lost to Princess Beatrice.

Some of Queen Victoria's children are said to have actively disliked John Brown. Certainly this was the case with the Prince of Wales, and not without reason. The story goes that on the death of his mother he smashed with his own hands a collection of plaster statuettes of the gillie that were unearthed at Osborne. The Duke of Edinburgh also had cause to complain of Brown's behaviour on occasion.

But to Princess Beatrice he was the ever-present faithful servant. To her, and the Ladies who were constantly in attendance on the Queen, no other position could have been tolerated. In addition, his services must have been of considerable help and relief to them.

The loyalty which Brown held for Princess Beatrice is glimpsed on the occasion of the building of the cairn to commemorate the Duke of Connaught's marriage, in 1879. After all the toasts had been given, it was Brown who stood up and said that the health of Princess Beatrice should be drunk.

Like her mother, she had come to rely on Brown. It was he who pinned Arthur O'Connor to the ground

7

when he pointed a pistol at the Queen in 1872. Ten years later Brown was first at the door when Maclean fired at the royal carriage. And it was Brown who always took charge if the way was lost on Highland expeditions, or the carriage was involved in an accident. At moments of domestic crisis, such as when the Queen's luggage was lost and she was staging a royal tantrum at the thought of retiring without her night clothes, Brown settled matters by bluntly telling her that she must make the best of things and go to bed without them. If crowds became too pressing, or reporters too inquiring, it was Brown who kept them off.

As a small girl, Princess Beatrice had assimilated from her mother the fact that one was safe if Brown was there. If he was on the box, there was no need to worry. When the Queen went for a drive, mention had to be made that he was there. Brown was almost part of the scenery to Princess Beatrice.

In the Queen's own words, his presence reassured her. While driving through crowds, he would sit on the rumble because, as the Queen, sitting with Beatrice, commented, 'it is safer under such circumstances to have a person close behind you'.

Apart from his capabilities as a watch-dog, Brown was not always an asset on the trips which he made abroad with the Queen and Princess Beatrice. Restricted in his travels until the time that he became personal attendant to the Queen, he was insular in his outlook, had little time for foreigners, and mistrusted them. He was often rude. He felt uneasy at not being able to understand what was said by those around him, and at losing some of the control that he was able to exercise at home.

The Queen, thinking that she would die before Brown, had built him a house at Craig an Gowan, on Deeside. It was completed and furnished, and into it went all the gifts which he had received from the Queen and the Royal

Family. All the silver had been given to him, and the walls were covered with signed photographs and pictures presented to him by royalties. Outstanding among the pictures were engravings, bearing messages of warm friendship, and signed 'Alice'.

Brown never lived in this house, for he caught a chill, and died from erysipelas on the 27th March.

The Queen was at Windsor, and ten days previously had had a fall which left her very lame. She slipped on the steps and it was Brown who helped her up and half carried her to her room. It was to be his last act of service.

The coffin containing Brown's body was laid on the bed of his room in the Clarence Tower at Windsor, where the funeral service was held. Slowly, leaning on the arm of Princess Beatrice, the Queen made her way there to take part in the prayers. On 2nd April, the coffin was placed upon a bier, at the start of its long journey to Scotland.

General Ponsonby was at Balmoral and there met the Queen returning from a visit to Crathie kirkyard. He wrote afterwards:

'Wreaths from Princesses, Empresses and Ladies-in-Waiting are lying on Brown's grave. He was the only person who could fight and make the Queen do what she did not wish. He did not always succeed nor was his advice always the best. But I believe he was honest, and with all his want of education, his roughness, his prejudices and other faults he was undoubtedly a most excellent servant to her.'

The Queen ordered a life-size statue of her servant to be executed by Boehm, and this was put up at Balmoral, by the small wooden building where she had worked at her despatch boxes, guarded by her faithful gillie. Thereafter, on her arrival at Balmoral, her first visit was always to this statue, and she laid flowers on the pedestal and on

his grave. She dedicated to his memory her second Highland diary, upon which she worked throughout the re-
mainder of 1883, and was hardly restrained from writing
a personal memoir of him.

The death of John Brown not only ended a chapter in
the life of Princess Beatrice—it brought upon her more
work and responsibility. So accustomed had the Queen
become to the constant attention and screen of Brown, that
she expected its continuance. Once more, the burden fell
largely upon the shoulders of her youngest daughter.

4

The Battenbergs

TWINGES of rheumatism began to plague Princess Beatrice early in her life, and on a holiday in Scotland when she was only twenty, she was suffering very severely. As with the years the pains became increasingly troublesome, it was decided in the summer of 1883, on medical advice, that the Princess should take a cure at Aix-les-Bains.

The Queen, still feeling the loss of Brown, was deeply upset at the absence of her daughter even for the three weeks that the cure demanded. Very seldom had they been parted for more than a few days, and, in a letter to Empress Augusta, she showed clearly how sincerely she missed the Princess:

'Beatrice's absence is very grievous and unpleasant, and increases my depression and the horrible ever-growing feeling of emptiness and bereavement, which nothing can ever really remove. But recently she had been suffering a great deal from neuritis, especially in the hand and right arm, which was a great inconvenience to her in writing, and especially in playing the piano, and before that she had had it in the knee and foot too. So we thought it would be advisable to try a thorough cure for three weeks.'

Thus began the royal association with Aix-les-Bains. Princess Beatrice returned with her rheumatism so much improved by the cure and so delighted with the beauty of the town and its surroundings that the Queen was eager to accompany her on a visit the following year. Thereafter the visits became part of routine.

The years 1883–1884 were both difficult and sad for the Queen. Princess Beatrice was handicapped by rheumatism, she herself was still very lame, the result of her accident at Windsor, and there was no John Brown to administer to her.

The Queen and Princess Beatrice, who shared her mother's strong and direct views on Imperial matters, were also worried and indignant over the Government's attitude to affairs in the Sudan, where the people, under the leadership of the fanatical Mahdi, had risen against Egyptian rule and were threatening the frontier. The Queen urged immediate action to settle the uprising, but little attention was paid to her words. Then a section of the Press joined in on the side of the Queen and at length the Government decided to send General Gordon to negotiate with the rebels.

Despite Gordon's experience and his influence with the natives, the Queen watched his single-handed advance with many misgivings, which proved all too well-founded when the General found himself besieged in Khartoum by the Mahdi's forces.

The Queen expressed her indignation, which was reinforced by public opinion, and in the autumn of 1884 a British army, under the command of Lord Wolseley, left for the Sudan to rescue the hard-pressed General. But it arrived too late, and Gordon's death was the price of the delay.

The Queen's indignation and fury knew no bonds. She wrote to Gordon's sister: 'Some day I hope to see you again, to tell you all I cannot express! My daughter Beatrice, who has felt quite as I do, wishes me to express her deepest sympathy with you.'

Miss Gordon gave to the Queen the Bible which her brother had with him in Khartoum, and later showed her the diary which Gordon had kept, describing the agony of his last days. A marble bust of 'Chinese' Gordon was ordered and placed in the corridor at Windsor.

Another sorrow was the sudden death of Prince Leopold, Duke of Albany, whilst on holiday in the South of France.

In April 1884, three weeks after the death of Prince Leopold, the Queen and Princess Beatrice went to Darmstadt. It needed an event of some importance to draw the Queen out of her retirement during a period of family mourning, but Princess Alice's eldest daughter, Victoria, now grown into a lovely girl of twenty-one, was to be married to Prince Louis of Battenberg. The Queen felt that the motherless bride should have the support of her grandmother and her aunt.

During the preceding six years the Queen and Princess Beatrice had kept in close touch with the Hesse family and in 1880 had visited Darmstadt for the children's confirmation service. Each year from 1879 the Grand Duke had brought his son and daughters to stay at Osborne, Windsor, or Balmoral, his preference being for Balmoral because of the shooting.

The children's English governess, Miss Jackson, who had been with them when Princess Alice died, reported monthly to the Queen on the educational and general progress of her charges. In order to keep an even closer eye on her grandchildren and ensure that there should be no mistakes in their upbringing, the Queen sent out another English governess, a Miss Pryde.

Miss Pryde was typical of that wonderful tribe of Victorian governesses, who carried out their lone tasks all over the globe and in their unselfishness became loved and indispensable. Her mother was the widow of an army officer. Left with daughters to educate and very little money, she herself became a governess, and later launched her daughters on the same career. Miss Pryde held the Queen in considerable awe. Every day she had to submit a progress report from Darmstadt, and even the patterns of the girls' frocks had first to be sent for approval.

In the early 1880's Miss Pryde brought her charges on a holiday to Windsor. One evening, while changing her clothes in her bedroom, a loud knock came at the door. Miss Pryde asked who was there, and there came the firm and unmistakable reply of Her Majesty, 'It is I.' Not daring to hesitate, the governess opened the door. The Queen marched in, and looked around her. She saw, sheltering behind the door, the blushing and embarrassed Miss Pryde, wearing only a red flannel petticoat, with nothing below it and nothing above. Queen Victoria took one look, collapsed into an armchair, and burst into fits of laughter. She then produced a beautiful inscribed locket which she had brought the governess as a token of her appreciation.

Princess Victoria's two younger sisters, Ella and Irene, were both of a marriageable age. A few years previously it had been thought that the Queen's eldest grandson, William of Prussia, might wed Ella, but from childhood her heart had been given to her Russian cousin, the Grand Duke Serge. She ignored William's advances, and in 1881 he married Princess Augusta Victoria of Augustenberg. In his way he had loved Ella, and never forgot her, as he was to show thirty years later, when he tried, without success, to save her from the horrors of the Russian Revolution.

Of Princess Alice's remaining children, Ernest was sixteen and studying at the University at Leipzig, and Alicky was only twelve.

Prince Louis of Battenberg was already well known to the Queen and Princess Beatrice. In fact steps had been taken to see that he did not become too well known. He was the eldest son in the family referred to by the German Emperor as the most handsome in Europe. Bismarck, unimpressed by looks, regarded the family with a sus-

picion akin to that which he had held for the Coburg
dynasty, or for that matter any person or group who
seemed capable of handling the reins of power.

Louis was thirty, an officer in the British Navy, clever,
gay, and with a gift of impersonation that could be
wickedly funny at the expense of his victim. As a young
officer, he had sat between Queen Victoria and Princess
Beatrice at dinner one evening at Osborne. Something
about the undoubtedly attractive young man's manner
suggested to the Princess that he held, at the back of his
mind, ideas that their futures should follow the same
path. It was a plan which she was not inclined to share,
and she put into action her customary method of defence
—silence. Not a word did she speak to the young man
beside her throughout the meal. The upshot was that the
First Lord of the Admiralty received word from the
Queen that Prince Louis was to be kept on foreign
stations, well out of the way.

The Queen was always fond of the Battenberg boys,
from the time that they used to play with Princess Alice's
children at Darmstadt, until her death. She would have
nothing of Prussian and Russian criticism of their mixed
breeding and newly-created title. She knew too much
about the antecedents of other notable European families
to tolerate that.

Queen Victoria had watched the Battenberg story from
its very beginnings. In fact, if two young hearts had
harboured a deeper and more constant emotion, there
might not have been a Battenberg story. In May 1839 the
conversation of the British people had turned on the
finding of a husband for the young Queen. There were
plenty of candidates, and Princes from Prussia, Denmark,
Holland and Belgium arrived at frequent intervals, with
the weakest of excuses and the most obvious of purposes.
The one-time favourite, George of Cambridge, had
proved a non-starter and had taken himself off to the

Mediterranean until the matter was settled. As yet hidden in the field was Albert of Coburg.

Then the Grand Duke Alexander, eldest son of the Tsar of Russia, arrived at Windsor. He had eyes that shone with energy and fun, his manners were perfect, his uniforms resplendent. He partnered the Queen at a ball, went with her to the theatre, and, most telling of all, taught her to dance the Mazurka.

The Coburg supporters became quite worried by her obvious enthusiasm, especially when shortly afterwards she wrote to Uncle Leopold to tell him that he must not consider that she had made any definite promise regarding Albert and that it all depended on whether she liked him more than one likes a brother.

But with such an owner, and a trainer as wily as Stockmar, success was certain, and before the year was over Albert had cantered home the winner.

Grand Duke Alexander found his bride in Darmstadt, a quaint and quiet old town of minor importance in which other Romanoff young men were to seek partners, mostly with tragic results. Despite Russian opposition, he married Princess Marie, daughter of the Grand Duke of Hesse, in 1841.

Princess Marie was delicate. She could not withstand the climate of St. Petersburg, nor could she face up to the enmity that she met at Court. She found herself in a position not dissimilar to that which faced seventeen-year-old Victoria, Princess Royal of England, when she arrived in Berlin in 1858. But 'Vicky' was a fighter, and Marie was not.

To Marie's delight her brother, Prince Alexander, accompanied her to Russia, and was given a commission in the army. He was a gay young man and, the antithesis to his sister, revelled in the grandeur and brilliance of life at St. Petersburg. Flirtatious by nature, he was soon in trouble for attempting to make love to the Grand Duchess

Olga. When he eloped with one of his sister's ladies-in-waiting, he was promptly banished from Russia.

The Polish beauty who so captured Alexander's heart that he was prepared to incur the Tsar's anger was Countess Julia Theresa von Hauke, who was twenty-six years old at the time of the marriage in 1851. Five children were born to them, a daughter, as lovely as her mother, and four sons. The three who were to be most closely connected with Queen Victoria and Princess Beatrice were Louis, the eldest son, born in 1854, Alexander, in 1857, and Henry, in 1858. *Entre nous*, as the family said, Alexander was called 'Sandro' and Henry 'Liko'.

A title which had lapsed for over five hundred years was revived in 1851, and the runaway lady-in-waiting became Countess of Battenberg. Seven years later she and her children were elevated to Princes and Princesses of Battenberg and entitled to call themselves Serene Highnesses.

In 1855 the delicate Princess from Hesse became the Empress Marie Alexandrovna of Russia. Still devoted to her brother Alexander, she bought for him the estate of Heiligenberg at Jugenheim, a few miles to the south of Darmstadt. Here the Battenberg family settled down.

The children of Princess Alice often went to Heiligenberg to play with the Battenbergs. They met the sons of the Empress Marie, and there Serge made Ella his childhood sweetheart. Prince Arthur of Connaught was another young visitor, and Queen Victoria received a favourable report on the Battenberg boys from his Governor.

It was through the efforts of Princess Alice that young Louis Battenberg was able to achieve his ambition of joining the British Navy. He arrived at Gosport in 1868, became a naturalised British subject, did very well in his examinations and reached the rank of Commander by 1885.

The second son, Alexander[1], more easily distinguished by the name of Sandro, was less known to the Queen and Princess Beatrice, although he had paid them a visit. Declared Prince of Bulgaria in 1879, the young ruler of twenty-two had by 1884 already endured a series of troubles and crises. To add to his burden foreign politics were interfering with his private emotions. He had fallen in love with Princess Victoria, daughter of Crown Princess Frederick, and she was deeply in love with him. The Emperor and Empress of Germany, Bismarck and Prince William were dead set against the marriage, Queen Victoria and the Crown Princess being equally determined that it should take place.

The third Battenberg son, Henry, the Queen and Princess Beatrice had not met since he was a boy.

So, journeying towards Darmstadt in April 1884 for the wedding of Victoria of Hesse to Louis of Battenberg, was a collection of royalties with very mixed feelings.

Queen Victoria was thinking of her dead son, Leopold, and of the motherless children whom she was on her way to visit, children whom she had once hoped would be put under the care of Princess Beatrice.

The latter was thinking of the young man whom she had once rebuffed and who was now to marry her niece.

The Empress Augusta of Germany was pondering what she could say to put an end to the romantic ideas of her granddaughter and Sandro. She was also thinking up some hard things to say about Ella, who had not only rejected her grandson William as a selfish, egotistical and impossible suitor, but had also refused point-blank to marry the Hereditary Grand Duke of Baden, all because she thought she was in love with the Grand Duke Serge.

The Crown Princess was spoiling for a fight over the thwarted love of her daughter for Sandro.

The Prince of Wales, on the same journey, was also a

[1] See Appendix B.

worried man. His mother, he knew, was under the impression that the Grand Duke of Hesse had been faithful to the memory of Princess Alice. The Prince of Wales was aware that this was not the case.

For some time past the Grand Duke had been on intimate relations with a Madame Alexandra de Kalomine. She was the divorced wife of a Russian diplomat, and has been described as one of the most beautiful and accomplished women of her time. The children, particularly Princess Ella, liked Madame de Kalomine, and the elder daughters thought it a good thing that there would be someone to look after their father when they had married and left Darmstadt.

When asking Queen Victoria to attend the wedding of his daughter, the Grand Duke should, out of bounden duty, have informed her of his liaison. This he omitted to do, for any of a number of reasons—fear of upsetting his mother-in-law at a time when she was mourning for Prince Leopold, lack of moral courage, or knowledge of the plans which the Queen had held to introduce Princess Beatrice into his family life. And the Prince of Wales knew that there would be a 'scene' of some magnitude when his mother found out the truth.

As the trains bearing the various royal personages trundled across Europe towards Hesse, there was little mental comfort for any of the passengers. Nor was there physical comfort. There was no electric lighting, and no sleeping-cars. Queen Victoria had the power to take her own bed with her, but the others had not. There were no restaurant cars and, although the royalties had lunch brought to them at their seats, those less lucky had to collect whatever snacks were available at the stations where they stopped. Progress was somewhat slowed by the Queen's kindly insistence on a forty-minute halt so that the guard and the crew of the engine could eat in peace.

There were no toilets in the coaches, and the ladies had to notify a member of the Household who asked the railway authorities to arrange that the train should come to a halt at the next station. There it was often discovered that a red carpet had been laid down from the platform edge to the 'ladies', and the Royal passenger had then to endure the embarrassing ordeal of waiting whilst the engine driver carried out the delicate manoeuvre of placing the relevant carriage door in line with the red carpet.

The Grand Duke, with his daughters, Ella and Irene, met the Queen and Princess Beatrice at Darmstadt station, and together they drove to the New Palace. Despite his secret, the Grand Duke was in high spirits. Rarely had the town sheltered so important a collection of royal personages. The streets were gay, the Hessians in holiday mood, and there was a heavy and splendid pre-marriage programme. The Queen, however, did not feel like festivities and kept herself in seclusion. Deep in her sad thoughts, she did not notice the troubled looks on the faces of other guests as they pondered on the Kalomine situation, but she noted the immediate and mutual attraction that had sprung up between Princess Beatrice and Prince Henry of Battenberg.

This officer of the *Gardes du Corps* was attracting considerable attention in Darmstadt. He was good-looking and well-built and had the charm and perfect good manners native to this family. Without, perhaps, the intelligence of his gifted brother, he succeeded where Louis had failed. Now there was no defence by silence from Princess Beatrice.

Talk among the guests was centred on the possibility of a romance between these two. Then the Grand Duke of Hesse made the announcement that the Grand Duke Serge was engaged to his daughter, Princess Elizabeth, and interest switched. The wedding was to be in St.

Petersburg, in June. This early date Serge had insisted upon. Since his father's assassination three years before, he had become taciturn and embittered. Convinced that he too would be assassinated, he was determined not to be robbed of his days with Ella. Correct as his fear turned out to be, little can he have guessed of the end towards which he was leading his childhood sweetheart.

The announcement angered the Empress of Germany, who saw in it a slight to her own family. To increase her ill-temper the romance between her granddaughter Victoria and Sandro Battenberg stayed very much alive, and both Queen Victoria and the Crown Princess were adamant in their opinion that the marriage should take place.

The wedding of Princess Victoria of Hesse to Prince Louis of Battenberg took place on 30th April and for a while all the royal relations were able to forget their differences. Not for long, however, for that evening the Grand Duke of Hesse was married in secret to Madame Alexandra de Kalomine. It was three days before the news leaked out but, when it did, the Empress Augusta quickly gathered her entourage around her and stamped out towards Berlin in a flaming temper.

The Crown Princess told the Prince of Wales, and it therefore became his unfortunate duty to tell his mother. The Queen was furious, and to make her son's lot even harder she ordered him straightway to interview this Madame de Kalomine. She also peremptorily ordered the Grand Duke to put an end to the marriage. It was unthinkable that a man who had been married to one of her daughters should ever marry anyone else—or even want to. Madame de Kalomine must sign a paper agreeing that the marriage was null and void. On the point of whether this was legal or no, the Queen had a precedent. Her own father's marriage to Julie de St. Laurent had been annulled, and what had happened before could happen again.

The Prince of Wales went, as he was bid, from the fury
of his mother to the hysterics of Madame de Kalomine.
All his tact was required to cope with the entreaties, the
floods of tears, the threats of suicide, but Queen Victoria
had her way. The marriage was duly annulled, and a son
born of the union was adopted as a brother by the Empress
of Russia.

The Queen allowed no sign of her anger and disappointment to show on her face, nor did she mention
the matter except to those directly concerned. She did
not advance her day of departure, and decided to take
Princess Ella back to England with her for a quiet holiday
and some helpful talks before the marriage with the
Grand Duke Serge.

Poor Darmstadt. Its fortnight of splendour and festivity
had ended in melodrama. Ministers suddenly found themselves called away on urgent business, officials were struck
down with strange illnesses that took them to their rooms.
The very streets lost their gaiety.

Princess Beatrice said her goodbyes to Prince Henry,
and the train steamed out towards Frankfurt. Her thoughts
at least were happy. Fortunate indeed that she could not
peer into the future and know that, as the flowers on her
grave faded and died, the old town that she saw dis-
appearing into the distance would be flattened by Allied
bombs, her sister's homes gutted and the dead and
wounded lie in their thousands in the ruins of the quaint
old streets.

Whilst the Queen and Princesses were in Darmstadt
a fifth, and last, child was born to Prince Alfred and his
wife—the Duke and Duchess of Edinburgh. The Edinburgh family already consisted of Alfred,[1] and three
charming girls, 'Missy',[2] 'Ducky'[3] and 'Sandra'.[4] The

---

[1] Died in 1899.   [2] Marie, Queen of Roumania.
[3] Victoria Melita, Grand Duchess Cyril of Russia.
[4] Alexandra, Princess of Hohenlohe-Langenburg.

latest addition was also a daughter and it was decided to call her Beatrice,[1] after her aunt. 'Baby B' the child was nicknamed, and it stuck to her just as it had to her aunt. Her future, too, was to be tied to Spain.

Princess Ella, having accompanied Princess Beatrice to the christening, hurried off with her father and sisters for her June wedding in St. Petersburg.

The Queen now entered upon one of those strange and enigmatic moods. Having learned from Princess Beatrice of her considered wish to marry Prince Henry of Battenberg, Queen Victoria at once severed verbal relations with her beloved youngest daughter. Week in and week out, month after month, she would not speak to her. Essential information for the day reached the Princess in the form of notes pushed across the breakfast table. It would appear that the Queen even went so far as to cut out references to her daughter in her letters and Journal. In the six months, June to December, 1884, there is but one reference to Princess Beatrice, and that in a postscript to a letter of condolence that the Queen sent to Lady Ampthill on the death of her husband. Suddenly, there was silence.

One can only imagine the misery through which Princess Beatrice passed that summer. It must be remembered that she had never been allowed to be alone in a room with a man, not even a brother. Her romantic experience was, simply, zero. She saw marriage as a natural goal, and one which all her sisters had reached at a much earlier age. When they had found the man whom they wished to marry, Princess Beatrice had been told that love was a wondrous thing and made in Heaven. Now that she had found 'Liko', she was being made to suffer. It must have all seemed most incomprehensible and unfair.

Although many mothers of the period considered it

[1] The Infanta of Spain.

8

their right to take their daughters' lives in their hands, Queen Victoria seldom acted without a reason, selfish though that reason might appear to be. In her attitude to the engagement of Princess Beatrice to Prince Henry of Battenberg, light is thrown on the previous meetings of the Princess with Prince Louis and the Prince Imperial. The night when Princess Beatrice would not speak to Prince Louis of Battenberg at dinner—was it her own wish or had she been prompted by her mother? Could it not have been Queen Victoria who was solely behind his transition to foreign stations, well out of the way? Recalling Disraeli's remark about how obstinate the Queen had been over the Prince Imperial being allowed to go to Africa, could it not also have been that she wanted him out of the way? Certainly she could not have foreseen the tragedy that was to befall him, but certain it was that, in some quarters in France, she was held responsible for his death.

Queen Victoria was determined upon one thing—and that was to retain the services of Princess Beatrice as companion and helper. She had lost her main prop—her husband. She had lost Brown, and she had lost Disraeli. Her sons could not play the rôle while she was Queen. Of her daughters, her eldest was tied up with Prussia and had early shown that she would not do what she was told. Princess Alice had also proved her independence, but in a more tactful way. As the wife of Prince Christian, Princess Helena did not fit the bill. Princess Louise was far removed from the Queen's idea of a dutiful daughter and there were times when Princess Beatrice had to use her power of persuasion to ensure that her sister was asked to the Queen's homes at all. There was left—Princess Beatrice; her mother had no intention of losing her, for there could be no replacement.

It was not that Queen Victoria had finally decided against the marriage of Princess Beatrice to Prince Henry.

The point of the silence was that she could make her own position strong, and only be persuaded out of it if she were allowed to lay down conditions. The main condition was that the home of Princess Beatrice and Prince Henry should be the Queen's home. If she was to talk to her beloved daughter again, those were her terms.

In due season the persuaders arrived, in the persons of the Prince of Wales, Grand Duke Louis of Hesse, and Prince Louis of Battenberg. The Prince of Wales, with his own experiences behind him, thought that his mother's attitude was intolerable. That delightful man, Grand Duke Louis, put the same thing in a different way. Elevated now to being a grandson by marriage, Prince Louis spoke for his brother. Queen Victoria allowed herself to be persuaded—when she had won her terms.

Mother now spoke to daughter again across the breakfast table, and the normal preamble to royal marriages was resumed.

For Christmas, 1884, Prince Henry came to stay at Kent House, Osborne, with his brother Louis and sister-in-law Victoria, who was expecting a baby.[1] As was their custom, the Queen and Princess Beatrice were at Osborne and on 23rd December the Battenbergs were asked over for dinner. In the festive days that followed, Princess Beatrice and Prince Henry were able to see much of one another and on the 29th the Queen wrote in her Journal:

'Received a letter from Liko Battenberg saying that my kind reception of him encouraged him to ask my consent to speaking to Beatrice, for whom, since they met in Darmstadt eight months ago, he had felt the greatest affection! I had known for some time that she had had the same feelings towards him. They seem sincerely attached to each other, of that there can be

[1] Princess Alice, mother of Prince Philip, Duke of Edinburgh.

no doubt. I let Liko know, to come up after tea, and I saw him in dear Albert's room. Then I called the dear child, and gave them my blessing; Lenchen was so delighted that all was satisfactorily settled, and poor Helen,[1] so pleased too, though it must be very trying for her.'

That evening there was a large, and most cheerful dinner party at Osborne. Beatrice was very quiet, her mother noted, but she looked very happy.

[1] Duchess of Albany.

5

Marriage

THE engagement of Princess Beatrice to Prince Henry met with wide, and largely unexpected, criticism. It was the Princess's first experience of being involved in a dispute concerning her actions, and the first time that criticism had been levelled at her. She remained calm and unruffled. Her mother, on the other hand, became very angry indeed.

The engagement now suited the Queen very well. In the first place she was delighted that her 'Benjamina' had found a man with whom she was genuinely in love. In the second, she was relieved beyond measure that 'Liko' was prepared to resign his commission in the Prussian army and make his permanent home with her and Beatrice, so that life could go on much as before.

Criticism of the engagement came from Britain, Russia, Germany, and even France. At home the announcement was received with disappointment, as it had been hoped that Princess Beatrice would follow the lead of her sister Louise and find another Marquis of Lorne. The people had seen their Princess Royal go to Prussia, there to meet the enmity of the Emperor, the Empress and Bismarck, and have her loyalties torn in three wars. They had watched Princess Alice leave for Darmstadt, there to endure the devastation of Hesse by Prussian hordes, and to die at thirty-five. Princess Helena had brought back to England an unknown German princeling, a good man perhaps, but with strong German connections, and as a personality of little interest to the man in the street. Recalling that the sons of the Queen had found their brides in Denmark,

Germany and Russia, people began to ask, what was wrong with the noble lords and ladies of Britain?

It was not an easy question to answer, particularly when bearing in mind the Queen's own words in criticising Continental marriage rules: 'In England . . . if a King chose to marry a peasant girl, she would be Queen just as much as any Princess'. There was also the rooted objection of the British people to paying dowries and annuities, part of which might line German pockets.

The engagement was not well received in Russia for the reason that Prince Henry's brother, Sandro, Prince of Bulgaria, was defying Russian domination and making himself very unpopular in St. Petersburg.[1]

In Paris the news was greeted with ill-natured gossip among the minor royalties and so-called social set who played along the boulevards. It was said that Prince Henry had been for some time 'on the books' of old 'Maman' Lacroix and even she, the best marriage-maker in Europe, had failed to find him a bride. Mme Lacroix had found wealthy wives for a number of impoverished princes and nobles, and was obviously only too pleased to enhance her reputation by coupling her name with that of Prince Henry. But the story that the most handsome son of the 'most handsome family' in Europe should have to seek her aid in finding a bride had its amusing side.

From Berlin came the greatest weight of opposition to the proposed marriage. This deeply hurt Queen Victoria as it involved her friend, the Empress Augusta, and her own son-in-law, Frederick, the Crown Prince.

Immediately after she had seen Prince Henry in Albert's room at Osborne and given her blessing to the engagement, the Queen had sent a telegram containing the news to the Empress. She expected in reply an expression of gladness that Beatrice was so happy and that the Queen would not be deprived of her support and would have a

[1] See Appendix B.

young man whom she liked about the house. Princess Beatrice was her ninth child, and, although two were dead, it would need a series of ghastly tragedies before she even approached the position of one day being Queen. The parentage of Prince Henry was thus of little real importance.

Berlin did not see it in that light. There, breeding was more important than friendship, and love and happiness did not enter into it. The Prussian royal family picked up their guns and sniped at Prince Henry. Even the Crown Prince fired a shot, and that deeply wounded Queen Victoria, who was very fond of 'Fritz'. The Crown Princess raised no objections. Even had she wished to, she could hardly have done so, as her dearest wish was that her own daughter, Victoria, should marry Henry's brother, Sandro.

Sir Sidney Lee summed up the position: '. . . the comparatively low rank of the Battenbergs was held to unfit them for close relations with the Queen'.

'Unamiable' was how the Queen described the reply of the Empress, and the same applied to a letter from 'dear Fritz'. The Crown Prince made the mistake of criticising Prince Henry's 'stock', rather, the Queen commented, as if one were talking about animals. But it gave her an opening, and when Prince William and his wife, 'Dona', joined in the attack, the Queen fired back a volley against their insolence.

Nor was the Empress of Germany spared from castigation, the Queen pointing out that the father of her son-in-law and his brothers and sisters were 'the children of a Fraulein von Geyersberg, a very bad woman, and they had been acknowledged by the whole of Europe as Princes of Baden'. She added the veiled threat that, if one were to look carefully enough, there were black spots to be found in the background of most of the royal families of Europe.

The Queen's last shot was reserved for her eldest grand-son, William of Prussia who, as a child, it will be recalled, had called the British Royal Family a 'pug-nosed lot', had thrown his aunt's muff out of the carriage window on to a Windsor street, and had bitten his uncle Leopold in the leg during a marriage service. She dismissed him as a foolish, undutiful and unfeeling boy.

Against such an attack, the opposition to the marriage petered out. It did not die, but lay dormant, and showed life again years later when the time came for the marriage of Princess Beatrice's daughter. But the inter-*Schloss* chatter could not be silenced and many queries were raised over Queen Victoria's attitude to marriage. Why, it was asked, had she taken into her arms the children of the Countess von Hauke and at the same time demanded the annulment of the wedding of the Grand Duke of Hesse to Madame de Kalomine?

Inconsistent as the Queen may have been in her attitude towards marriage, allowing convenience and affection to guide her decisions, one of the answers in this case was that Madame de Kalomine was a divorced woman and Countess von Hauke was not. The Queen was resolutely opposed to divorce. In Germany different views were held, as was clearly shown (in 1900) by the abrupt ending of the marriage of Princess Marie Louise in a curt letter of annulment from her father-in-law, exercising his mediaeval prerogative as Duke of Anhalt.

The German gossips even went further. They declared that the Queen was engaged in a campaign to ease the unwritten ruling, so that she might herself marry a man of her own choice. Her brother-in-law, Duke Ernest of Coburg, whom the Queen had cut off her visiting list because of his attitude to John Brown, came out with the wild theory that she herself wished to marry a Scotsman.[1]

[1] Here one can only suppose that the Prince Consort's brother was somewhat confused over the Queen's relations with the Fifes. The fifth

Prince Henry returned to Hesse in January, promising to come back in March and escort the Queen and Princess Beatrice to Darmstadt for the confirmation of Ernest, Princess Alice's son, and then go on with them to Aix-les-Bains. But the death of the Grand Duke's mother caused an alteration in plans and the Queen decided to take her holiday at Aix first, and call in at Darmstadt on the way back.

It was the Queen's first real holiday abroad since John Brown's death and, though she missed him, she found that she was now able to see much more and move about more freely. The weather was perfect, the scenery entranced her, and Princess Beatrice was in high spirits and much less troubled by rheumatism. Together they visited Geneva, took long drives to see the places of interest around Aix, and went for steamer trips on the lake.

Although the visit was a private one, and the Queen was travelling as the Countess of Balmoral, the people of Aix and visitors to the town could not let the Princess's birthday pass by unfêted, especially in view of her forthcoming marriage. The warmth of the celebrations must have come as a very pleasant contrast to the bitterness from Germany.

The streets were decorated, the church bells pealed and the night sky was lit by the brilliance of fireworks. A band played in the gardens of the villa in which the royal guests were staying. Flowers and bouquets from officials, societies and visitors streamed into the Princess's room.

Earl of Fife (1814–1879) who married the granddaughter of King William IV and Mrs. Jordan in 1846, was on friendly terms with the Queen. He was one of the few men who could tease her and escape with impunity. His son, Viscount Macduff (1849–1912), later Duke of Fife, was a great favourite of the Queen, and in 1882 she sent him out to Germany to invest Albert, King of Saxony, with the Order of the Garter. 'Macduff' married the Prince of Wales's eldest daughter, Louise (Princess Royal), in 1889.

During an afternoon drive with her mother she was cheered by large crowds all the way.

A week later the Queen and Princess were welcomed to Darmstadt by Prince Henry. There they attended the christening of Prince and Princess Louis of Battenberg's baby daughter.[1] Fittingly, she was named Alice. The stay was short, but it gave Princess Beatrice the opportunity of visiting Heiligenberg, the home of her future parents-in-law.

Prince Henry came once more to England before the wedding, and now took his place for the first time in the tapestry of the Royal Family's life and duties. With Princess Beatrice he visited wounded soldiers back from the Sudan and was beside her at receptions. There were many people whom he had to meet, and much work to be done in acknowledging presents and congratulatory messages. Also there were details of the wedding ceremony to be settled.

This had been arranged for 23rd July, to be held at the little church at Whippingham, in the Isle of Wight. It was believed to be the first instance of a daughter of the Sovereign being married in a parish church.

The limitations of space gave the Queen, Princess Beatrice and Prince Henry an excellent excuse for not sending invitations to those whom, for one reason or another, they did not wish to attend, but it brought a number of other problems. There were a considerable number of relations and chosen friends from abroad who must of necessity stay on the Island, and the available accommodation at Osborne and suitable houses nearby was soon filled. To cope with the overflow, the royal yachts were called in to serve as floating hotels.

Many guests were coming down by train from London for the ceremony, returning that evening, and the problem of seating became difficult. With energy the Lord Cham-

[1] Princess Andrew of Greece.

berlain's Department and Canon Prothero, Rector of Whippingham, set about their task of improvisation and decoration. A passageway, roofed with canvas, was erected from the gate to the entrance of the church, and benches, in tiers, were built up on either side of the path. To avoid the inconvenience, and possible danger, of the existing steps, a wooden floor was laid down from the porch to the chancel.

The decoration of the church was a matter which occupied the particular attention of the Canon. For the great day he was determined that St. Mildred's should look its very best. To be married was not only a daughter of the Queen, but a parishioner and a regular member of his congregation since her childhood days. In this connection he was fortunate to have a co-operative Lord Chamberlain.

The final result proved a triumph for the Canon and the gardeners. Evergreens, lightened by lilies and roses, wreathed the gate. Inside the church lilies and roses also predominated, and the gardeners skilfully erected walls of greenery and colour, and cones of hothouse plants.

The Service was to be taken by the Archbishop of Canterbury, assisted by the Bishop of Winchester, the Dean of Windsor and Canon Prothero. The organist and the choir were to be imported from Windsor, and a pointer to the strained resources of Osborne and Whippingham was that a message had to be sent to the organist that no refreshments would be available for the boys, who would have to be fed somewhere en route.

For the chosen guests, the question of dress was a problem, particularly for the ladies. While they knew full well what they should wear at St. George's Chapel, Windsor, or Westminster Abbey, a royal wedding in a parish church posed unprecedented problems, especially for those who had to make the long journey from London.

Members of the Household were plagued with queries,

but none was prepared to take the risk of giving opinion until the Queen had made up her mind—and this she was slow to do. In the meantime, ladies had to be content with the somewhat vague instruction that '*demi-toilette*' should be worn. At last the Duchess of Buccleuch, Mistress of the Robes, approached the Queen, and thereafter was able to send these rulings to the Lord Chamberlain:

> 'Ladies staying in the Isle of Wight to wear long dresses with *demi-toilette* bodies, cut down on the back, and with sleeves to the elbow. Jewels to be worn on the dress and in the hair as for full dress evening party.
>
> 'Only those ladies who travel down to Osborne for the day are to wear bonnets and smart morning dresses.
>
> 'In case it may be any help to you I will desire my dressmaker, Miss Metcalfe, 111 New Bond Street, to make my "body" at once, so that any one who cares to see it can do so by calling there.'

Thereafter there was a pilgrimage to New Bond Street to see 'the body'.

There were to be ten bridesmaids[1] for Princess Beatrice —all nieces. To one of them it was a particularly important occasion. The bride's godchild, Alix of Hesse ('Alicky'), was allowed to start her summer holidays early so that she might reach the Isle of Wight in time.

On the invitation list, which covered the usual sphere of those holding responsible positions, there was one very obvious omission. The name of Mr. Gladstone did not appear.

'The Grand Old Man', who had known the Royal children since their nursery days, who had been taken to see 'Baby' Beatrice in her nursery in those sad times after

---

[1] Princesses Louise of Wales; Victoria of Wales; Maud of Wales; Marie of Edinburgh; Victoria Melita of Edinburgh; Irene of Hesse; Helena Victoria of Schleswig-Holstein; Alexandra of Edinburgh; Alix of Hesse; Marie Louise of Schleswig-Holstein.

the Prince Consort's death, who had been present when, at last captured, she had had a tooth extracted by Dr. Jenner, and who had so often met her since, was not even asked if he would like to attend her wedding.

Indignant supporters flooded Gladstone with letters asking if, in fact, he had been snubbed. He answered none of them, but he was deeply hurt.[1]

Prince Henry and his family arrived at Osborne on 20th July, followed in the next two days by the important guests who were to stay on the Island. These included, besides the bridegroom's parents and brothers, the Prince and Princess of Wales, the Dukes and Duchesses of Edinburgh and Connaught, the Grand Duke of Hesse, Prince and Princess Christian, Princess Louise and Lord Lorne, the Princesses Louis of Battenberg, Louise of Wales and Irene of Hesse, the Prince and Princess of Leiningen, the Princes Albert Victor, Edward of Saxe Weimar and Philip of Coburg, and the Duke of Cambridge.[2]

The Order of the Garter was conferred upon Prince Henry, the Duke of Connaught and Princess Beatrice being present with the Queen at the Investiture, which was a private one. It was also announced that the Queen had been pleased to confer the dignity of Royal Highness on Prince Henry.

The guests came to an island garlanded with flowers and decorations. Sailing craft of all types speckled the Bay, flags and streamers playing with the breeze. Hotels and clubs were in rivalry to proffer the brightest display and everywhere the letters 'B' and 'H' could be seen

[1] Gladstone's Government had fallen in June, and the Queen did not conceal her elation. She offered him an earldom, which he declined. It was not until some seven years later that Gladstone discovered that the probable cause of the slight originated in the Queen's invitation to Lord Hartington to form a Government in April 1880 and his failure to do so.

[2] No members of the ruling dynasties of Germany were present.

entwined in flowers. Stands were being run up along the bridal route and fields opened as parking places for carriages. The one essential ingredient needed to ensure the success of the day was the continuance of the fine weather, and in this regard Princess Beatrice shared her mother's good fortune. As a lady-in-waiting once said, if the Queen were to visit a town where it had been raining solidly for days, the sun would come out as her train pulled into the station. So it was 'Queen's weather' on the 23rd July 1885.

Princess Beatrice's wedding dress was of white satin, trimmed with orange blossom and lace, the lace overskirt held by bouquets of the blossom entwined with white heather. There was lace, too, on the pointed neck line, and on the sleeves, for the Princess was a lover of, and an expert on, lace. One of her most treasured possessions was a tunic of old *point d'Alençon* which had belonged to Catherine of Aragon.

Knowing her daughter's love of lace, the Queen now bestowed a signal favour upon her. She allowed Princess Beatrice to wear the Honiton lace which she herself had worn on her wedding day forty-five full years away. It was a very precious possession to the Queen, and Princess Beatrice was the only one of her daughters to be given the opportunity to wear it. The Queen's wedding dress had also been of white satin, trimmed with orange blossom. Thus, in the marriage of her best-loved daughter, the Queen was able to recapture for a space the deep emotion of the moment when she saw Prince Albert, beside Queen Adelaide, waiting for her by the altar at the Chapel Royal.

A guest on that occasion, Prince George of Cambridge, may have had some similar reflection as the large procession of carriages left Osborne for Whippingham Church. True there was strange contrast between St. Mildred's and the Chapel of St. James, but there was much in common in both dress and character between the brides of then and now, and a like streak in a Coburg and a Battenberg. But Prince Henry was more strikingly dressed than had been Prince Albert. The Queen insisted upon his wearing the white uniform of the *Gardes du Corps*, which was somewhat overwhelming for a parish church and caused the Princess of Wales to refer to him as 'Beatrice's Lohengrin'.

All the way along the quiet country road carriages were parked in adjoining fields, and the hedge tops showed smiling faces and waving hands. From the crowded stands by the church a great cheer went up as the procession came into sight.

The music broke out, drowning the acclamation, and the four Chamberlains began their reverse steps up the aisle. Slowly, the bride followed them. On her left was the Queen, wearing the new dress which she had ordered for the occasion. On her right was the Prince of Wales, in the uniform of a Field-Marshal. Calmly did the Queen give her daughter away, and watch her kneel beside Prince Henry before the altar. There was no trace of the sadness that had shown on her face at other Royal marriages. This time she knew, in truth, that she was not losing a daughter, but gaining a son.

To an even greater reception than it had received on its outward journey, the procession returned to Osborne. Now followed the important ceremony of signing the Register. To avoid problems of precedence, a list showing the order of signing had been prepared beforehand. In all there were forty-four signatures, the first being that of the Queen, and the last, that of Canon Prothero.

'At 5', the Duke of Cambridge wrote in his diary, 'we saw the young couple drive off for their honeymoon to Lady Cochrane's Villa[1] near Ryde. . . . We all dined

[1] Quarr Abbey, where a modern house had been built on the site of the historic ruin.

in uniform in the two large tents. The Queen was again present and seemed wonderfully cheerful and well. The Gardens were beautifully illuminated and the *Hector* and Royal Yacht, besides being illuminated, gave a very pretty display of fireworks.'

The festivities continued far into the night, the Queen giving a dinner and dance for her tenants and servants, the latter very smart in the new uniforms which had been ordered for the occasion. As the fireworks exploded in the sky and the music of the band surged from the gardens, a mother sat at her desk writing from her heart, of her feelings at the marriage of her youngest daughter:

> ·'A happier-looking couple could seldom be seen kneeling at the altar together. It was very touching. I stood very close to my dear child, who looked very sweet, pure and calm. Though I stood for the ninth time near a child and for the fifth time near a daughter, at the altar, I think I never felt more deeply than I did on this occasion, though full of confidence. When the Blessing had been given, I tenderly embraced my darling "Baby".'

The honeymoon was neither long (two days) nor isolated, Ryde being but a few miles from Osborne. A week after the wedding Prince Henry was at the House of Lords to take the Oath of Allegiance. It was remembered too late that he was not yet a naturalised British subject and a Bill had to be rapidly prepared and passed. Another misunderstanding came over the manner in which the newly-married couple should be addressed. It was eventually decided by the Queen that, when their names were used together, the style should be, 'Their Royal Highnesses Prince and Princess Henry of Battenberg'. The Princess, when alone on official occasions and when addressed by letter, was to be styled 'Princess Beatrice, Princess Henry of Battenberg'.

Princess Christian

The Princess of Battenberg, mother of Prince Henry of Battenberg (*by permission of Her Majesty Queen Victoria Eugenia*)

Prince Alexander of Hesse, father of Prince Henry

Hulton Picture Library

Wedding-day photograph of Prince and Princess Henry of Battenberg

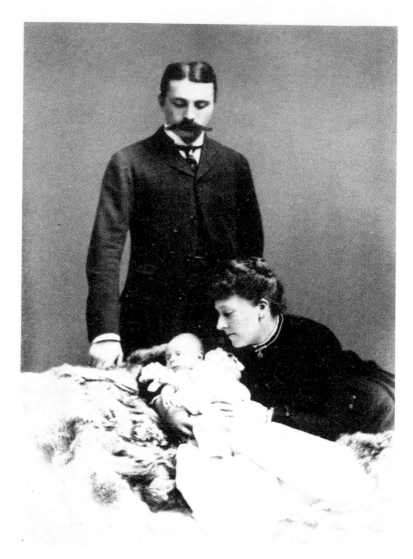

Princess Beatrice and Prince Henry, with Prince Alexander, 1886 (*from the album of the Empress Frederick at Friedrichshof*)

August was spent at Osborne, Prince Henry happy with the sails around him, for he loved the sea. He drove with the Queen and Princess Beatrice to watch the procession of yachts of the Royal Yacht Squadron, the final parade of the 'white wings' which scatter in August.

In September came the customary royal migration to Balmoral, and a jubilant reception was given to Deeside's favourite Princess and her husband. There a new experience awaited Prince Henry—the wearing of the kilt. No dispensation was granted from donning the Highland dress for dinner—John Brown would have sworn from his grave at the mere idea—but some murmured that the unaccustomed garb did not suit the former first lieutenant of the Prussian *Gardes du Corps*.

When Princess Beatrice and Prince Henry reached Windsor Castle in October 1885 married life began for them in earnest. The months intervening since their wedding had seemed like a long honeymoon, although they had not been away from the Queen for more than a few days. From the sun and the sails of the Isle of Wight they had moved to the autumnal beauty of Deeside, and a round of shooting parties, picnics and expeditions in the hills.

Windsor was different. Not only was it the centre of the Queen's life, ruled by etiquette, tradition and memories of her long reign, and of those who had ruled before her, but it was truly a stronghold of the British people.

Prince Henry's position was not an easy one. He was half of Germany, half of Russia, and neither country was popular with the public. His task was to find his place in a Castle that stood for everything British, ruled by a Queen-matriarch whose word was law and whose every whim had to be met. He was married to a woman of twenty-eight, capable and talented, who had a most

9

important job to do in support of her mother and who, since the age of four, had been infused with the duty which she had to undertake.

Marriage brought Prince Henry few of the assets of normal married life—a home of one's home, being master of one's own house, being able to start afresh with personal memories and treasures, or even carving out a career. He had stepped into a routine where every coming and going was pre-ordained, where meals were parades, dress dictated, and the final authority on any problem was the man who had died a quarter of a century before.

From the start Prince Henry tackled the problem with a kindness, tact, understanding and gaiety which enabled him not only to become a great favourite with the Royal Family and Household, but also to lead a most happy married life. Yet those advisers close to the Queen followed the progress of the young Prince with some misgivings. How long, they wondered, would this former officer of the Prussian *Gardes du Corps* be prepared to play a minor rôle, tied to the apron strings of his mother-in-law? How long would he remain content with days of leisure and the ties of family life? He was only twenty-seven, and these Battenbergs were an ambitious tribe. Louis was already proving his forcefulness and capabilities in the British Navy, and Sandro had been a Ruler by the time he was twenty-three.

A suite had been prepared for the Prince and Princess at Windsor. Some of the rooms were in the south turret, and close by the Queen's own sitting-room and private audience chamber. One of them was the schoolroom which had been used by Princess Beatrice and her brothers and sisters, and was now luxuriously furnished and filled with her treasures and photographs, the walls covered with her paintings and sketches of birds and favourite animals and Scottish scenes. All her rooms faced south and overlooked the Long Walk. In the Victoria Tower, above the

Queen's own rooms, space had already been allocated for an expansion of the Battenberg family.

Here, at Windsor, Prince Henry was introduced to the existing way of life. He was shown the twelve-piece Burmese tea service, with raised gold design, which was often used by Princess Beatrice. It was very fragile and he was warned to be careful at tea-time. He learned that the Princess, when at Windsor, always had the same candlestick. It was small and flat with a strange long handle. But he found at least one thing in the Castle to which he could lay part claim, for, in pride of place in the 'China and Glass Room', were the splendid Wedgwood flowerpots which had been especially made for his wedding.

Although Prince Henry did not meet his wife until she was twenty-seven, there was no excuse for not knowing what she looked like at all ages, particularly as a baby. There were pictures of her everywhere. In the Queen's private sitting-room hung a portrait of Beatrice aged ten months, dressed in a white lace frock and lying on a satin cushion. In the dining-room was Lauchert's picture painted in 1863, showing her in half-mourning for her father and holding a miniature of him in her hand.

Prince Henry had to make acquaintance with a host of birds and animals. First in importance came the Princess's cage of canaries, from which she was seldom parted. Next her white doves. Then there was the peacock belonging to Lord Beaconsfield which had been sent from Hughenden soon after his death. A sheltered spot by the Royal Aviary was a favourite place with Princess Beatrice for having tea, watching the while the white Jacobin pigeons, and the ducks splashing on the pool.

One of the first signs that Prince Henry was developing an influence with the Queen was when he managed to persuade her to relax some of her stern regulations about smoking. The Queen hated tobacco. She could tell on receipt of a letter whether the writer had been smoking.

In a room which, to ordinary nostrils, smelled sweet and fresh, she would declare that the hated weed had burned there; and she could not be fooled. Thus it was that prominent and elderly men would squat on the hearth so that the chimney draught would draw away the tell-tale fumes, or endanger their health by leaning out of windows and puffing their pipes out into the cold evening air.

Prince Christian, otherwise representing all that was good, had the obnoxious habit of smoking. In time the Queen came to accept the fact that if men must do it, it must be done well away, in some room hidden and distant, rather as a servants' lavatory might be. A cubby hole was allocated to Prince Christian, where he could indulge his vice in seclusion. To reach this place he had to traverse the servants' quarters and cross an open yard. On the bare boards of the cubby hole a wooden chair and table were placed.

Prince Henry managed to alter that. He wheedled a bigger and more conveniently placed room out of the Queen, and had writing-tables and easy-chairs installed. Although he managed later to have the regulations relaxed at Osborne, there was no easing of the rule at Windsor that smoking was to be confined to the billiard room after eleven at night.

Prince Henry's eldest sister-in-law had been married in the same year as he was born, and the Prince of Wales was seventeen years his senior. It was only natural that the elder children of the Queen should look down with a certain condescension, gained from the superiority of their years, at the man who was a year younger than their 'baby' sister whom he had married.

In middle age Princess Beatrice's brother, Alfred, Duke of Edinburgh, had, in the opinion of certain people, turned into what can only be described as a bore. In the billiard room to which men longing for a smoke were at last allowed to retire, the Duke would either make a frightful noise on the fiddle[1] or, occupying a prominent chair, hold forth about himself for hour after hour, being convinced that his qualities were not sufficiently appreciated. It was more than Prince Henry could stand. For a time he even sacrificed his smoking.

A pleasant and genial man, and full of fun, Prince Henry was also a fine all-round sportsman, being first-rate with a gun, on a horse, on skates or at the tiller. Riding and tennis were two loves that he shared with Princess Beatrice. Soon to be installed at Windsor stables was the weight-carrying bay of over seventeen hands which was to become his favourite hunter, a painting of which was shown at the Land and Water Exhibition. It had for company at Windsor two blacks, 'Gloaming' and 'Midnight', and two bays, 'Noon' and 'Dawn', owned by Princess Beatrice. These she drove either as a team or in pairs. Also there were her two favourite ponies 'Tarff' and 'Wave', which had been bred at Hampton Court.

Prince Henry had already had opportunity at Balmoral of proving to his wife and his mother-in-law that he was an excellent shot. One had to be very good to satisfy the Queen, who had the disconcerting habit of having her gillies report on the accomplishments of the guests who went out stalking. While Prince Henry passed the test with flying colours, his brother Francis,[2] on a subsequent visit, to Balmoral did not. He was not a good shot (the cooks could always recognise the victims of his gun) and on his return one evening, when quizzed by the Queen, began, not unnaturally, to exaggerate both bad luck and

---

[1] The Duke fancied himself as a violinist and was a member of the Stock Exchange Orchestra. Lord Goschen asked Joseph Joachim, head of the Berlin Academy of Music, if the Duke could have made his living as a professional violinist. Joachim replied: 'Yes, on the sands'.

[2] Prince Francis Joseph, who married Anna, daughter of Nicholas I, Prince of Montenegro, in 1897.

range. Slowly it dawned upon him, from the nature of the
questions, that the Queen had been apprised of every
detail of the day's sport. He took refuge in silence.

Christmas of 1885 was spent at Osborne, where
Princess Beatrice and Prince Henry were to be given a fine
suite in the New Wing and with the use of the rooms on
the top floor which had once been nurseries. One reason
for the addition of this new wing was that Osborne could
not stand up to the demands that were made upon it.
When the French or German fleets put in, there simply
was not space to entertain the officers.

It was a gay Christmas, with Princess Beatrice and
Prince Henry celebrating the first anniversary of their
engagement. The Duchess of Albany was there with her
children, and the Connaught family, and throughout the
holiday beech logs burned in the polished steel grate in
the Queen's sitting-room.

Princess Beatrice had one engagement in the Isle of
Wight, a small one, but most important. As was done each
year, she, with her husband, went to Whippingham School
to give presents to the children who studied there. As they
had been married in the parish, the people of Whippingham held, and rightly, that they had a special claim on the
Royal couple.

There now came along other engagements which
presented more difficulty. With marriage the status of
Princess Beatrice had completely changed. Accustomed
to appearing in public beside her mother, she had always
been the shadow, the somewhat shy, unmarried girl who
had played the supporting rôle. Now suddenly she was
the star, and had to take the stage alone, or with the
uncertain support of her husband, who was a 'new boy'
in the school of behaviour at public appearances. On one
of his first trials he was undecided whether it was required
of him to join in the National Anthem, or not. Accordingly
he sang very, very softly indeed, in the hope that, if he

was not supposed to sing, the audience would think he was not doing so, and vice versa.

Princess Beatrice also had her teething troubles. She attended a charity gathering, at which her duty was to make a speech and receive purses. The speech was somewhat of an ordeal, and, having made it, she was so relieved that she forgot the rest of her duty, and sat down. Those who had looked forward to the honour of presenting their purses were somewhat upset that there was no Royal hand waiting to receive them.

Now that she was Princess Henry of Battenberg (outside the Palace), requests came in plenty that she should be the patron of this or that society, or lend her support to campaigns that, however worthy they might be, were beyond the boundaries that marked royal impartiality. In this connection the Princess needed no prompting – she had been beside her mother too long for that.

In view of the forthcoming Jubilee celebrations, the President of the Royal Institute of Painters in Watercolours wrote to the Princess suggesting that it would be fitting that an Order be instituted for bestowal on those who had distinguished themselves in the Arts and Letters, and that the honour should be extended to women. The answer, at Princess Beatrice's request, was made by Sir Henry Ponsonby, who pointed out that such a suggestion could not be considered by the Queen until it had been discussed by the responsible Ministers.

At Windsor, in the winter months, there was skating for Princess Beatrice and her husband. This was a pastime at which Prince Henry excelled, and which he loved. Daily he was to be seen on the shallow, asphalt-lined rink, which Queen Victoria had had made after the occasion when Prince Albert went through ice that covered deep water and was nearly drowned. In fact, having her son-in-law near was becoming more and more like having Albert back.

It was being noted that, more and more often, the Queen was accompanied by 'Prince and Princess Henry of Battenberg'. They were with her on that great day in May of 1886 when the Queen opened the Colonial and Indian Exhibition at South Kensington. The Prince of Wales, who was President and had been busy with the organisation for months past, received his mother and the Royal party in the Colonial Hall. They then passed through the Indian Hall and Bazaar, where an Indian workman who was a hundred years old pressed forward with a carpet so that the Queen might touch it; through a section made up to look like an old London Street; through the Australian Colonies section and into the Albert Hall itself. Here, before a vast crowd, the Queen made her speech and thereafter Madame Albani sang 'Home, Sweet Home' and 'Rule, Britannia'.

Much interest was taken in the 'new' Prince Henry and favourable comment made about the manner in which Princess Beatrice had blossomed out in the past year. Very becoming indeed she looked in her grey velvet and yellow, feathered hat.

It pelted with rain when the Queen, the Duke of Connaught, Princess Beatrice and her husband went to Liverpool for the International Exhibition of Navigation and Commerce. The carriages available would not shut, so there was nothing for it but for the Royal party to put on mackintoshes, raise umbrellas and make the best of things. For nearly a mile they drove through the lines of the Trades Processions, showing the banners of their guilds. Liverpool did not seem to mind the rain, every house being decorated and the cheering tremendous. The Queen commented that she had never heard anything like it, and her head ached with the noise. On the ferry steamer, on which they took a trip among the giant liners lying in the Mersey, a cabin had been fitted out for the Queen and her daughter, and there they were able to get

rid of their dripping coats and sip a much needed cup of
tea.

The summer sports of the Battenbergs were tennis and
sailing. Princess Beatrice, like her brother of Connaught,
was a fine tennis player and there was plenty of opportunity
to practise at Osborne and Windsor, where both grass and
asphalt courts lay below the East Terrace. Sailing was the
love of Prince Henry's life. The *Sheilah* was a fine
schooner, given to him by the Queen, and he and his wife
spent much of their time aboard. In subsequent years he
was to sail as far away as the Mediterranean, though his
favourite waters were those off the West coast of Scotland
and in particular, around the Hebridean island of Iona,
where St. Columba landed in A.D. 563.

When the white wings on the Solent folded in August
1886, the Queen, Princess Beatrice and Prince Henry
set out for Balmoral, stopping on the way to visit the
international exhibition at Edinburgh. Unhappily, this
year their Scottish holiday was to be quite spoiled by the
news from Bulgaria.

The Queen was alone on the afternoon of 22nd August
when the telegram saying that Sandro[1] had been kidnapped reached the Castle. Princess Beatrice, who was
expecting her first baby in November, was resting in her
room. Prince Henry had driven over to Birkhall with his
four-in-hand. The Queen waited for confirmation from
a second telegram before she disturbed her daughter.
They were talking about it and what might be the conse-
quences both for Sandro and Princess Victoria, when
Prince Henry returned. He was completely shattered,
asking to be excused dinner, and took it alone with his
wife in her room.

The anxieties, the insults and the exasperation that
followed in the next few weeks might well have upset

[1] See Appendix B.

many a woman about to become a mother, but fortunately Princess Beatrice was very even-tempered, and proved a great support to her husband. Sandro referred to by the Russians as the 'Prisoner' and condescendingly released by orders from St. Petersburg! He and his brother Francis (who had been kidnapped with him) without even a servant to look after them, and being ordered to return by rail! Surely, the Queen thought, these monstrous happenings were without parallel in modern history! Her sleep was being affected by her anxiety.

All through those autumn months the Queen fought to save the fortunes and good name of the deposed ruler of Bulgaria, but she could not get to grips with those who were pulling the strings in Russia and Germany, nor force the politicians and diplomats to fight as she would have liked them to fight. It was not only because she liked Sandro and thought him a good ruler, but also because she saw in the chain of events an insult to her own daughter and the husband she loved.

Letter after letter she wrote but on Thursday, 25th November, she had to apologise to Lord Salisbury for being tardy in replying to a message from him. She had intended writing before, 'but the *event* of Tuesday morning so absorbed her, and the letters and telegrams she has received and written have been so overwhelming, that she could not do so . . .'.

The event referred to was the birth of a son to Princess Beatrice.

6
'Gangan'

PRINCESS BEATRICE and Prince Henry had four children, born to them in the five years 1886–1891. The four, in order of age, were Alexander, known as 'Drino'; Victoria Eugénie, or 'Ena'; Leopold; and Maurice.

Halcyon days were these for the Queen and Princess Beatrice, and so were they to remain until Prince Alexander was nine. Irreverently known in certain quarters as the 'Battenberg kids', the little tribe, backed by Prince Henry, certainly brought to their mother a happiness far beyond anything she had as yet experienced. And not only to their mother, for the Queen was now happier and more light-hearted than at any time in her widowhood. In her heart, perhaps, she was also more at peace, for her years with Prince Albert had been overcharged with emotion and challenge, and she had never been as much at ease with her own children as she now was with her grandchildren.

Being so much with the Queen, Princess Beatrice's happiness was affected by the state of mind of her mother. There were other reasons, beyond family ones, for the Queen to be more contented. Having overcome her aversion to appearing in public, the enthusiastic reception accorded to her on her visits to various parts of the country was ample proof of the hold that she had on the hearts of the people of Britain. The pendulum had swung fast, for but a very few years before Republicanism had been accounted a danger to the firm standing of Royalty.

The Queen's popularity was increased by the harvest of prosperity being reaped from Empire development, mechanical progress that was making communication with dim corners of the world more swift, and the freedom now allowed to the Dominions that did away with much of the friction that had disrupted Parliament for the best part of the century.

Jubilee spirit, too, was in the potion with which the people now toasted the health of their Queen. All through the land, plans were being made for festivities and gaieties to mark the fiftieth year of Victoria's reign.

Yet, even on this crest of jubilation, criticism of the cost of Royalty did not completely cease—it had been too profitable a subject to the cartoonists since the days when the sons of George III poured away their incomes. With the Queen no longer such a suitable subject, jibes were aimed at lesser targets, notably the Prince of Wales and Prince Henry. When Parliament, on Gladstone's motion, had voted Princess Beatrice a dowry of £30,000 and an annuity of £6,000, passed by 337 votes to 38, the opportunity had been too good to miss.

A full-page cartoon came out showing Princess Beatrice dressed as a cook, rolling pastry on the kitchen table. The flour bin had '£30,000' written on the side. Prince Henry is sitting on a wooden chair, peeling potatoes. Princess Beatrice says to her husband: 'Well, Harry dear, this is Holy Matrimony'. To which Prince Henry replies: 'No, Trixie darling, not *wholly* a matter of money'. The approaching birth of Princess Beatrice's first child was also seized upon by the cartoonists to stress how Prince Henry's fortunes had prospered by marrying the daughter of the Queen. But Princess Beatrice, universally popular and admired for the duty she performed at her mother's side, was spared these savage pleasantries.

The news that Princess Beatrice was expecting her first child had an importance for the majority of British women that may be difficult to appreciate to the full one long life later. By 1887 the Regency school had been swept clean.

The new discipline of Victoria and Albert had, after a noisy rebellion, come to be accepted. In the solid square houses, with often a touch of Albert about them, that were spreading around the rapidly expanding towns, in the farm houses by the country roads, deserted now that the railways had taken the traffic away, newspapers often arrived but once a week, and a magazine once a month. That magazine took the place that is jointly occupied to-day by the radio, the television, the cinema and a pile of newspapers and glossy periodicals. And that one magazine was devoted to God, to Queen Victoria, to etiquette, to adage, to humility, to the blessings of facing up to life's burdens with a smile, and to the general omnipotence and kindliness of the British Empire.

To women in the middle and lower income groups Princess Beatrice now stood for all that a young matron should be. Her clothes became the subject of full-page fashion plates. Her hobbies and her talents were described in the monthly magazines, and writers held her up as an example for daughters to follow. Songs and music dedicated to her—'The Beatrice Waltz', 'The Royal British Rose Bud', 'The Princess Beatrice Bridal March', which had been composed by Karl Kahn for her wedding —had pride of place on the upright cottage pianos.

Princess Beatrice's life held all that was necessary to fill this popular rôle. Robbed of her father at the age of four, she had comforted her mother as a child and supported her constantly as a young woman. She had studied hard, and become accomplished at drawing, music, singing and dancing. She was a good cook and housekeeper. No breath of scandal had ever touched her name. The fact that she had not married as early as her sisters was attributed to the fact that she had placed her duty towards her mother before her own happiness. When at last she had decided to marry, she had chosen a most handsome Prince.

In addition, Princess Beatrice was better known in her
own country than were her sisters, and her name was more
closely associated with that of the Queen and with Palace
life. Nearly thirty years had passed since the Princess
Royal left for Germany, and she had, in part, lost her
identity. Princess Alice had died eight years before.
Princess Christian was playing an increasing part in public
life, but she did not live with the Queen and her husband
lacked the gay personality and looks of 'Liko' Battenberg.
Princess Louise, the royal bohemian, had been away with
her husband in Canada, and at home was apt to keep in
the shadows. And she and Lord Lorne had no children.

When it was announced that Princess Henry of
Battenberg was expecting a child, the interest shown
throughout the country was outstanding, and even took
the Queen by surprise.

The baby, a son,[1] was born at five o'clock on the morning of 23rd November 1886, thus thoroughly upsetting
the strict routine of life at Windsor Castle. Both mother and
child fared well and, when Sandro of Bulgaria arrived at
the Castle a fortnight later, Princess Beatrice was able to
greet him with her son on her knee.

If there was one thing that irritated the Queen more
than any other it was having to alter her set way of life
or postpone her settled comings and goings. Christmas
was always spent at Osborne, and no event had yet arisen
serious enough to alter this arrangement. But one had
come now, and the Queen, considering that it would be
unwise for the Princess and her son to undertake the
journey, decided that she would stay on at Windsor,
merely commenting that it would be rather strange. The
christening was arranged for 18th December.

In the speculation as to what names would be chosen,
Punch, under the heading 'Little What's-His-Name?'
suggested that 'the Battenberg Baby should be called

[1] The Marquess of Carisbrooke.

Prince JUBILEE'. In the event the more traditional ones of Alexander Albert had been decided upon.

The gold font, with the figures of naked children playing round its base, from which all the Queen's children had been christened, was placed in the White Drawing Room. To the delight of the parents, the Prince of Bulgaria was at Windsor, and he was asked to be sponsor to the child who was to bear his name. Others to undertake the duty were the Queen, the Prince of Wales, Prince Alexander of Hesse, and Princess Irene of Hesse, the third daughter of Princess Alice. There was a great and cheerful concourse of royalties at Windsor on that 18th of December.

Although the Queen had become a grandmother on thirty-six previous occasions, no addition to the family had given her more pleasure than the arrival of Alexander Albert. She seemed to gain a new lease of life and was much more cheerful. When a small boy ran beside her carriage at Windsor she ordered the coachman to stop, and gave her admirer a florin. She did the same for a blind man who was singing 'Abide with me' by Windsor Bridge. And when the news was given that she had commanded the Royal Box at Drury Lane for the Carl Rosa Opera Season, the Press came out with the headline, 'What a surprise'.

The reason for the change of heart lay in the proximity of the baby. There he lay, in the nursery right above her private sitting-room. The demands he made were immediate and brooked no delay, and she had to give way to them. She had always had first call on Princess Beatrice. Now she was content to have second.

Recent events had called upon Queen Victoria to work even harder than usual. She was very tired. After tea she would doze off in her chair, a luxury which she had never before allowed herself, and in March she caught a feverish cold. She decided to spend a quiet holiday in France before tackling the strenuous Jubilee programme. So in April fond farewells were paid to the baby Prince, and the Queen, Princess Beatrice and Prince Henry set off for Cannes.

Prince George of Wales was serving in Mediterranean waters at the time, under the command of his uncle of Edinburgh—'the Admiral' he called him—and the two were waiting to receive the Queen and her party and conduct them to the Villa Edelweiss, where they were to stay.

One of the reasons why the Queen had chosen Cannes for her holiday was so that she could see the Church of St. George, built in memory of her son Leopold, Duke of Albany, who had died so tragically and suddenly in the town three years before. Her first visit was alone with Princess Beatrice, but on the following Sunday a memorial service was held and all available members of the Royal Family attended.

While at Cannes a message came from Windsor for Princess Beatrice that her son was unwell. However, a following report read that there was no cause for alarm, and, upset as she may well have been, Princess Beatrice felt that she could safely accompany her mother on the next stage of the trip to Aix.

Once again the Princess was in the white town, under the mountains and by the lake, for her birthday—her thirtieth—and once again the bands played in the garden outside her window.

During this visit Princess Beatrice and the Queen made history, for they became the first women of Protestant faith to explore the monastery of the Grande Chartreuse. The Empress Eugénie, the first Roman Catholic woman to have the privilege, had extolled to them the wonders of the monastery, and, after long planning, the Queen and her daughter now had the opportunity to see for themselves.

Slowly, on a perfect day, they drove up into the mountains towards the Monastery, where a monk, in white habit and cowl, and with shaven head, stood waiting to receive them.

After the sunshine, the cloisters struck cold as the monk led his visitors into the presence of the Grand Prior. A genial man, he took them to the Chapel, where Vespers were being sung, to the Chapter Room, to the new library and to the burial ground where, in the shade, the snow lay hard across the graves of the monks.

One other door the Grand Prior unlocked, and that the door of a cell. In the two small rooms behind that locked door a young Englishman spent his days. He had passed the five years since he was eighteen at the Monastery. He was tall, good-looking in a delicate way, and there was a rapt expression on his face. He told his Queen how proud he was to be her subject, and in answer to her query, said that he was very happy.

Before they left Grande Chartreuse the Royal visitors were offered wine. The Queen asked instead for the Monastery's own liqueur. Their guide agreed but, as the Queen later commented, by mistake he gave her some of their strongest!

Back in London Princess Beatrice found that every hour of the day was crowded. Apart from the attentions demanded by her son, she had to attend the rapidly increasing Jubilee engagements of her mother, and ensure that she did not become overtired. In addition she and Prince Henry had their own engagements in various parts of the country, as the demand for Royal appearances was exceeding the supply.

Early in May, the Queen, Princess Beatrice and Prince Henry had a very novel experience. They went to a private showing of Colonel Cody's Wild West Exhibition at Earl's Court. After the riding and the shooting and the shouting were over, 'Buffalo Bill' was presented to the Royal

10

audience, but the Queen also insisted on receiving the other performers.

Another London engagement was the opening of the People's Palace, and Princess Beatrice and Prince Henry accompanied the Queen on the long drive to Whitechapel through cheering crowds. The only dampener on the day was that, at intervals, small groups of Irishmen gave vent to boos.

A few days later the Queen and the Battenberg family, in full strength, left Windsor for Balmoral, and here the Jubilee brooches, designed by Princess Beatrice, were distributed to the tenants and servants. The Queen's sixty-eighth birthday was on 24th May and the Princess, as she had done every year since her father died, came down early to her mother's room to wish her joy. This time things were different, for with her she brought her baby, firmly clasping a bunch of lilies of the valley in his hand.

London was not reached again until 20th June, the eve of the great day of the Procession. And what a wonderful London it was! Every Royal home was bulging with royalties and rulers. Seats on the route were being sold for fabulous prices. Everywhere carpenters and decorators were busy putting up balconies and triumphal arches, fixing Venetian masts, flags, scrolls and pennons, and hanging festoons of evergreens and banners across the streets. All through the night of the 20th the hammering and banging went on, as the crowds took their pavement seats under the starlit sky.

One of the personal problems facing Princess Beatrice and her sisters was how to encourage their mother to wear clothes suitably *chic* for the occasion. They solved it by calling in the Duke of Connaught, who could say things to the Queen that the others might fear to say. His comment was simply: 'Now, Mother, you must have something really smart.' And she did. There were white feathers above the diamonds on her bonnet, and white in the rich brocade of her frock. Princess Beatrice had chosen a dress of pale pink, shown off by her beautiful lace, and a bonnet all of rosebuds.

To the Princess, expecting her second child in October, those full and wonderful June days proved a considerable strain. Although in the pageantry she had to give precedence to those who ranked above her, it was her duty to be always near her mother, to see that she was not unduly tired, to snatch her away from the bustle to rest and have tea in a quiet corner of Buckingham Palace garden, and to help her to read the spate of telegrams and letters.

In the Jubilee Procession, the Crown Princess of Germany and the Princess of Wales were with the Queen in her carriage. Princess Beatrice drove with the Duchess of Edinburgh and Princesses Christian and Louise, the last named being much upset as her husband had been thrown from his horse as the Procession began. Fortunately, Lord Lorne had landed on soft ground and was unhurt. Borrowing a more sober means of conveyance from an Artillery officer, he took a short cut to the Abbey via Birdcage Walk, to the great relief of his wife and sisters-in-law.

Four reigning Kings and five Crown Princes figured on that Jubilee tapestry. In the Queen's Procession was a cortège of thirty-two Princes, yet of all the mounted escort the man who stole the thunder was suffering from cancer—the Crown Prince of Germany. His uniform was wholly white, his breast-plate of silver, and on his burnished steel helmet a silver eagle outstretched its wings. Towering, Wagnerian in his majesty, he rode the eighteen-hand charger which, after his death, the Queen was to have brought to Windsor with orders that no one was ever to cross its back again.

It was four o'clock before the King of Saxony led the Queen into luncheon at Buckingham Palace. Thereafter she felt so faint with fatigue that she had to be wheeled to her room. Yet later that evening she attended a State Dinner. Next day there was a fête in Hyde Park for 26,000 school children and, on her return to Windsor, came a drive to Eton, ending with fireworks and illuminations. Thereafter Princess Beatrice took charge, for she saw how spent her mother was as they breakfasted at beloved Frogmore on the morning of the 23rd.

After more busy weeks, the Battenbergs went with the Queen to Osborne and were able to sail again in the *Sheilah*. To the Isle of Wight also came the Crown Prince and Princess of Germany. Anxiety over them was to cloud that Jubilee year for both the Queen and Princess Beatrice. British and German doctors disputed whether the growth in the Crown Prince's throat was cancerous, or no. Bismarck shouted that the Crown Prince's place was in his own country, particularly as the Emperor was so very old. The Crown Princess argued that her husband should be where it best suited his health, and for the moment she considered that to be England. And Prince William behaved almost as if he were already Emperor.

To afford Princess Beatrice the necessary period of recuperation, the Queen decided to extend the autumn holiday at Balmoral. On 24th October, after a severe confinement, a daughter was born. Once they had learned that mother and child were well, the cottars went wild with delight, and more so when they heard that the christening was to be on Deeside.

Beatrice was 'their own Princess', she was the mother of the first Royal child to be born in Scotland since 1600, and there had not been a Royal christening there since that of Prince Henry, son of James VI, in 1594.

The christening took place on 23rd November, and was a quiet, family affair, the Queen holding the baby. The service was taken by Dr. Cameron Lees, of St. Giles's Cathedral, Edinburgh, and the water came from the River Jordan. The Empress Eugénie was sponsor to the child.

She had been staying at Abergeldie earlier in the autumn
and was now represented by Princess Frederica of
Hanover, daughter of blind King George. Victoria
Eugénie Julia Ena were the names given—but this was
not the exact intention. Princess Beatrice had written
'Eua'[1] on the documents, but Dr. Lees misread a 'u' for
an 'n' and, before the mistake was discovered, the little
girl was 'Ena' for ever. And, in the years to come, a great
many Enas would, but for the slip of a cleric's tongue,
have been Euas.

Christmas that year was spent at Osborne, and the
fortunate children at Whippingham school had both
Lornes and Battenbergs on the platform to hand them
their presents.

On 9th March the German Emperor, William I died,
and the Princess of Wales, remembering the war over 'the
duchies that belonged to Papa', announced that she would
not attend the Memorial Service. The 10th was the Silver
Wedding day of 'Bertie' and 'Alix', and that morning the
Queen, with Princess Beatrice and Prince Henry, drove
round to Marlborough House to give them a splendid
silver vase. In the evening, the three went again to
Marlborough House, for a family gathering and dinner.
As a surprise all ten bridesmaids who had taken part in
the wedding suddenly appeared. Said one of them, sadly,
'We all look old ladies', but added that the Princess of
Wales appeared more like a sister than a mother beside
her daughters.

On 22nd March the Queen, Princess Beatrice and
Prince Henry began their visit to Florence and Berlin,
with all the upsets and misunderstandings over the
engagement of Princess Victoria of Prussia and Sandro,
Prince of Bulgaria[2]. Apart from this distraction, there was
much to fill the days. The King and Queen of Italy paid
a call on the Queen at the Villa Palmieri, and the following

[1] An old Gaelic name.   [2] See Appendix B.

day Princess Beatrice accompanied her mother on the return visit to the Palazzo Pitti. Other visitors were the Emperor and Empress of Brazil.

Prince Henry had taken the opportunity of being in Italy to visit the Duke of Edinburgh at Malta, but he was back for the Saturday in Passion Week when, by custom, the ox-drawn cart, garlanded and laden with fireworks, entered the Piazza del Duomo. The ceremony was watched by the Royal Family. They saw the model of a dove, propelled by a rocket ignited by the holy candle, fly along its cord, stretched from church to cart. The fireworks went off, and their explosions punctuated the voices of the choir singing '*Gloria in excelsis*'. Then the church bells pealed out. It seemed a far cry from the Presbyterianism of Crathie.

The journey to Berlin took the Royal party through Modena and Verona, during the night, and by breakfast time they were in the Alps. On the platform at Innsbruck the Emperor Francis Joseph of Austria was waiting to greet them, and at Munich the mother of mad King Ludwig of Bavaria.

It was a year of deaths among German Royalties. Two Emperors[1] passed away, and in December a message came to Windsor that Prince Henry's father was very ill. Princess Beatrice hurried to Darmstadt with her husband, the fear of the '14th' in her heart, and in her mother's. Prince Alexander died on the 15th. It was a sad Christmas at Osborne, with the Empress Frederick there, widowed, heart-broken, defeated, aged.

Recognition of the services of Prince Henry came in the New Year when the Queen appointed him Governor and Captain General of the Isle of Wight and Governor of Carisbrooke Castle. Having been married there and being such a keen yachtsman, the appointment was most popular on the island.

[1] Emperor Frederick died on 15th June.

In March Princess Beatrice passed a milestone in her life when she visited Spain for the first time. It was on the recommendation of the Empress Eugénie that she, with her mother and husband, decided to spend an early holiday at Biarritz. The holiday had to be somewhat earlier than was the usual custom, as the Princess was expecting a third child in May. On the 27th the Queen, with the Princess and Prince Henry, drove on to Spanish soil, on a visit to the Queen Regent at San Sebastian. No British Sovereign had ever been to Spain, with the exception of the two Charles's, who journeyed there as Princes. There was to be another point of interest. The widowed Queen Christina had three children, one of them called Alfonso.

Princess Beatrice's second son, Leopold, was born on 21st May at Windsor and, three days later, the Queen celebrated her seventieth birthday. Early that morning Princess Beatrice sent her two elder children to the Queen's bedroom. They sat on her bed and 'Drino', proffering a nosegay, kept repeating: 'Many happy returns, Gangan'.

Fittingly, Princess Louise was the godmother to Prince Leopold. She had been the closest of companions with her brother of that name and missed him deeply. There was to be a tragic similarity in those two Leopolds.

In July Princess Beatrice became concerned over the quarrel which was going on between the Prince of Wales and his nephew, Emperor William of Germany. William's new power had gone to his head, and he was taking exception to the fact that the Prince of Wales appeared to treat him more like a nephew than an Emperor.

William made a number of remarks calculated to annoy. 'He is boating with a grocer', he observed, when he learned that his uncle had been aboard Sir Thomas Lipton's yacht. The climax came when William refused to meet the Prince of Wales when both were to be in Vienna together at the invitation of Emperor Francis

Joseph. The British Ambassador, Sir Augustus Paget, found the position particularly difficult. His wife, 'Wally', came to England in July and one evening sat between the Queen and Princess Beatrice at dinner. Lady Paget, who had been responsible for the Prince of Wales meeting his wife, tried to pour oil on the troubled waters, saying that William had the greatest love for Queen Victoria, but was apt to be a little excitable and irritable. The Queen was immovable in her anger and thought that William should apologise for the annoyance he was causing his uncle.

The Kaiser came to visit his grandmother at Osborne in August, arriving at Cowes in his yacht, *Hohenzollern*, accompanied by twelve warships. There was a naval review and, in the uniform of a full admiral, he visited the more important British vessels. He was accompanied by his unforgiving uncle, by Prince George of Wales and Prince Henry. Striving to placate his grandmother, he made her honorary colonel of his first regiment of Horse Guards.

A contrasting engagement was the visit to Wales at the end of August. Palé Hall, near lovely Lake Bala, had been placed at the Queen's disposal, and from here Princess Beatrice and Prince Henry journeyed to Ruabon and descended a coalmine, the Princess trying her hand at cutting coal.

At the end of the year Prince Henry sailed off in the *Sheilah* for a cruise round the Mediterranean and did not return until February, 1890. At home Princess Beatrice concentrated on the translation that she was making of *The Adventures of Count George Albert of Erbach*, from the German of Emil Kraus, a work that was to be published that year.

In the spring of 1890 the Queen and her inseparable Battenbergs again visited Aix-les-Bains—for Princess Beatrice it was becoming routine that she should spend her birthdays there. Feeling the pains of rheumatism once more, she had a course of thermal treatment, her mother being content with the attention of a *masseuse*.

The return journey was made via Darmstadt, and there the German Emperor and his wife came to visit them. It was the first time they had met 'insignificant little Dona' since her elevation, and it may not have been easy to forget the uncalled-for remarks she had made at the time of the engagement of Princess Beatrice and Prince Henry. But much had changed in five years—William had jumped from Prince to Kaiser, and had but recently disposed of Bismarck—and he was doing his best to be nice to Grandma, at least in her presence. Though the H.R.H. status of Prince Henry was not fully accepted in certain quarters of Germany, he was travelling with the Queen as her son-in-law, and it was he who greeted the Emperor and Empress at Darmstadt station.

Back at Balmoral an interesting visitor came to the Castle in the person of Queen Isabella of Spain. She was met by Princess Beatrice and Prince Henry, and they asked after her grandson, the young King Alfonso, who had been born in their marriage year. It seemed as if a path into the future was already being laid.

Princess Beatrice's fourth child, and third son, was born at Balmoral on 3rd October 1891. The birth of a Prince in Scotland was the signal for great celebration. Up from the south came the gold font, and a battery of Artillery to discharge the royal salute. A bonfire was built on the top of Craig Gowan, and a procession of gillies, cottars and keepers, led by pipers with flaming pine torches in their hands, marched up the hill and lit a blaze that showed for miles around Deeside. With whisky to encourage them, they set about dancing on the flat, rocky space reserved for such occasions.

The christening took place at the end of the month, in the drawing-room of the Castle. Dr. Lees, Chaplain to the Queen and to the Order of the Thistle, once more took the

service, and Sir George Reid was present to paint the
scene. The Queen held the baby, dressed in the historic
christening robe which had clothed so many princes and
princesses before him, and by her side stood Prince Henry,
wearing the Royal Stuart tartan. The names given were
Maurice Victor Donald, the last in compliment to
Scotland.

The 'tribe' of Battenbergs was complete. From now on,
as the babies turned into children, there was to be a
change in the existence of the Queen—and their mother.
With the nursery at Windsor just above her private
apartments, the Queen was never to be safe from their
childish raids. There might be a wooden horse with
damaged paint or a ragged doll resting in her chair. A
hair-covered steed was stabled outside her door, its course
the length of the corridor. It was 'Gangan this' and
'Gangan that' from rising to bedtime, and feet scamper-
ing where statesmen softly trod. The school children of
the new century were chasing out the ghosts of the old,
and a fig for Bismarck, Palmerston, Stockmar and
Baroness Lehzen.

The Queen revelled in the change. After thirty years
of hiding in the shadows of the past, she had come out
into the sun. The years seemed to fall from her, and she
laughed. Brown study gave place to Indian summer, and
she recalled some of the forgotten smiles of spring. Ena,
with her golden hair, was like her own 'Baby' Beatrice,
and just as pert and mischievous. And when the young
Connaughts came to play, she could watch the sets of
grandchildren she knew best, the offspring of her favourite
son and her favourite daughter, Arthur and Beatrice.

In the upbringing and education of her children
Princess Beatrice followed in the main the lines which
had been adopted by her mother and father, but with considerably more leaven in the dough. Having been so much

with her mother, it was natural that she should do this, and the method had proved most satisfactory for learning, manners and discipline. With happy memories of the plays and *tableaux vivants* of her own childhood, she used the same means to give her sons and daughters poise, and at the same time to practise them in French and German. And so, just as forty years before the Queen and Prince Albert had been bidden to attend some surprise showing, now the message came that her presence was required in the Indian Room of Osborne's new wing, and a new generation would pose the same scenes.

The Princess, whose duties became more onerous as the years passed, encouraged her children to be much with the Queen. While they amused her and lightened her days, her influence and wisdom were beneficial to them. But, however close they were to their grandmother, they were never allowed to forget that she was Queen.

To them, 'Gangan' was a fount of perpetual interest and 'treats', and there were many excitements to break the long-established routine of Windsor, Osborne, and Balmoral. Breakfast at the Tea House at Frogmore on a summer's morning, and the 'cock-and-hen' egg cups and salt cellars that Brown had given her. . . . Tea on a winter's afternoon and being allowed to pour out from the small silver teapot inscribed with a 'V' and 'May 24th, 1827' and grieving over the butterfly with the broken wing which rested on the lid. . . . Picnicking, when it rained, in the Lower Alcove at Osborne and watching the raindrops splashing into the fountain. . . . Playing Mounted Escort to Her Majesty as a gillie led the pony carriage around Balmoral. . . . Before going to bed, watching 'Gangan' making a mouse from a handkerchief and jumping with delight as it ran over her hand and up her arm.

At Osborne the nurseries of the Battenberg children were those which had been occupied by their mother, immediately above the Queen's rooms and with direct access to them. Gay with flowered wall-paper and matching chintzes, the day nursery was fully carpeted and free of furniture in the centre so that games could be played unimpeded and without danger.

Toys were everywhere, both in the nurseries and in the Observatory Tower. Preference seemed to be for the well-worn article, though there were toys of the more expensive kind, such as the beautiful organ which had been made for Prince Maurice.

Some of the happiest days of the Battenberg children were spent at Osborne, with the sea so near and the young Connaughts to share their summer holidays with them. There were tea parties in the Swiss Cottage. There was swimming in Osborne Bay and attempts, under parental instruction, to play tennis, with the Queen coming along to watch.

Riding was taught in the School at Windsor. One of the Princes' ponies was fittingly called 'Prince'. Also in the stable, and sometimes used as a mount, was 'Jacko', a donkey which the Queen, out of pity, purchased in France, and a pretty Albino pony bought from Hengler's Circus for the Battenberg boys.

The new generation had inherited a love of animals and liked nothing better than going to the Aviary to feed the birds at the appointed hour. 'Drino' had a pen of gold-spangled Hamburg poultry, of which he was very proud.

Other, and stranger, animals came to Windsor. At the bidding of the boys two dancing bears arrived to give their act, but Ena did better than this. A monkey attracted her attention in Windsor town, and its owner, complete with barrel organ, was ordered to the Castle. The command performance took place in the Quadrangle below the windows of the Oak Dining-room. To the delight of the Princess the monkey escaped from its owner, climbed the portico and attempted to get through the window at which the Queen and the children were sitting.

'Punch' was also bidden, to make his dastardly attack on 'Judy', and Hengler's Circus arrived to give its turns in the Great Riding School. The Queen was vastly intrigued with the wisdom of Whimsical Walker's donkey and after the show ordered that he be presented. For greeting she poked the animal with her walking-stick. The donkey, being accustomed to the reverence due to star status, took strong exception and lashed out. The Queen was heard to say that she was afraid it was not a very loyal subject.

In June, 1892, Pinder's Circus was ordered to Balmoral to amuse the Battenberg Princes and Princess. In its day Pinder's had been a most successful circus, but it had fallen on hard times and was left with only a few shabby caravans, from which the gilt was peeling. In the course of its circuit, the outfit arrived at Ballater and set up camp on the moor. The Queen, on her way to Braemar, saw the tawdry tents and the tethered ponies, and forthwith issued her summons. A field near the river was duly placed at Pinder's disposal and invitations were sent to all the children living on the three Royal estates.

Pinder, with a new lease of life, put his all into the show and the Battenbergs spent two entranced hours from their ringside seats in the carriage. Once again it was the donkey which stole the thunder, but Pinder would not sell. The Queen gave him a jewelled scarf pin, and the circus went on its way richer not only by a generous fee, but by the fact that it could now announce that it had performed before Her Majesty the Queen.

At the entreaty of the Battenberg children, a number of travelling minstrel troupes sang their repertoires at Balmoral. Of all the songs they heard, the one the Queen liked best was Charles Bernard's rendering of:

'Just before the battle, mother,
I was thinking most of you.'

7

Sunbeam and Shadow

LINKED by a dual connection with Hesse, through Princess Alice and the marriage of the latter's daughter, Victoria, to Louis Battenberg, Princess Beatrice and Prince Henry had many family affairs in common. The family that had begun with the marriage of the only daughter of the Duke of Kent to the younger of the two sons of the Duke of Saxe-Coburg had multiplied vastly, and a list of the home railway stations of the descendants and their in-laws read like a Continental Guide.

In the years between the Jubilee and Prince Henry's death in 1896 there was a flush of weddings, and subsequent christenings, of close interest both to the Princess and her husband. Four of the Empress Frederick's children had married. Henry, the sailor, married Irene, daughter of Princess Alice, thus strengthening the ties between the Battenbergs and the Royal House of Prussia; Victoria, recovered from her romance with Sandro, married Adolphus of Schaumburg-Lippe; Sophie married Constantine of Greece, a country with which the Battenbergs were shortly to have another connection; and Margaret married Frederick Charles of Hesse-Cassel. Princess Margaret, known as 'Mossy', was a great favourite of Queen Victoria. Her mother sometimes called her 'Benjamina', as the Queen had called Princess Beatrice. Also a youngest daughter, Princess Margaret offered the Empress Frederick, in her last years of agony, the same wonderful support that her aunt gave to Queen Victoria.

Two of the daughters of the Prince and Princess of Wales had married; Louise, Princess Royal, to 'Macduff', Duke of Fife, and Maud to Haakon of Norway. In the Edinburgh family there were weddings for three of the daughters, Marie to Ferdinand of Roumania, Victoria Melita to Ernest of Hesse (Princess Alice's son), and Alexandra to Ernest of Hohenlohe-Langenburg.

Of special interest to Princess Beatrice was the marriage of her godchild, Alix of Hesse, to an infatuated Nicholas, Tsarevitch of Russia. Also that of her niece, Marie Louise, Princess Christian's daughter, to Aribert of Anhalt. The ideas of this pert, cosmopolitan Princess, nicknamed 'young Mrs. Aribert', soon came to clash with those of the cold dowagers of German discipline. She arrived in time to be caught up in the web of anonymous letters which tangled the German Court in the 'nineties, letters which purported to know every secret behind every bedroom door. As we have noted, the marriage ended in annulment as had that of the other Louise, mother of Prince Albert.

The wedding of the greatest importance during these years, both to the Royal Family and the people of Great Britain and the Empire, was that of George, son of the Prince of Wales, to Princess 'May' of Teck.

As for births, the four youngest of the German Emperor's children had arrived on the scene. His brother, Henry, and Irene of Hesse had two. Sophie had three children, two boys, who were to become Kings of Greece, and a girl, Helen, who was to marry King Carol of Roumania. Margaret had four boys.

Louise of Fife had two daughters, Alexandra and Maud. To Victoria of Battenberg were born a daughter, Louise, and a son, George, who joined Alice, born in 1885. Victoria Melita and Ernest had a daughter, to be their only child. Marie of Roumania had a son and a daughter, Carol of Roumania, and Elizabeth, who married George II of Greece. In Russia Alix gave birth to a daughter, Olga. Two sons, 'David' and 'Bertie', were born to the future King George V and Queen Mary.

It was a complicated, and somewhat topsy-turvy, genealogical table that was being unfolded before the Battenbergs. For example, Princess Beatrice's son, Maurice, was still in his nursery when his mother became a great-great aunt.

During this period one death overshadowed all others in its tragedy. Prince Albert Victor, Duke of Clarence and Avondale, eldest son of the Prince of Wales, died shortly after the announcement of his engagement to Princess 'May'. On 5th December 1891 Princess Beatrice drove with the Queen to Farnborough to lunch with the Empress Eugénie. On their return to Windsor they found Prince Albert Victor waiting for them. He told the Queen: 'I have some good news to tell you; I am engaged to May Teck'. He had proposed while dancing with her at a ball at Luton. The Queen, not greatly taken by surprise, was nevertheless delighted, for she was very fond of this pretty and amiable great-granddaughter of George III.

At Osborne, on 13th January, Princess Beatrice had the unenviable task of taking into her mother a telegram announcing that Prince Albert Victor was very, very ill indeed. Next day, another 14th, he died. The Prince of Wales wrote to his mother: 'Gladly would I have given my life for his, as I put no value on mine. . . .'

He wished the funeral to be held at Windsor and the Queen placed the Castle at his disposal. Terribly shocked by the death of her eldest son, the Princess of Wales wanted the service to be as private as possible, and that no ladies should attend. Even the Duke of Cambridge, who had not missed a family occasion for half a century, received a message that his presence would not be necessary.

The Princess of Wales was particularly anxious to avoid

The Duchess of Connaught in the undress uniform of the 8th Branden-
burg Regiment, 1890

Queen Victoria at Osborne in 1893, with her grandchildren Princ
Prince Maurice of Battenberg (*by permissio*

exander, Princess Victoria Eugénie (Ena), Prince Leopold and
Her Majesty Queen Victoria Eugenia)

Prince Alexander of Battenberg in Queen Victoria's sitting-room, Windsor Castle. Barber, 1887 (*by permission of the Marquess of Carisbrooke*)

Prince Alexander and Princess Victoria Eugénie of Battenberg, with Queen Victoria's Indian orderly officer. Long Corridor, Windsor Castle. Barber, 1889. (*By permission of the Marquess of Carisbrooke*)

a cavalcade of family mourners from Osborne. In the case of the Queen the matter was settled by the doctors backing up the Prince of Wales in his opinion that her attendance would expose her to a risk, owing to the bad weather and the spreading influenza epidemic. She gave in reluctantly, but was not prepared to flaunt usage and custom by allowing her other children to stay away. Princess Beatrice and her sisters duly journeyed to Windsor.

Unfortunately, at the end of the service, the door of the pew in which they sat could not be opened, to the irritation of those within. Sir Henry Ponsonby later raised the matter with one of the Prince of Wales's Equerries and received the following reply:

'... The Prince of Wales desires me to say that—the harem of Princesses was *not* locked into the further Zenana pew closet but the door got jammed, and adds that they were none of them wanted at all. No ladies were to attend, and the Princess of Wales especially requested privacy—and to avoid meeting her Osborne relations. So they all came.

'If Princess Beatrice was annoyed it cannot be helped and she must get over it—as she likes! ...'

Here, at a moment of great stress, is glimpsed the underlying irritation of the heir to the Throne at the close trust and confidence that the Queen gave to her youngest daughter and her husband. Already a man of fifty, and surely within a few years of becoming King, the Prince of Wales sensed that there was much that his mother did not tell him, and that the Battenbergs received on occasion confidences denied to him.

Yet Princess Beatrice had won her position after a long and faithful apprenticeship and, though the brother had the more splendid façade, the rooms behind were better furnished in the case of the sister. However much the

11

Queen may have loved her son, always tucked away at the back of her mind was the memory of his affair with the girl in Cambridge and the fateful journey of the Prince Consort to the University. Then there were detractions such as the Mordaunt divorce and the baccarat at Tranby Croft, and the fact that 'Bertie' was apt to be biased over foreign affairs, particularly when it came to Germany.

As for Prince Henry, he was in a cleft stick. If he played what was considered too small a part in Royal affairs, or went off on a cruise in the *Sheilah*, he was accused of living an indolent life at the expense of the British tax-payer. If it was thought that he was too close to the ear of the Queen, he was regarded as a German intruder and a dangerous influence. One magazine writer observed severely that Prince Henry spent much of his time at Windsor playing billiards with Ponsonby.

True, Prince Henry did have time on his hands, for there were many duties in which only Princess Beatrice could support her mother. Then, very rightly, he occupied himself with the many sports he loved. A true Battenberg, he was always anxious to try anything new. When bicycling became the craze, he bought himself a machine, and small ones for his children, to whom the finding of balance came more easily than to their father. Prince Henry chose a quiet summer's evening at Windsor to put in a practice ride, but it was also a night out for the insects, and very shortly a cloud of them was moving with him. The Prince dared not take a hand from the bars for fear of upsetting, and had to pedal furiously for home, his attackers feasting undisturbed.

Even worse was the fate of the Duke of Connaught on one of his first spins. Advancing along the road towards him he glimpsed a private soldier. To salute or not to salute was the question. Duty and tradition triumphed. The Duke snapped up his hand; the soldier, also a learner, had no option but to do the same. Vertigo to the right set in, and the two ended in the road on top of one another.

One of the changes in palace life during the married days of Princess Beatrice was the now frequent musical and dramatic entertainment. The first such performance for forty years came with the staging of 'The Gondoliers' at Windsor in 1891, and it set the pattern for many more happy evenings for the Queen and the Battenbergs in the Waterloo Gallery. Eleanora Duse sang there, and Irving played opposite Ellen Terry. Beerbohm Tree and John Hare acted before them, and the Comédie Française delighted them. There were also performances of 'Il Trovatore' and 'Carmen'.

Princess Beatrice and Princess Louise both loved amateur theatricals and in 1890 they put on an ambitious programme at Osborne. The only trouble was that the Princesses were not too good at remembering the words and considerable prompting was necessary. On one occasion when they were alone on the stage together, neither could remember what to say next, and there was no one to help. A few moments of absolute silence followed. Their dilemma was solved for them by the audience of members of the Household and servants applauding enthusiastically, and the dropping of the curtain by a tactful carpenter.

The Queen loved watching these theatricals, but in her delight was apt to forget that, even as Queen, she was not entitled, as a member of the audience, to give advice and a running commentary about what was happening on the stage. Once Princess Beatrice had sternly to bid her mother to stop talking, at which the Queen hid her face in her hands and meekly cried, 'I will be good! I will be good!'

The Queen also took upon herself the duty of Censor, ensuring that the proprieties due to Royalty were observed, and she was not above re-writing a play if it did not suit her. When Princess Beatrice's part ended in the first act, the Queen ordered a reconciliation between her and her stage husband so that the Princess might make another appearance. When, in a French piece, the Princess was to have been referred to as a 'degraded woman', the Queen firmly exercised her veto, as she did when her daughter was called upon to describe her marital relations and was to say, 'I had nothing to offer as a dowry but my virtue,' to which the male reply was, 'Ah, little enough!'

In a play in which Princess Louise and Beatrice played leading parts, Frederick Ponsonby had to chuck Princess Louise under the chin. The Queen saw that act during rehearsal and gave her opinion that it was altogether too familiar. On the next try Ponsonby left out the personal touch altogether, only to be told that he was overdoing it the other way. Whereat, with the Princess convulsed with laughter, the two worked out a middle course.

Prince Henry was also called upon to appear on the stage, and among the *Tableaux* presented at Osborne in January 1892 was 'King Richard among the Saracens', with the Queen's Indian servants appearing as the Saracens and Prince Henry as Saladin, their leader. 'Willie' Clarkson provided the costumes and wigs and, talking with him afterwards, Prince Henry remarked that the diamond in his turban had been brought specially from Windsor.

'Pardon me if I am wrong, Your Royal Highness,' said Clarkson, 'but surely the jewel is a paste one of mine.'

'Certainly not,' said the Prince. 'It is genuine.'

He was wrong. He had put down the diamond on a tray on which lay stage jewellery, and later picked up one of Clarkson's imitations as the best diamond there.

On one evening in the year the Queen forgot all about the proprieties and the power of her veto, and that was when the annual Gillies' Ball was held at Balmoral. To the Queen there was something of a primitive rite in this carousal, and those who slipped from the narrow path were, for once, able to pick themselves up without the steely eye of disapproval.

The Balls had been started at John Brown's proposal and the Queen had always danced with him several times. Now they were in part sacred to his memory, and also to the far-off days when she had first come to Scotland with her husband. She always insisted on being at Balmoral for that particular evening, and would not postpone it even for a family death.

The drinking and the dancing began at seven o'clock and by the time the Queen sat down to dinner the lights were already sparkling in the eyes of many of the staff. If a little wine was spilt over a guest's trousers, the guest pretended that it had not happened. Stewards unsteady on their feet were quietly exchanged for more sober substitutes, and the distant crash of crockery falling on to stone corridors was ignored. It was the rule of the table that nothing unusual should be noticed, and to this end the Queen kept the conversation going and told story after story.

Prince Henry, unlike certain of the more sedate and elderly among the Household, enjoyed these evenings. In 1891, when the birth of Prince Maurice had given occasion for special gaiety, he led the Queen, then aged seventy-two, on to the floor. She dropped her stick, forgot her rheumatics, and carried out every step of the dance perfectly.

There were, of course, the usual crises that come to upset family life. Prince Henry had a fall whilst out with the Atherstone near Rugby, injured his leg and was laid up for the rest of the season. At Osborne, Ena's pony crossed its legs, fell, and rolled on her. Princess Beatrice saw the groom leading the little girl back by the hand, crying, and very quickly had her in bed. Later Prince

Henry saw the Queen, telling her that the doctor said that their was some indication of suffusion of blood on the brain, and a second doctor was sent for. Fortunately, there was no injury to the spine.

A nurse was summoned from London and interest in the progress of the golden-haired Princess was not confined to the Isle of Wight. A month passed before she was fully recovered.

The round of public engagements and appearances for the Battenbergs continued. One of the most important of these was the opening of the Imperial Institute at South Kensington on 10th May 1893. The majority of those who chronicled the events of the day dwelt on its splendour and dignity, but that was not exactly the impression of all the spectators. Lady Emily Lutyens recalls that her family had been given places in Knightsbridge Barracks:

'We sat there from 10 until 2, and all for the mere purpose of seeing the Queen and a few other Royalties drive by. It is astounding what human beings will do, and the only thing about it which was good was the luncheon, of which I ate largely. The Procession was poor and the crowd very cold. One thing was rather comic. The band played a few bars of God Save the Queen as each carriage drove by. The first carriage contained Lord Suffield, and as the band struck up he put his head out and made violent signs of disapproval. The finest part of the Procession were four Indian soldiers. They had splendid faces and rode magnificently—it was all a frightful waste of time.'

On 6th July 1893 the Duke of York was married to Princess Mary of Teck in the Chapel Royal at St. James's Palace. Princess Beatrice, with Prince Henry and her eldest son, Alexander, sat behind the Queen. For the Princess there was special interest in the bridesmaids, for among them were her namesake, 'Baby B.,' nine-year-old

Beatrice of Edinburgh; Alice Battenberg;[1] and her own daughter, Ena.

Princess Beatrice was with her mother and husband at Coburg the following April for another family wedding, that of Princess Victoria Melita of Edinburgh to Ernest of Hesse, Grand Duke since his father's death two years previously. The Queen was not only attending a wedding, she was visiting a son who was a reigning prince. The Prince Consort's brother, Ernest, had died in 1893 and by long-standing arrangement the Duchy of Saxe-Coburg-Gotha passed to Prince Alfred, and the family so long known as 'the Edinburghs' were now 'the Coburgs'.

There was a great gathering of royalties for the wedding, but some speculation as to why the Tsarevitch Nicholas had travelled so far to attend. The reason became clear when he announced his engagement to Alix of Hesse, youngest surviving daughter of Princess Alice and god-child of Princess Beatrice. The Queen was breakfasting alone with Princess Beatrice when the news became known, and she sent for the couple immediately. 'She is too good for me,' said the Tsarevitch, who was infatuated with the ethereal 'Alicky'. This was the most important union yet made by any of the Queen's children or grandchildren. It was soon to prove even more impressive, for Nicholas's father died on the 1st November and, on her marriage three weeks later, the little girl, who had been a brides-maid to Princess Beatrice, became Tsarina of Russia.

That November at Windsor the interest swayed between the marriage of Princess Alix and the floods. Up came the Thames until people in low-lying houses had to take refuge on the first floor. The Queen and Princess Beatrice, carrying her camera, drove out as far as the water would allow to see how much damage had been done, and carts were ordered out from the Royal farm to carry people and their belongings away from the advancing tide.

[1] Mother of Prince Philip, Duke of Edinburgh.

In March 1895 Prince Henry set off on one of the sailing trips that he loved, while the Queen, with Princess Beatrice and the children, sought the sun in the south of France. The Queen had been worried as to whether it would be advisable for her and the Princess to take their spring holiday there, owing to bad feeling and the talk of bombs, but the French authorities had assured her that she would be safe and welcome. There were certainly no signs of ill-feeling when she attended the Battle of Flowers at Nice, and, prompted by her grandson, Leopold, threw flowers at French officers on a decorated cart.

On the way back visits were paid to the Hesse relations at Darmstadt, and to Kronberg, to see the new house, Friedrichshof, which the Empress Frederick had built in the Taunus Forest. With her husband, Princess Beatrice went again to Kronberg in August, the Queen remaining at Osborne to entertain the Emperor William. It was to be the last holiday together of Beatrice and 'Liko'.

Meanwhile, trouble had flared up in far-off Ashanti. It had been hoped that, after Sir Garnet Wolseley's expedition of 1874, and the subsequent treaty, conditions there would remain peaceful and ordered. Under the rule of young King Prempeh, human sacrifice became a commonplace and raids were being made upon the tribes across the Gold Coast border, members of these tribes being taken back to Ashanti territory to be sold as slaves. The British Government demanded that Prempeh should adhere to the terms of the 1874 Treaty and, on his refusal, it was decided to send out an expedition to restore order.

The expeditionary force was put under the command of Colonel Sir Francis Scott, Inspector of the Gold Coast Constabulary, and was to be made up of West African native troops, and a contingent of specially-selected officers and men of the British Army.

The expedition became of personal interest to the Queen when, on 11th November, Lord Wolseley asked if it would be in order for Prince Christian Victor to serve in it. Prince Christian, twenty-eight years old and in the King's Royal Rifles, was Princess Helena's eldest son, and a close friend of the Battenbergs. The Queen asked the Prince's parents and, on hearing that they were agreeable, gave her consent.

There may well have been collusion between Battenbergs and Christians, for six days later, as they were finishing breakfast, Prince Henry suddenly told his mother-in-law that he also wanted to go to Ashanti. Astonished and concerned, the Queen said that such a course would never do—and that was that. But that was not that, for she had reckoned without Princess Beatrice.

The Princess was firmly behind her husband in his decision. She told her mother that he had set his heart upon going, that he was smarting under his enforced inactivity, and that all his brothers had been on active service. She recalled Sandro of Bulgaria's short, but brilliant, military career, and stressed that the Ashanti force presented a unique chance for Henry, as he could volunteer without stepping into anyone else's shoes.

The Queen, dwelling upon the dangers of fever, called upon the medical evidence of Sir James Reid to support her case, but the Princess answered that, while she appreciated the dangers, the campaign would be short and that Henry would take care of himself.

Still the Queen protested. She was thinking of the Prince Imperial sailing for the Cape. . . .

Then Prince Henry wrote to the Queen. 'I hope, by volunteering in a national cause, to prove my devotion to my adopted country.' The Queen gave in.

A section of the Press greeted the news that the Prince was to join the expedition with comments that were far from kind, and drew an erroneous conclusion as to his motive. Prince Henry made that motive perfectly clear when, a few days before he sailed, he told Lord Harris:

'I am an Englishman, and I want to show the people of England that I am ready to take the rough with the smooth. I know there is no glory and honour to be got out of it, and I know of the danger of subsequent ill-health and perhaps death from malaria, which I know is so great in that country.'

On 6th December, at Windsor, he went in alone to the presence of the Queen, to say farewell. He knelt before her, kissed her hand, and she embraced him. Princess Beatrice entered sadly and shortly afterwards husband and wife left for Bagshot, where they were to stay the night with the Connaughts. Next morning, at Aldershot, the Duke of Connaught reviewed the Force. As Princess Beatrice returned to Windsor, Colonel Prince Henry of Battenberg was on his way to join the transport, *Coromandel*, lying at the Royal Albert Dock.

With two gay Princes on their way to Africa, the news came from York Cottage, Sandringham, that a second son had been born to the Duke and Duchess of York, and that he was to be called Albert. From Las Palmas soon came a message that Prince Henry had arrived there safely.

A very excited Princess Ena also received a letter from her father. Prince Henry had taken advantage of a break in the voyage out to Cape Coast to do some sight-seeing in Spain, and from there he wrote to his daughter, with strangely prophetic words: 'Always be a good girl and love your mother. If you do this, when you grow up and are big, you too will travel, and you will come to this beautiful country. You will see for yourself that you will like it and how happy you will be here.'

On 27th December the main column of the Expeditionary Force, Prince Henry with it, started its march towards Kumasi. There were a number of cases of fever among the troops by the time the River Pra was reached on 4th January. At Prahsu, Prince Henry went for an evening stroll with Major Ferguson, the camp commandant, the Prince noting that his companion had signs of fever. Two days later Ferguson was dead. The Prince, considerably upset, continued with the column to Kwisa, some forty miles from Kumasi, reached on the 10th. Here Prince Henry was attacked by malaria and doctors ordered that he should be carried back to the coast immediately. At Prahsu hope of saving his life was almost given up, but he rallied and reached Cape Coast Castle on the 17th. There, despite his protests that he wished to stay on African soil until Kumasi was occupied, he was induced to go on board H.M.S. *Blonde*, and the journey began back to England.

It was a Friday afternoon and, after a good night, the Prince was talking about a stroll on the deck on Sunday. On that day came a turn for the worse. The Prince, worrying about the unkindly comments about him in the English Press, sent a last message to Princess Beatrice: 'In case I die, tell the Princess from me that I came here not to win glory but from a sense of duty.' He died quietly on the evening of Monday, 20th January 1896, as H.M.S. *Blonde* steamed off the coast of Sierra Leone. On the same day, at Kumasi, King Prempeh made submission to the Governor of Cape Coast.

Meantime, life at Osborne went on without an inkling of the shock that was so shortly to break upon it. Sir Henry Ponsonby was dead, and the Queen missed him sorely. Her eyes were troubling her, and she could not find glasses to suit. As a result, Princess Beatrice's duties increased considerably. News then came of the Jameson Raid on Johannesburg, and Emperor William's telegram of congratulation to Kruger, and no one could talk of anything else.

Lord Wolseley reported faithfully to the Queen and Princess all the news which he had of Prince Henry but, as he said, the newspapers seemed to get the information before the War Office. He had received a report that the Prince had been a universal favourite on board on the journey out, had sprained his ankle slightly but recovered before landing. On 3rd January the Princess heard that her husband had been appointed Military Secretary to Sir Francis Scott and that his presence was of great help when dealing with native chiefs, who were much impressed at meeting a man married to a daughter of the Great Queen. On the 10th she received a telegram from Sir Francis saying that her husband was suffering from an attack of fever, slight, but enough to prevent him going further. Next day she heard that he was returning to Cape Coast, with a medical officer and his servant, Butcher. A later message said that the fever was declining and that there was hope that he might get back to the Force in time for the entry into Kumasi. The telegrams still gave little cause for anxiety and, on the 16th, one came from Prince Henry himself, at the hospital at Cape Coast Castle, saying that he had arrived there safely, thanks to the care of the doctor and his servant.

On the 22nd another telegram arrived. The Princess was expecting this to give the news that her husband had arrived at Madeira. There it had been planned he should stay awhile, the Princess hoping to go out and join him during his convalescence. Instead the telegram announced that Prince Henry of Battenberg was dead.

Princess Beatrice read it with half-seeing eyes. 'The life is gone out of me', she said, and turned away. The Duchess of Connaught led her to her room.

Later in the day the Queen went to sit with her daughter, and tried to comfort her. There had been no tragedy that touched her so deeply since her own husband had died in 1861. Knowing how devoted the couple had been, she found the Princess's talk of her vanished happiness heart-rending, but Beatrice remained firm in her belief that her husband had been right to go.

On board *Blonde* the problem was how to preserve the body of Prince Henry in the equatorial heat. The solution was found by placing it in a tank fashioned out of biscuit tins and filled with rum.

At Madeira Prince Henry's body was transferred from the *Blonde* to the *Blenheim*, which reached Portsmouth on the morning of 4th February.

The Royal Yacht, *Alberta*, carried Princess Beatrice, the Prince of Wales, the Duke of Connaught, Princess Christian, Princes Louis and Francis of Battenberg, and Grand Duke Ernest of Hesse across the Solent to where *Blenheim* lay. The coffin had been placed in the Captain's cabin and there a short service was held, conducted by the Bishop of Winchester and the naval chaplain. The coffin was then transferred to the *Alberta* and Prince Henry's last journey to the Island began.

As soon as the *Alberta* was sighted, the Queen left Osborne by carriage for Trinity Wharf, Cowes, with Princess Louise, Prince Alexander and Princess Ena, the two younger children following with their governess and nurse.

It was a perfect, still afternoon and the sun was going down. Above the booming of the minute guns and the tolling of the bells on the ships, no sound came from the *Alberta* as she glided up to the pier. The Queen walked to where the flower-covered coffin lay, between the funnels and the saloon. Veiled entirely in black, Princess Beatrice stood at the coffin's head. The Queen laid her wreath and looked at her daughter. It was the most poignant moment that had ever passed between them.

At nine o'clock next morning Princess Beatrice came back to the pier, alone but for her children and the Duke of Connaught. The anchor wreath of orchids and lilies was placed, and she said her last goodbye.

Along a road lined with troops, men of the Princess Beatrice's Volunteer Battalion led the gun-carriage on its way to Whippingham. Behind the coffin walked a groom leading the Prince's favourite hunter, the Captain of the *Sheilah*, and Butcher, the servant who had been with the Prince in Africa, and was with him when he died. Prince Alexander walked between his uncles, the Prince of Wales and the Duke of Connaught, Princess Beatrice riding in the Queen's carriage with her mother and the younger children.

Once again the choir of St. George's Chapel, Windsor, had journeyed to the parish church at Whippingham, as they had ten years before on a very different occasion.

The Princess busied herself with plans for the monument to be placed at Whippingham. The sarcophagus was to be surmounted by a recumbent statue, and the tomb ornamented at the sides and corners with columns of green and white marble from Iona, an island which her husband had loved to visit.

With the Ashanti affair over and the men home, all manner of stories soon began to circulate about Prince Henry's part in the campaign—tales of his cheerfulness, his energy; of the manner in which he impressed the Chiefs; and of how he had jumped into a fight between native troops and saved a man from being murdered. Now, tragically late, the pendulum had swung.

Noting the wide expression of national feeling, Queen Victoria expressed her appreciation in a letter published in the *Gazette*, in which she referred to Prince Henry as 'a bright sunbeam in my Home'.

8

Diamond Jubilee

MOTHER and daughter were widowed at the same age. For a quarter of a century the Queen had wailed her grief from behind a wall and demanded close support. Princess Beatrice chose a very different course. She decided to do what she had never done before, and would never do again—to spend a whole month alone with her children away from her mother and royal routine.

The occasions since 1861 when she had been parted from the Queen for more than a week could be counted on the fingers of one hand. There had been the trip to Aix to take a cure for her rheumatism . . . there had been several short visits with Prince Henry to Germany to stay with relations . . . and that was all.

She was determined to face her problem squarely, and to fight it on her own. With her children playing round her, she hoped to mitigate the force of the shock. She chose to go to the south of France.

On the 13th February Princess Beatrice went into her mother's bedroom to say goodbye, until they met again at Cimiez in March. A few days passed before the Queen returned to Windsor, days of unbroken gloom for the Isle of Wight. The 'sunbeam in her home' was dead, she missed her grandchildren, and felt lost without the support of her daughter. In *My Memories of Six Reigns* Princess Marie Louise called back to life a few moments of one of those days:

'. . . a dark, dank afternoon in February—the Queen was at Osborne, and she went out for her customary drive with Lady Errol, who was then in waiting. These dear elderly ladies, swathed in crêpe, drove in an open carriage, called a sociable. The Queen was very silent, and Leila (Lady Errol), thought it time to make a little conversation. So she said, "Oh, Your Majesty, think of when we shall see our dear ones again in Heaven!"

"Yes," said the Queen.

"We will all meet in Abraham's bosom," said Leila.

"I will *not* meet Abraham," said the Queen.'

At Windsor, also, Prince Henry was seldom out of her thoughts. Although opposed by the War Office, she persisted in her demand that a decoration should be given to all who took part in the Ashanti Expedition and that this decoration should be a memorial to Prince Henry. A Star was eventually decided upon.

Prince Christian Victor came to the Castle to give his grandmother a first-hand account of what had happened on the march from Cape Coast to Kumasi, and he brought with him, as a present for her, King Prempeh's umbrella and stool.

Countess Feodora Gleichen called to show the statuette she was doing of Prince Henry in uniform, and the Queen heard with great interest that Rowland Prothero, son of the former Rector of Whippingham, had begun work on a memoir of her son-in-law.

Hidden away from the world in the Villa Liserb at Cimiez, Princess Beatrice was not allowed to be lonely. Her two brothers-in-law came to see her, and then Princess Louise arrived. She was just the person to have near one at a time like this. Sympathetic, gay, a brilliant conversationalist, she adored children, though she had none of her own.

The Empress Eugénie was also a great comfort. She was staying at her villa at Cap Martin and with her came her bathing partner, the Empress Elizabeth of Austria.

Seventy now and a very splendid *grande dame*, there was little of the old lady about the Empress Eugénie—in the event she had still quarter of a century of life before her.

And despite the contrast in their ages, in their up-bringing, in their religion and in their experience, a very real friendship blossomed between Princess Beatrice and the Empress.

In the second week in March, Queen Victoria arrived at Cimiez, staying at the Grand Hotel Excelsior, and gradually Princess Beatrice was drawn back into the routine she knew so well. Comings and goings were reported once more. Calls upon the Queen had been made by the Emperor and Empress of Austria, the King of the Belgians, the Empress Frederick, the Empress Marie of Russia and the Empress Eugénie. The Queen had visited Lord Salisbury at his villa at Beaulieu. She had also received a deputation of eight fishwives, who presented her with a basket of roses.

Part of Princess Beatrice's problem was her conviction that she must make her own grief take second place to duty. The Queen was an old woman, and in the years ahead she would need ever-increasing help—help with reading, help with writing, help with remembering. She would be able to undertake less physical effort and the greatest care would be needed to conserve her energy. That meant that everything must remain as it had always been: everything must be to hand. Princess Beatrice knew how essential it was that she and her children should stay with the Queen. She would continue in the supporting rôle which she had so long played. She had told her mother that she was going to Cimiez to find the courage to go on. She had found it.

Yet, as the months slowly passed, the Princess found that the pain in her heart grew worse, and harder to bear, as she moved round homes which had become so indelibly

12

connected with Henry—the sea at Osborne, the moors round Balmoral and the stables at Windsor. She showed her true feelings in a letter of sympathy written to Lady 'Wally' Paget that summer, after the sudden death of Sir Augustus:

'How terrible for you to be fetched in that way, and yet I envy you having been with your beloved husband at the last moment. I am sure you also feel how the blessed hope of reunion is the only thing that helps one to bear this most awful of all losses, as well as the memory of all you have been to one another. But the blank in your life will, I fear, as time goes on, make itself more cruelly felt, as I only know too well. . . .'

The 22nd of September 1896 was a most important date for the Royal family, for on that day Queen Victoria's reign equalled in length that of any previous English sovereign, and at eight in the evening the Tsar and Tsarina of Russia arrived at Balmoral for a stay of a fortnight. The Queen seemed equally excited by both events.

Princess Beatrice stood with her mother at the Castle door, and watched the procession approach. Retainers bearing flaming torches had been waiting at the Gates and now marched beside the escort of Scots Greys, and the carriages. There were bonfires on every hill from Ballater, church bells rang out through the night, and the pipes were playing. The red tongues of the torches darted in the breeze, throwing strange shadow pictures of horses and men, and flickering lines where the carriage wheels turned.

'Alicky', dressed all in white, stepped from the carriage into the hall and embraced her grandmother and god-mother. The last of the Romanoffs had arrived in all their splendour amid the dark hills and fields of Deeside, where every cottager was the Queen's friend.

So great was the entourage of the Tsar and Tsarina

that a whole village of temporary huts, imported from Scandinavia, had been erected to house them. Every bed in the Castle was wanted, and the Battenberg children were sent to stay with the Connaughts at Abergeldie.

During the visit there was an event which intrigued all those at Balmoral. Mr. Downey, the photographer, arrived to take the first moving pictures of the Royal Family. The Queen found it very strange that she was asked to move about in front of the camera and that she had not to bid the great-grandchild[1] on her knee to be still and 'watch the birdie'. 'Animated pictures' she called them, and when the result was shown to her in November she found, to her amazement, that people looked as if they were *alive*.

The affair of Princess Beatrice and the German 'anarchist' also gave her family much amusement in 1896. The Empress Frederick was visiting Osborne and, a few days before her arrival, a tall German, with a very wild look in his eye and speaking broken English, presented himself at Osborne and asked that arrangements be made for him to see the Empress immediately she arrived. He would not be content with waiting until he could approach the head of the Empress's Household—he must see her at Trinity Pier. Frederick Ponsonby was acting Equerry and, guarding against the possibility of the man being either an anarchist or a lunatic, he arranged for a detective to follow him and keep in touch with his movements.

Ponsonby was a worried man as he drove with Princess Beatrice to meet the Empress. As he feared, there at the Pier was the tall German, trying to persuade the officer in charge to let him on. The Equerry had no option but to tell the Princess the story. She was horrified, and not without grounds, considering that in 1882 she had looked down the barrel of Maclean's pistol outside Windsor

[1] The Tsarina's daughter, Olga, whose sister, Anastasia, was later to be the subject of a more widely circulated film.

station. She was far from content with the precaution that this wild-looking man was being watched by a police officer, and considered that he should have been locked up.

As they talked the Empress arrived, and there was no time to take further steps to guard her safety. A perspiring Ponsonby hurried off to support the policeman in his watch. To his amazement he saw the Empress wave and blow a kiss to the suspect! He turned out to be a well-known sculptor whom the Empress had promised to see the moment she set foot in England. He had taken the words literally.

Before the year was out preparations for the Diamond Jubilee were well advanced, though it proved to be something of a nightmare for the planners. The whole excited nation wanted to celebrate and to see the little old lady, with failing eyesight and tired legs, who had passed through sixty summers since her crowning. She was being asked to face a programme that would have taxed a woman of half her age, and it was part of Princess Beatrice's responsibility to see that arrangements were kept within the limits of her mother's strength.

The original idea that the Queen should enter St. Paul's in her carriage, horses and all, had been dropped, as it was considered that some people might be shocked at finding horses among the congregation. It was decided that the service should be held outside, by the steps of the Cathedral. But here the statue of Queen Anne somewhat impeded the view, and the Queen was asked if the statue could be moved. 'Move Queen Anne?' she said sharply. 'Most certainly not! Why, it might some day be suggested that *my* statue should be moved, which I should much dislike.'

To save the Queen from undue strain it was decided that no crowned heads should be asked to the Jubilee. This upset the Emperor William considerably. He had been looking forward to flashing the might of Germany in the London streets, and to this end had been sending most affectionate letters to his grandmother, tactfully asking after the health and spirits of his Aunt Beatrice. He put the case that an exception should be made as far as he was concerned and even persuaded his mother to use her influence to get him an invitation. He had reckoned without the Prince of Wales who was absolutely determined that his nephew should not swagger in a procession which was the perquisite of the British Empire. He warned the Queen that, if 'Willy' were allowed to come, he would certainly arrive with an enormous suite, try to arrange things himself and that endless trouble would follow. The Queen needed no support—she had already decided.

Space was another limiting factor in the issue of invitations. Apart from the vast number of Imperial representatives who had been asked to attend, the Queen had the best part of a hundred direct descendants, counting in their husbands and wives. In the 'nineties frequent crises had occurred in the Royal Homes over the finding of bedrooms on the occasion of State visits and family gatherings. Sometimes the device of switching rooms was resorted to, the less important being banished to some obscure spot.

This happened to Princess Beatrice's Equerry. While he was out one evening, the immediate necessity arose of requisitioning his room. A valet moved his clothes elsewhere and a message was given to the night porter to be handed to the Equerry on his return, explaining what had happened. The porter forgot, and the Equerry went up to what he thought was still his room, and placed his top hat on what he took to be the bed. It was a lady's stomach. The resultant squeal, such as certainly had not been heard in Buckingham Palace in Victorian days, made him race for the safety of the corridor. As he paused for a moment to collect himself, insult followed mental injury. For a brief instant the door opened, and he ducked as his top hat sailed by.

The Queen and Princess Beatrice went to Cimiez again in March, a restful visit, the highlight of which came when Sarah Bernhardt, who was also staying at the Grand Hotel, performed a short piece before the Royal visitors in the drawing-room. Princess Beatrice spent much of her time sketching, and a water-colour she did of the *place* in front of the Monastery was a present to her mother on her seventy-eighth birthday.

Throughout the Jubilee celebrations Princess Beatrice never left her mother's side, except when the giving of precedence demanded it. She was so much part of her mother's life that when the Queen, chronicling the comings and goings of her large family, wrote 'All left at six . . .' that did not refer to her youngest daughter. The Princess now discarded her black and appeared dressed all in white, but thoughts of Prince Henry were ever present. It was the same with the Queen. Her first words on the morning of 20th June were how sad it was that her beloved Liko was not there. Always, on great occasions, she craved the support of the favoured men in her life—Albert, Brown, Disraeli, and finally Henry of Battenberg. . . .

The Queen came up from Windsor on the 21st and, as she drove with Princess Beatrice from Paddington to Buckingham Palace, she had a foretaste of her reception on the morrow. It was a hot night and sleeping bodies already lay thick in the parks.

The head of the procession had passed by the time the Queen and Princess breakfasted in the Chinese Room. They watched for a while. At a quarter to eleven, eight creams drew Queen Victoria in the State landau out among the millions for the greatest drive of her long reign. Six miles of jubilant route—the Strand, St. Paul's, the Mansion House, London Bridge, Borough Road, the

Houses of Parliament, the Horse Guards. The Queen thought that no one had ever received such an ovation. There were few hitches, though the heat and the acclamation upset some of the horses. Lord Dundonald, who rode close to the State landau, kept repeating 'Steady, old lady', and the Queen was somewhat puzzled as to whether he was referring to herself or his fretful mare.

So many people had crowded into a refreshment tent erected in the Palace gardens that there was fear of wholesale fainting. A gallant gentleman drew his sword, with the intention of cutting an emergency window in the fabric. Unhappily the point of it pierced the thigh of a maid who was standing against the tent on the outside.

Of all the Jubilee celebrations, that with the most personal interest for Princess Beatrice was the review of the Indian and Colonial troops in Windsor Park. Among those on parade were the Hausas from West Africa, most of whom had taken part in the Ashanti Expedition. Before the review started she went alone to talk to these men, meeting those who had come into close touch with Prince Henry. Then she joined the Queen in her carriage and, with Lord Roberts beside them, they drove round the ranks.

Although the Queen's mental capacity had lost little in the course of the years, her physical infirmities were a mounting handicap and an irritation to her. She became a little 'difficult', and Princess Beatrice had to adopt firm tactics, as Brown had done during the Queen's other 'difficult' period—after the Consort's death. She was particularly touchy about her failing sight and anxious to prove that there was still little that could escape her eagle eye. Kind beyond measure as she was to her servants, she was now apt to catch them out.

Although her appetite was failing, the volume of food that came up from the royal kitchens did not diminish. Seldom did the Queen touch cold meat, but there must always be a chicken on the sideboard. These chickens were choice birds from the home farms, and each made six portions. The servants were very fond of a cold leg before they went to bed, and one night they overtaxed the supply. There was only half a chicken on the sideboard at lunch next day—and the Queen spotted this at once. She sent a whispered message to Princess Beatrice and the other ladies present ordering them to ask for chicken. Long remembered was the rocket which subsequently exploded in the Windsor kitchens.

Dirt was a fetish with the Queen. Coming across an unpolished cabinet in a suite off the Grand Corridor at Windsor, she wrote 'Victoria R' with her finger through the dust. Next morning she found the signature still there; so she wrote below it the name of the maid responsible for the cleaning. On the third morning she looked again. Both signatures had gone, and so had the maid. In the evening shadows, as the lamp trimmers went their rounds, the frightened girl had stolen from the Castle and run for the station. She was fetched back, of course, and the Queen sent for her and was very kind.

Princess Beatrice was a great favourite with the servants and always most solicitous of their welfare. In 1898, a few weeks after M. Gabriel Tschumi[1] joined the kitchen staff at Windsor as an apprentice, he met Princess Beatrice in a corridor. As he was a cousin of a dresser to the Queen, the Princess showed particular interest and asked how he was getting on. Newly arrived from Switzerland, Tschumi was unfamiliar with the Royal Family and mistook the Princess for a lady of the Household. He answered her questions frankly, told her he was happy, and that he liked the food, for now he ate meat three times a day whilst in Switzerland he had only had it once a week. He added that there was so much chicken that some of the servants were sick of the sight of it!

[1] The well-known chef whose last Royal position was with Queen Mary at Marlborough House, from 1948–1952.

One of the Princess's questions he evaded. She wanted to know if the apprentices had pillow fights at night. They did—but he was not letting on about that.

That evening a startled apprentice learned from his cousin that the lady who had talked with him in such beautiful French was Her Royal Highness Princess Beatrice.

The Princess was much pleased when she was appointed to succeed her husband as Captain and Governor of the Isle of Wight. This office had once held both military and political importance, but by this time was little more than honorary. Prince Henry had taken his duties most seriously, spending many hours studying the Island's history, an interest which his widow shared. Her happiest childhood days had been spent at Osborne; she had been married from there, and her husband lay buried at Whippingham. To add to the connection with the Island, the 'Life'[1] of her husband had now been written by the son of the Rector of Whippingham.

Princess Beatrice's last visits to the Continent with her mother took them again to Cimiez. Restful as these visits may have been whilst in the south of France, the journeys back and forth meant much work and worry for the Princess. A most immobile old lady had to be transported up and down gangways and along piers—and the Queen disliked the public seeing her rolled about in her chair. The Royal party alone would number upwards of a hundred and, further to complicate the move, railway and

[1] *H.R.H. Prince Henry Maurice of Battenberg, K.G., A Memoir*, by Rowland E. Prothero, printed for private circulation, 1897. When Labouchere, proprietor and editor of *Truth*, asked the author to send him a copy, Prothero replied that he could not, as it was printed only for private circulation. 'You must ask Princess Beatrice,' he said. 'You know that I could not do that,' answered Labouchere, whose barbed criticisms had often irritated the Royal Family.

steamship directors, port authorities, generals and admirals, all thought it their duty to fuss around. Sirens hooted, bands played, guards presented arms and the crowds roared their approval and tried to evade the police so that they might get a better view.

Often the harassed daughter-cum-secretary-cum-nurse could hardly make her directions heard. In addition the Queen was prone to seasickness. In 1898 the weather forecast proved very wrong and the *Victoria and Albert* ran into a gale. The sea broke through the porthole of the Queen's cabin and the Princess, aided by maids and stewards, had to wheel her away quickly.

Princess Beatrice's epic of self-sacrifice and devotion was now reaching its climax. The Queen was beset by such national and personal anxieties and tragedies that the strain must have told on the length of her days. The Princess was never off duty. Helped as she was by her brothers and sisters, particularly the Prince of Wales, the Duke of Connaught and Princess Christian, she still had little time for the normal life of a mother with young children.

Meanwhile, British troops were engaged in many parts of the world. There was trouble on the Indian frontier. Kitchener was fighting in the Sudan. There was the Fashoda incident, and, in October 1899, came the Boer War. Engagements now were concentrated on the military, and three times in a year the Queen and Princess Beatrice visited the wounded in Netley Hospital, taking with them quilts which they had made themselves. There was a continual round of presentation of Colours and inspection of Volunteers.

Princess Beatrice suffered a loss in the Boer War, for her a peculiar tragedy. A third Prince died in Africa. Prince Christian Victor, her nephew, who had been with Prince Henry in Ashanti, died of fever at Pretoria. He was serving with the 60th King's Royal Rifles. Africa had claimed the Prince Imperial . . . Prince Henry . . . and now Prince Christian Victor. . . .

The Prince's sister, Helena Victoria, was staying at Balmoral with the Queen and Princess Beatrice when the news arrived. Young Maurice Battenberg was much upset to hear of the death of the soldier-cousin who had been with his father in Ashanti and that evening, in his dressing-gown, went to Princess Helena Victoria's room and said: 'Cousin Thora, it may comfort you to know that I have decided to join the 60th when I am old enough.' In 1914 his mother was to have strong reason to remember those words.

There were a great many other deaths to sadden the last years of the Queen, and upon Princess Beatrice usually fell the unenviable task of breaking the news. Many were contemporaries of the Queen and their course had ended, as her's was to do, with the turn of the century. There was more sadness, perhaps, at the passing of the humble ones, such as Annie Macdonald the dresser, the old lady who kept the shop at Balmoral, and Princess Beatrice's nurse, than at the demise of world figures like Gladstone and Bismarck.

Another tragedy was the illness of the Queen's eldest daughter. In her widowhood, the Empress Frederick had come much closer to her mother. Until that time there had been, deep down, a touch of competition, even of jealousy, between them. 'Vicky' also drew nearer to her sisters, in particular Helena, and Beatrice's frequent visits to Friedrichshof proved the tie between the eldest and youngest of Victoria's girls. It was there that she and Prince Henry had spent their last holiday together.

In the autumn of 1898, when riding in the Taunus woods, the Empress's horse shied at a threshing machine. She was thrown, and dragged for some yards. She made light of her injuries, but soon afterwards complained of pains in her back. In due course the diagnosis proved to be cancer.

Despite the strain and the sorrows, the Queen retained her mental alertness and powers of conversation until the last six months of her life, when a loss of memory began to worry her. When the Aga Khan sat at dinner between Princess Beatrice and her mother, then in her eightieth year, he said of the Queen: 'The vigour of her bearing and the facility and clarity of her conversation were astonishing.'

Few guests were now asked to stay, and those who did found that Princess Beatrice usually acted as hostess. One of the most important visits of the last years was that of Emperor William and his Empress, 'Dona', to Windsor in November 1899. William was trying to put right some of the bad feeling engendered between Britain and Germany over the Boer War, and he gave three hundred pounds to the bereaved families of men of the 1st Royal Dragoons, of which he was Colonel-in-Chief.

At times like this, Princess Beatrice had to hide her own feelings in duty to her mother. She had to forget what 'Dona' had said about the Battenbergs at the time of her marriage, and how badly William had treated Sandro. She met the guests at the station when they arrived, and dutifully saw them off when they left.

Meanwhile, the news, much of it bad, was pouring in from South Africa. The Queen was so busy and worried that, for only the second time in fifty years, she did not spend Christmas at Osborne. The other occasion was when Princess Beatrice had her first child.

At Windsor, on Boxing Day, there was a party for the wives and children of the men of the regiments stationed there. Princess Beatrice and her children helped to pour tea and the Queen handed out presents from her wheel-chair.

Shafts of sunlight that lit the last year of the Queen's reign, and the first of a new century, were the Royal visit to Ireland, the relief of Mafeking, and the Garden Party at Buckingham Palace.

The Queen had been planning to take her spring holiday at Bordighera, on the Italian Riviera, but the feeling in France was such that it was judged better that she should not cross that country. She was not perturbed, for already she had another idea. She would instead visit Dublin. It was nearly forty years since she had last crossed the Irish Sea. Displeased, amongst other reasons, at the Mayor of Dublin's refusal to erect a statue to the Prince Consort, she had not paid another visit, for she was slow to forget.

Fired now with enthusiasm over the bravery of the Irish troops in South Africa, she had sent them a special message of congratulation, giving them permission to wear the shamrock on St. Patrick's Day, and decided that, on her visit, she would announce the formation of the Irish Guards.

Princess Beatrice and Princess Christian accompanied the Queen on this visit, which began early in April. Out from Holyhead, the old *Victoria and Albert* bucketed about in a fresh wind, and soon there were casualties among the Royal party. But they could retire and lie in privacy: their retinue could not. Down in the larder, below the paddle wheels, young Tschumi thought that the yacht would founder at any moment, and, while he was sure that a place would be found in a lifeboat for the Queen, he was not so sure of the fate of an apprentice-cook below.

Dublin's reception was terrific, though every now and then the boo of a Nationalist would be heard above the cheers. Although it had been intended that the visit should be quiet, the Irish would not have it so. The Princesses were with their mother on enthusiastic State drives, on visits to hospitals and convents and the

Zoological Gardens, and at a gathering of 52,000 school-children in Phoenix Park.

Every afternoon the Princess sat with her mother on long carriage drives, of twenty miles or so. They were like those in Scotland in years gone by, except for the number of people in attendance. These included mounted Equerries. The carriage always proceeded at a slow jog trot, and before the stay was over the backsides of three Equerries were quite worn out.

On these drives the Queen was apt to doze off. As it would certainly not do for the groups of people who gathered by the roadside to see her asleep and have their acclamation pass unacknowledged, a drill was arranged between the Equerry and Princess Beatrice. When the Princess saw the Equerry spur his horse up to the carriage she knew that there were people ahead. She then nudged her mother, who was thus ready to smile and bow as she passed.

On the morning of 19th May Princess Beatrice and her mother were visiting 'friends' in the kennels at Windsor when the news came through that Mafeking had been relieved. This was a wonderful day for the whole country —and doubly so for a fourteen-year-old schoolboy at Wellington College, where Prince Alexander was eagerly awaiting a visit from his mother and grandmother.

Princess Beatrice made her separate way to the school, the Queen with the Duke of Connaught following by carriage. All the way along the road the crowds were 'quite mad with excitement' and there were pictures of Baden-Powell in every window.

The headmaster, with the Princess and her son, was waiting to receive the Queen when she arrived. She was shown the Chapel, the library and the dining-hall, and introduced to one of the masters in 'Drino's' house. Tea with the headmaster followed. As the Queen and Princess drove away, to the cheering of wildly excited boys, they passed an arch bearing the inscription, 'Welcome to the Queen of Mafeking'.

The swan-song of Queen Victoria proved to be the Garden Party at Buckingham Palace on 11th July 1900. It was the last time many of her subjects were to see her. The Queen's long reign, the reaction from the Boer War, and admiration for her courage and tenacity, all combined to create an emotion that brought many near to tears.

It was a brilliant day, and hot. The Palace gardens were at their best and the sunlight picked out the cluster of white marquees and the scarlet uniforms of the watermen as they rowed on the lake. Five thousand guests had come in from the Mall and now, on the green lawns, flashed a tapestry of uniforms and picture hats and long, muslin dresses of grey and white and pastel.

The centre-piece was the Queen, her carriage with the two white horses moving at a walking pace. Behind came her family—the Prince of Wales, in a white hat—the Duke and Duchess of York—the old Duke of Cambridge— Princess Beatrice with Princess Ena, long fair hair hanging down her back. There were white feathers and a rose in the Queen's bonnet, pearls around her throat, and she carried a white parasol, lace-covered.

At twenty minutes to seven the Queen left. Lady Monkswell described the scene:

'. . . Princess Beatrice sat beside her, the little girl Princess Ena sat back to the horses, and off she went to Windsor—we heard the crowd cheering her as she drove up Constitution Hill. I was glad to notice that though she wanted a good deal of help she was able to walk of herself and was not carried. Perhaps this is the last time I shall see her. God Save the Queen.'

In September the Queen's health began to decline. She had lost weight, slept badly and her failing memory caused her to exert additional mental effort.

But still she travelled, to Osborne in August, to Balmoral in October, to Windsor in November. Her energies now were reserved for her returning soldiers. She inspected the Life Guards and Canadian troops.

The 21st November was Vicky's sixtieth birthday. The last days of two Empresses were ticking away, and it was in doubt which would outlive the other. The Empress Frederick, racked with such pain that she could no longer write, now sent messages to her mother in the hand of her own 'Benjamina', Margaret, her youngest daughter. She did everything to conceal the agony in which she lay.

Princess Beatrice was torn between divided loyalties. Feeling that she must see her sister and know of her condition for herself, she hurried out to Friedrichshof for a few days early in December. She was deeply upset at how suffering had altered the beloved face and at the constant pain that racked the stricken woman.

Preparations for that Christmas proceeded with even more care than usual. It was particularly difficult to think of anything to give the ailing Queen, and yet important that she should have things she liked which might cheer her up. The Prince and Princess of Wales hit upon the idea of giving her a miniature of her two Pomeranians, Marco and Turi, of which she was very fond. The idea was splendid, but the problem was how to do it? The dogs were seldom away from their mistress's side, and accompanied her on nearly all her airings. They were only left alone at the Castle when the Queen went out for drives or on some official duty, and that was seldom now. Yet it was essential that the present should be a surprise. There was only one thing to do—call on Princess Beatrice to help.

The Prince of Wales had chosen Mrs. Gertrude Massey to be the artist and in due course she received a telegram from Windsor to report to the Castle and ask for Princess Henry of Battenberg.

The Court was in mourning for Prince Christian Victor,

Princess Victoria Eugénie (Ena) of Battenberg with Queen Victoria,
Osborne, 1897

At Osborne House, 1900. *Left to right:* Prince Leopold of Battenber
Windsor); Queen Mary, then Duchess of York, holding Princess Ma
ground, Prince Alexander of Battenberg; the late King George VI, th
Duke of York; Queen Victoria; Prince Arthur of Connaught; t
Connaught; Princess Beatrice; Princess Ena of Battenber

Harris Picture Agency

ncess Marie Louise; Prince Edward of York (now the Duke of
w the Princess Royal); Princess Margaret of Connaught; on the
nce Albert of York, being held by his father, King George V, then
chess of Connaught; on the ground, Princess Victoria Patricia of
ncess Helena Victoria; and Prince Maurice of Battenberg

Balmoral, September, 1857

The floods at Windsor, November, 1894 (*from Princess Beatrice's personal album*)

and Mrs. Massey had to borrow a black outfit before, in
considerable trepidation, she set out on her mission. At
the Castle no one seemed to know why she had come, but
after some enquiries she began a seemingly endless walk
behind a footman, up stairs, down stairs, along passages,
up steps, down steps, turn left, turn right, until she found
herself in the Grand Corridor. At the end of the Corridor
she was shown into a room, all gold and pale blue, and
filled with flowers.

Princess Beatrice came in, and in the words of Mrs.
Massey:

> 'She was very business-like and capable: she was
> extremely kind to me, but I had a feeling that I should
> not like to oppose her wishes. She rolled her R's freely
> in her speech, as when she invited me to use the
> r-r-room with the best light for my work. Considerate
> and thoughtful, she was anxious to know if I was tired,
> or could get anything for me.'

It was decided that Mrs. Massey should be ready to
work each day at twelve, in the hope that a chance would
come for her to see the dogs. She was given a room with
doors at each end and a table hidden behind a screen. If
the Queen were to come through in her chair, she was
quickly to take cover.

Sometimes Mrs. Massey would wait, and no one would
come near the room. A member of the staff might hurriedly
bring along Marco and Turi, and there would be a short
period of furious work, a look-out being kept for possible
intruders. Marco was old, brown, with grey on his face,
and a good sitter. White Turi was young and wanted to
play. If told to sit up, he would hold out a paw, and, when
tired of this, go to sleep.

Somehow the miniature was completed, but not without misadventure. Once, hearing the sound of voices, Mrs.
Massey ducked hastily behind her screen. A posse of

13

foreign Royalties sauntered into the room and, to her horror, stopped to chatter only a few feet away from her. An unwilling eavesdropper, she dreaded to think of how she would explain her presence were she to sneeze.

On 12th December Marco and Turi were left behind at the Castle while the Queen attended a sale of needlework by Irish ladies at the Windsor Town Hall. Princess Beatrice sat beside her mother in the open carriage, and opposite sat the Duchess of York.[1] It was the last public appearance of the Queen, and the last occasion on which she was photographed with Princess Beatrice. Christmas presents were bought at the stalls, one of them being a screen embroidered with the Napoleonic badge which was to go to the Empress Eugénie.

Wellington College broke up on 18th December and Prince Alexander was early back at Windsor, for the Christmas holidays were again being spent at Osborne and the Royal Family was leaving that day. He was at the station when his mother and sister arrived with the Queen.

In the Queen's own words, it was a terribly sad Christmas for them all, with little time for parents to spend with their children. The Princesses were very hard worked. Princess Helena Victoria took over the writing of the Queen's *Journal* and Princess Beatrice wrote her letters. The Queen could not sleep, and Princess Beatrice tried the experiment of sitting with her through the long hours, reading aloud, but this had the effect of only keeping her mother even more wide awake, so the experiment was dropped. Exhausted, the Queen would fall asleep in the early hours and then not awaken until noon, which infuriated her beyond measure. A final touch of sadness, Lady Churchill died suddenly at Osborne, thus ending fifty years of close association with the Queen.

On Boxing Day Princess Beatrice wrote to her dying sister at Friedrichshof:

[1] Later Queen Mary.

'Dearest Vicky,

So many thanks for the interesting old Japanese Brule Parfume you have so kindly sent me for Xmas, which I think might come in quite usefully one day for keeping a breakfast dish hot. I thought so much of you on Xmas Eve, wondering how you would be spending it. I trust in not too much pain!

'Dear Mama was able to come down for a short while to the *Bescherung*[1] but she was very depressed . . . and generally rather weak, her sight is so very bad and she could hardly see all her pretty presents, but she was very much pleased and particularly touched that you should have thought it out for her. It certainly is a most beautiful piece of workmanship. It was too sad, how many presents were mementoes of dear departed ones . . .

'Mama is so afraid that you may be worrying about her and about her inability to write to you, but I assured her you would not, though of course you were very sorry she was so uncomfortable and far from well. I do think she is a little better and able to take more nourishment, allowing herself to be fed every 2 hours, and she does not attempt to come to any meals, keeping quite quiet in her room, excepting when she goes out for a little,

Ever, dearest Vicky,
Your loving and attached sister,
BEATRICE.'

Next day the Queen dictated to Princess Beatrice a letter for her eldest daughter.

'Darling child,' she began, as was her custom. '. . . A thousand thanks for the most beautiful and tasteful magnifying glass which I shall always use in thinking of you. I have not been very well myself, but nothing

[1] Distribution of presents.

to cause you alarm, and I have not a bad pulse. I have been able to get out a little most days. . . .'

There were to be few more outings. On New Year's Day the Queen went with the Duke of Connaught to visit convalescing soldiers, and to Whippingham Church, while the Princesses Christian and Beatrice stayed at Osborne to answer a mountain of telegrams, letters and cards of congratulation for the beginning of 1901. Next day Lord Roberts arrived to meet the Queen, and Princess Beatrice, as Governor of the Isle of Wight, met him at Trinity Pier.

It was now a strain to talk to people, and the Queen liked best to hear music in her room. Young Prince Leopold played the violin, charmingly the Queen thought. His mother accompanied him, and also played duets with a lady-in-waiting. On 13th January the Queen's *Journal* ended, having been kept religiously for nearly seventy years. Her active life was over.

One more letter went to the Empress Frederick. The Queen wanted to tell her about the visit of Lord Roberts and of how Princess Beatrice had received him. Slowly the words drifted to her 'Benjamina', who wrote them down. The tired old lady, who could see no more, ended her letter in that most hackneyed of ways—she must stop now to catch the post. No, the postman could have waited, but she was in fact so weary that no more words would come.

9

End of an Era

ON Wednesday, 16th January 1901, the Queen went for a morning airing in her donkey chaise in the grounds of Osborne House. When the chaise came to the door again in the afternoon, Princess Beatrice sent it away empty.

The doctors said firmly that the Queen must transact no more business, and the despatch boxes began to pile up. Her three daughters, the Princesses Helena, Louise and Beatrice, took turns by her bedside. The Prince of Wales came to the Isle of Wight and, satisfied that all was well for the moment, returned to London. The Duke of Connaught was in Germany, representing the Queen in the celebrations taking place to mark the two-hundredth anniversary of the foundation of the Prussian Monarchy.

Randall Davidson, Bishop of Winchester, came to pray by the Queen's bedside. When he had gone she turned to Princess Beatrice and said: 'I think I ought to see Canon Clement Smith,[1] otherwise he might be hurt.'

On the 18th the Queen's condition deteriorated, and a telegram was sent to Berlin advising the Duke of Connaught to return. To the Duke's consternation, the Emperor decided to come to England with him. William postponed all functions, waved aside opposition, disregarded the feelings of the British Royal Family and the public, and personally undertook the arrangements for the journey. He wrote to the British Ambassador:

'I have duly informed the Prince of Wales, begging

[1] The Vicar of Whippingham.

him at the same time that *no notice* whatever is taken of
me as Emperor and that I come as grandson. . . . I
suppose the 'petticoats' who are fencing off poor
Grandmamma from the world—and I fear, often from
me—will kick up a row when they hear of my coming;
but I don't care, for what I do is my duty, the more so
as it is this "unparalleled" grandmamma, as none ever
existed before. . . . I leave with Uncle Arthur. . . . Am
sorry, very sorry.'

It happened to be the duty of the 'petticoats' to see
that their mother was kept quiet and unworried, and their
nephew had often proved that his presence and peace
were not synonymous. Relations were already filling every
available bedroom in the vicinity of Osborne. In addition
to their nursing duties, the Princesses were faced with
the task of replying to endless telegrams. It was certainly
very much in doubt if at such a time they would welcome
the usual theatricals from the 'All Highest'. On the
journey to Flushing the Emperor drove the special train,
apparently under the impression that the experience
would cheer up his uncle.

The news that the Emperor was on his way did in fact
cause consternation at Osborne. As the Queen had rallied
in the meantime, a telegram was sent off telling him to
stay in London. Princess Beatrice's message to her relations on the morning of the 21st read: 'The Queen's
condition is very grave, but not entirely without hope.'

That evening hope died, and the Prince of Wales and
Emperor William were summoned. They arrived early
next morning, and were met by the Princesses. The
Emperor said earnestly to his aunts: 'My first wish is not
to be in the light, and I will return to London if you wish.
I should like to see Grandmamma before she dies, but if
that is impossible I shall quite understand.' Thereafter
he behaved splendidly, though the wish was expressed

that some of the respect and affection that he now showed
for his grandmother could have been extended to his
mother.

The Queen hung on tenaciously to life. The Marquess
of Carisbrooke recalls that he talked with her at eleven
o'clock that morning, and her thoughts were still clear. But
at two-thirty in the afternoon the Princesses summoned the
rest of the family to the Queen's room. Like a sinking ship,
rising and falling with the waves, each rise smaller than the
last, she moved from consciousness to coma. For nearly
three hours her grandson William cradled her in his arms.
She thought for a while that he was 'dear Fritz', his
father. At five o'clock she whispered her children's names
—'Bertie', Helena, Louise, Arthur, Beatrice. She asked
that her white Pomeranian should be put on her bed, but
Turi was bored and would not stay there. At five-thirty
the Duchess of York[1] arrived. An hour later Queen
Victoria was dead.

Death did not bring an immediate end to the authority
of Queen Victoria. She had left detailed and explicit
instructions as to what was to be done after she died and
how the funeral was to be conducted, even down to the
music that was to be played. These instructions had been
given to Princess Beatrice, as her favourite daughter and
most constant companion; to Princess Beatrice and the
Duke of Connaught in their capacity as executors of her
will; and to Princess Beatrice and the Prince of Wales in
two papers addressed jointly to them and dated 25th
October 1897 and 21st January 1898.

There was no black to be upon her in her passing. She
was rejoining Albert. Now that she was dead, the wedding
veil that she had worn on the 10th of February 1840 was
placed over her face, and her bed was covered with flowers.

In due season the little woman, who had once weighed

[1] Later Queen Mary.

eleven stone and eight pounds, but was so much lighter now, was lifted by King Edward VII and the Emperor of Germany, and placed in her coffin. Her wedding dress, and a flag, were placed over her. The room in which Princess Alice had been married became a *chapelle ardente*.

So many years had passed since the death of a Sovereign that no one knew quite what to do. As if the rising of the sun and Queen Victoria were two eternals, knowledge of the ceremonial for the funeral, and the accession of the new King, were found to be far from complete. Old staff hesitated to give up their duties, and new staff to take them on. Almost as if the donkey chaise would suddenly appear in the drive and explanations sharply demanded. The Princess of Wales asked not to be called Queen until the funeral was over.

On 1st February, Princess Beatrice walked with her sisters and the new Queen as the coffin began its journey to Windsor. She was thinking of that other time she had gone in black to Trinity Pier, when her husband came back in the *Alberta*.

There was more to remind her of the Battenbergs before the funeral procession had ended its journey. At Windsor the horses, which were to draw the gun-carriage bearing the coffin, had grown restive in the cold, and broke their traces. Prince Louis of Battenberg suggested that the naval guard of honour should replace the horses, and so it was that sailors led Queen Victoria home to Windsor for the last time.

On 4th February the coffin was taken to the mausoleum at Frogmore, as the pipers blew their lament. The husband of Princess Louise, now Duke of Argyll, wrote:

' . . . and so . . . her children and grand-children and great-grandchildren following her, our dear Queen was brought to where she would be at rest beside her Prince.

In the tomb, sunk into the grey granite sarcophagus, his coffin was seen, and upon it lay the sword that he wore. Her own was lifted, and then slowly lowered by her faithful Life Guards until it lay by his. For thirty-nine years the loving spirits had been separated. How long it seems, and yet what an unfelt moment in the being of the Eternal!'

The Victorian age was over.

It was a strange and unreal situation in which the children of Queen Victoria found themselves in the early months of 1901. Until late middle age there had always been a guide. Now they were alone, although the echo of the past still sounded from the palace walls.

The new King and Princess Beatrice stood in strange contrast to one another. Edward, nearing sixty, was the eldest of the children, except for 'Vicky' who was dying. He was a grandfather. For forty years he had lived at Sandringham and his roots were firmly embedded in Norfolk. He had led a full and gay life, waiting long and patiently to enter into his heritage. Since boyhood he had had the lessons of the past rammed into him, and throughout manhood had had the example of Prince Albert held up constantly before him. Looking back through his life, King Edward had little reason to suppose that he would live to as ripe an age as had his mother. However much he revered her, he felt that he had as much right to make a name for himself as a Sovereign. He was a man of the present and the future, and there was much clearing up and alteration to be made in a short time.

His 'Baby' sister, on the other hand, was only forty-three. Her youngest son was the same age as the King's eldest grandchild. Yet, in the eyes of the public, she was indelibly connected with the past. Whilst the new King moved gaily into the future, clasping the new century by

the hand, the ghost of the nineteenth still held the
Princess tightly in its arms.

The Queen had guessed that things would change when
she was dead, but she had built such a long line of precedent to resist the attacks of time that she imagined many
of her ways and the things she loved were safe. She had
indeed built solidly, in bronze and stone and marble.
Plaques, statues, monuments, cairns and effigies by the
hundred honoured the great days, and mourned the passing members of her family and others who had served her.
Gravestones told the story of her every dog, and the likeness of her babies' hands was imaged in white marble. Her
every possession had been photographed and catalogued,
and every daily happening committed to paper. Every
wish as to what was to be done after her death had been
carefully recorded. One of those wishes was that her heir
should, as King, style himself 'Albert Edward'. That was
the first of her wishes to go by the board—and the title
of 'Edward VII' was not popular in Scotland.

The legacy of the past clung to Princess Beatrice as
executor of the will. She shared the duties with the Duke
of Connaught and the latest Keeper of the Privy Purse,
Lieutenant-Colonel Sir Fleetwood Edwards, while Prince
Louis of Battenberg had been appointed by the Queen as
a Trustee of her private money on the last day of 1900.

Queen Victoria had been a collector all her life, from
the days when, as an only child and with a mother who
had little money, she had treasured her belongings. Even
in those days it had been very much '*my* doll, *my* donkey'.
Now it was found that she had not parted with a possession
in eighty years. All her toys had been packed away in
trunks. Every frock she had ever worn had been carefully
wrapped up and put away, a note inside saying when the
frock had been made and when worn. Every gift (some
expendable) from tribal chieftains, from faithful servants
(particularly Brown), from children and grandchildren,

from visiting Royalties and notabilities, from societies and associations, had been stored away. There were photographs and drawings of everyone remotely connected with the Family. These were all housed in the four great repositories of Windsor, Balmoral, Osborne and Buckingham Palace.

There were, of course, the shrines to Albert. Nothing that was his was moved after his death. His walking-sticks, his despatch boxes, his paper-weights, everything had been frozen into immobility on the 14th of December 1861. The writing on the paper on his desk had faded, the ink in the wells dried up, but that was a process not even the Queen could alter. Every night before dinner water was poured out into his basin. Every bed the Queen slept in bore her husband's photograph, and there were his night clothes to clasp. She never slept alone.

At Sandringham, or Abergeldie, or Homburg, or Cannes, the Prince of Wales had seen little of these things. But Princess Beatrice was always in the next room. Now, if King Edward were to live his own life and be a King in his own right, much of this legacy of sacred cobwebs must go. There must be new drains, new plumbing, new lights, new decorations. Gone were the days when old newspaper squares were good enough for the lavatories at Windsor. In he stalked to his London Palace, which he had long called 'the Sepulchre', and back went the piles of old photographs to the army of distant German relations who appeared in them. Out went the *bric-à-brac*, some of it to old retainers of the Queen, and literally out with a bang went the collection of plaster statuettes of John Brown. This part of the clearance King Edward attended to personally. He smashed them on the floor.

One of the most difficult problems which faced the King in sorting out the legacy of his mother's expressed wishes and desires, was to decide the future of Osborne. The Isle of Wight estate had been left to him, as had

Balmoral. He was therefore provided with five residences, Windsor and Buckingham Palace belonging to the State, and Sandringham, Balmoral and Osborne to himself. He intended to spend much more time than his mother had in his London home and, for a man who liked his Continental visits, there were patently not enough days left in the year for him to make a home in four other places. Balmoral was a welcome gift, because of the shooting and his many friends in Scotland. Windsor had its own historic claim. Sandringham was where his heart lay, and he would never part with that. So Osborne became the odd house out. There was also the cost of its upkeep to be considered.

Yet Osborne had come to mean to Queen Victoria almost what Inveraray meant to the Argylls. As a child she had fallen in love with the Island; there, twenty years later, she and Prince Albert had found a secluded spot away from prying eyes and public departments, and had built their dream house. Albert had planned everything —the gardens, the stables, the trees, the shrubs. Their younger children, 'the Osborne set' (Louise–Beatrice) had known it as their real home, and had had much of their education there. For forty summers the Queen had taken her lonely teas in the shade of Albert's ilex trees, and her favourite son-in-law rested in Whippingham Church. She had made him, and his wife after him, Governor of the Island. She had indeed made it absolutely clear that she expected Osborne to become part of the life of the British Royal Family.

The Queen had already given properties to her three daughters, the Princesses Helena, Louise and Beatrice. Princess Christian and her husband had Cumberland Lodge, in Windsor Park. At Osborne, Princess Louise had Kent House and Princess Beatrice, Osborne Cottage. It was because of these last two properties that King Edward found himself in such a dilemma over Osborne.

He took legal advice and discovered that the wording of the will allowed him, if he so chose, to make a market garden or a new town of Osborne. Its fate was in his hands—always provided that his son and heir did not stipulate that he wished to live there when he came to the Throne. So the King asked the Prince of Wales, who replied that in no circumstances would he care to live there. So far so good, but to what useful purpose could Osborne be put?

That proved a simple problem. At Dartmouth the old training ship *Britannia* had had its day and the Admiralty were looking about for a suitable place to which to transfer the naval cadets. Lord Esher suggested that the stables at Osborne, and the land around them, would make an excellent site for a new Naval College. King Edward agreed heartily.

Officers invalided home from abroad had no place where they could go to convalesce. Netley Hospital fulfilled its rôle while they were ill, but for those without homes it was a real problem where to spend the recuperative period. Again King Edward at once fell in with the suggestion that the great wing of the house could be used.

There still remained the central portion of the house, and this allowed the King to fulfil, in part at least, the wishes of his mother. He decided that the rooms which she and his father had occupied should be kept closed and sacred to their memory. The umbrella, with 'Osborne' inscribed on it in large letters, which the Prince Consort had used on his last walk in the rain in the summer of 1861, was to be left untouched in the corner where it had been placed. Five rooms were to be sealed off with iron grilles and only the House Governor, the Matron, and a trusted cleaning staff were ever to see what lay behind them. Below, on the ground floor, the State Rooms would be open to the public.

The plan seemed convenient, advantageous to the

country and satisfactory in every way. But there were two obstacles—the views of the King's sisters.

To Princess Beatrice, Governor of the Island, executor of the will and owner of Osborne Cottage, the news came as a considerable shock. Osborne and its associations had become so entwined in her life that she saw it, like her mother, as a family home and a favourite one. To cross her mother's wishes was to trespass on holy ground. It was not that she quarrelled with the worthy aims to which the greater part of the estate would be put—it was simply that something was going that she thought would never go. It had been the Queen's intention to bestow on her daughters secluded and pleasant homes where they could, as they grew older, enjoy the same privacy that she had found on the Island. An influx of convalescing officers and high-spirited boys would break the spell and drown for ever the dim strains of Albert's organ as, with that strange look in his eyes, he had played towards the sea when the sun went down.

Tact was, however, an asset which the King had developed to a considerable degree. Fully briefed, he now put his powers to the test. He took his two sisters, Beatrice and Louise, for an afternoon stroll at Osborne. He put his case in all its strength, extolled the eternal sanctity of their parents' rooms, and offered to enlarge the grounds of Osborne Cottage. He won the day. Osborne was to be altered, the gift to the nation to take effect as from his Coronation day.

A consolation came to Princess Beatrice. Her great nephews, David[1] (nicknamed 'Sardine') and Albert,[2] went as cadets to the new training college, and enjoyed nothing more than having tea with their 'Aunt B.' at Osborne Cottage on Sundays.

A constant source of worry to Princess Beatrice and

[1] Later Duke of Windsor.   [2] Later King George VI.

her brothers and sister in 1901 was the illness and suffering
of the Empress Frederick. They visited her as and when
they could, but these were sad visits, for now only drugs
could bring back clarity to that brilliant mind. In February King Edward went to Friedrichshof, where he was
received by the Emperor.

Princess Beatrice paid her last visit to her sister in the
middle of July 1901 and found that, once relieved of pain,
her brain was still clear and that she wished to hear all
that was going on in London. Three weeks later, on
5th August, the Empress Frederick was at last released
from her long agony. As she died, a butterfly flew out of
the window and was lost to sight in the sky above the park.

10

Queen of Spain

SIX months after the death of her mother, Princess Beatrice moved into Osborne Cottage. Prince Alexander had passed from Wellington College to the old H.M.S. *Britannia*, and the younger boys took lessons with their sister. Prince Maurice was now ten, a good-looking and boisterous boy, set on joining the 60th Rifles. Prince Leopold, two years the senior, suffered from the handicap of haemophilia, just as his uncle, Leopold of Albany, had done. The bleeding disease was a burden to Princess Beatrice all her life. In childhood it had spoilt the fun that she could have had with the brother nearest her in age, and through girlhood his constant illness, and final death, haunted her. It had now appeared in her own child, and was to do so yet again in the next generation.

Princess Ena stole the limelight. Ever since her riding accident at Osborne, which had proved so much more serious than had at first appeared, the public had watched her tenderly. They had seen her in the carriage with the Queen and her mother, and admired the golden hair flashing against the black crêped background of her grandmother. And just as Queen Victoria had craved the presence of her 'Baby' after the death of the Prince Consort, so did Princess Beatrice treasure the relief that came from having her daughter by her side. Both mothers saw a reflection of the father in the child.

There was much of Prince Henry in his golden-haired daughter. She inherited his looks, his charm, his penchant for games, and she had some of the ethereal beauty of the Hesses. From her mother Princess Ena also inherited the gifts of drawing and music, the piano being her favourite instrument. In the field of sport, she was a first-rate horsewoman and excelled at tennis and golf.

There were happy days for the Battenberg children at their Isle of Wight home. There were visits to Bonchurch, so full of memories of Swinburne, picnics in the chine at Shanklin and voyages of exploration around Carisbrooke Castle. Princess Ena would often take a carrot to the donkey which worked the water-wheel there—the successor to that donkey to which the Prince Consort had likened himself in his last tired months.

The date of King Edward's crowning had been fixed for 26th June, and so few people could remember the last Coronation that the excitement was intense.

On the 14th the King attended a military tattoo at Aldershot. The rain poured down, just as it had when the Prince Consort visited Sandhurst on 22nd November 1861. As his father had done, the King caught a chill. He was put to bed, but was up two days later, looking very pale, but insistent that there should be no interference with the Coronation programme.

The main body of visiting Royalties arrived at Victoria Station on 21st June, and two days later there was a grand dinner at Buckingham Palace, but the King was not well enough to dine and the Queen did the honours. There were seven round tables, with only Royalty around them. Princess Ena was not yet old enough to attend, but her mother and her cousin, Princess Beatrice of Coburg, were able to tell her all about it. The pretty, eighteen-year-old Princess was taken in to dinner by the Duke of Cambridge.

Next day the announcement was made that the Coronation was postponed, and that the King was being operated on for appendicitis. Instead of driving to Westminster to see her brother crowned, Princess Beatrice went to St. Paul's to pray for his recovery. On the way she passed,

14

where Fleet Street begins, the monument which bears her likeness, marking that well-remembered day in 1872 when she had driven with her mother to the Thanksgiving Service for the recovery of the Prince of Wales. It seemed a happy omen.

The King again showed the same resilience and determination to get well. It was decided that the new Coronation date should be 9th August. By this time most of the official foreign visitors had returned home, one of the exceptions being the Abyssinian Mission, who feared, for their heads, to go back without achieving what they had set out to do.

The carriage bearing Princess Beatrice and her family was in the first procession to move from Buckingham Palace. After a short rest on arrival at the Abbey, the King and Queen passed to their Chairs of State, near the old Coronation Chair. On the north side, in their scarlet robes as Doctors of Divinity, were the prelates who were taking no part in the ceremony. On the south were the Royal ladies, the Princess of Wales, the daughters of the King, Princess Christian, Princess Louise, Princess Beatrice. The regalia was placed upon the altar. The service began with the 'Recognition'. The King stood within the Sanctuary, and the Archbishop of Canterbury loudly proclaimed: 'Sirs, I here present unto you King Edward, the undoubted King of this Realm . . .'

Princess Beatrice, exceeding proud of the embroidered copy of the Service which had been presented to her, turned the book this way and that as she savoured of its craftsmanship. On several occasions it was near to slipping from her grasp and falling from the Royal Box. At length the inevitable happened. It landed with a clatter among the Abbey's Church plate that was on show below.

A trip to Egypt during the winter of 1903–4 was a very necessary rest and change for Princess Beatrice. She took her children with her, and her godchild, Princess Beatrice of Coburg, as company for Princess Ena. The Princess had intended the visit to be private, but the Khedive would have none of that, and gave an official reception to the Royal tourists. After entertaining the Princess at Cairo, he put the royal yacht at their disposal and his A.D.C. went with them up the Nile. Also on board was Mr. Percy Newberry, the Egyptologist. It was a wonderful trip, with horses awaiting their use at anchorages.

At Aswan[1] the party had a suite at the Cataract Hotel. They were there for Christmas and, as a surprise, organised by the manager, native musicians surrounded the Royal table after dinner and gave their version of Christmas carols. Then presents were handed to the children.

A journey to the Sudan followed and in Khartoum the Princess laid the foundation stone of the Anglican Cathedral. Under the aegis of Sir Reginald Wingate, the Princess saw the terrain covered by the campaigns which she and her mother had followed so closely. Of particular interest to her, she saw, in the old palace in Khartoum, the spot where Gordon fell.

After an excursion to the shores of the Red Sea, the Princess and her family returned to England in April. This had been her first 'great' holiday. Such had been the price of being indispensable to Queen Victoria.

In 1903, Princess Alice of Battenberg married Prince Andrew of Greece. As far as the people of Britain were concerned, it was to prove one of the most important royal unions since Queen Victoria married Prince Albert, for eighteen years hence they would become the parents of Prince Philip, later Duke of Edinburgh.

Once again Princess Beatrice went to Darmstadt, to

[1] The Aswan Dam was opened by the Duke and Duchess of Connaught in 1902.

find that the people of the quaint old town were staging celebrations such as had not been seen since the bride's parents had married nineteen years before, those never-to-be-forgotten days when Queen Victoria was crossing swords with the Empress Augusta as to whether 'Sandro' should marry Victoria of Prussia . . . when the Grand Duke married Madame de Kalomine on the wedding night . . . and for Princess Beatrice, most important of all, the days when she met Prince Henry and fell in love with him.

That wedding of Prince Philip's mother and father was a day of the nineteenth century intruding into the twentieth. Radiant Queen Alexandra was there, for the bridegroom was her nephew. Princess Beatrice's godchild, the Tsarina of Russia, was present because the bride was her niece. For the Tsar, there were many connections between the Greek family and his own. King George had married the Grand Duchess Olga, while Prince Andrew's brother, Nicholas, had married the Grand Duchess Helen Vladimirovna, and his sister Marie, the Grand Duke George Mihailovich. And the Prussian Royal Family were there because the bridegroom's eldest brother, Constantine, had married Princess Sophie, daughter of the Empress Frederick.

They were all riding on the historic roundabout at Darmstadt. The bands played, and up and down bobbed the relatives of England, Russia, Greece, Prussia, France, Hesse and Hanover. It was to be the last time that gaiety would ride triumphant over tragedy and war. Forgotten were Japan, South Africa, Turkey, and Kaiser Wilhelm's growls and greed; and, glittering in her box at the Court Theatre, was the woman who had turned down the German Emperor—Ella, the Grand Duchess Serge, the most beautiful lady in all Europe.

There were two marriage ceremonies, in addition to the civil ceremony demanded by German law. The Tsar had brought his own choir for the Orthodox service and, although the bride had studied the complicated procedure very carefully, she became muddled in her excitement, saying 'No' when she was asked if she was marrying of her own free will, and 'Yes' when asked if she had previously plighted her troth elsewhere—mistakes which were quickly put right by Prince Andrew.

At the dinner afterwards, fun ran high. The servants were dismissed, and the Grand Duke Ernest and the bridegroom's brothers acted as waiters, assisted by the younger members of Princess Alice's family—not that the boy who was to become Earl Mountbatten was much practical help as he was only three.

As the couple drove away through a downfall of rice and satin slippers, someone suggested that, by taking a short cut, they could catch up with the carriage. Off rushed the guests, in their full wedding regalia, tiaras toppling, and children hanging on to the coat tails of the men. The Tsar of Russia caught up with the open carriage, threw a pretty slipper and managed to pour a bag of rice right over the bride. She caught the slipper and hit him over the head with it, hard. He stood in the crowd, roaring with laughter, while heavy German detectives, lost in the levity, sweated to keep touch with him and expected the bombs to go off at any moment.

Gloom soon came to Hesse with the death of Princess Elizabeth, eight years old and the only child of Grand Duke Ernest and Victoria Melita of Edinburgh. The divorce of the children of Princess Beatrice's sister Alice and brother Alfred had caused great upset in the Royal Houses of Britain, Germany and Russia, and the former Grand Duchess was living in the shadows at Coburg, waiting for the time when she could marry the Grand Duke Cyril. The Grand Duke Ernest took his daughter with him on a visit to Russia. There her sudden death took place. The rumour started that she had been poisoned

—a whisper which can still be heard in Darmstadt today. She was buried at the Rosenhohe.

The year 1904 opened with the marriage of another Princess Alice, again a niece of Princess Beatrice. On Queen Victoria's wedding day, at St. George's Chapel, Windsor, the daughter of Prince Leopold of Albany married Prince Alexander[1] of Teck, brother of the Princess of Wales.[2]

In March, the Duke of Cambridge died, and thus snapped one of Princess Beatrice's strongest links with the past. He had been an integral part of the Royal scene for as long as she could remember, and a good friend of Prince Henry. Older than Queen Victoria and Prince Albert, he was one of the last survivors of the reign of George III. He was a man of fads and fancies, as were his father and uncle, Edward of Kent, before him.[3]

During his last illness the weather was very wet, and the Duke instructed his valet, Mr. Dealtry, who had been with him for thirty-five years, that, if it was raining on the day of his funeral, his *second* best pair of boots was to be put on his charger.

The 23rd of October 1904 was Princess Ena's seventeenth birthday and in January she 'came out' at the Infirmary Ball at Ryde. Her Majesty Queen Victoria Eugenia recalls:

> '. . . the following month my mother and I were invited by King Edward to stay at Buckingham Palace for my first appearance at a Court, as he wished me to come out officially from our old home, which was a charming gesture, and touched my mother greatly.'

[1] The Earl of Athlone.   [2] Later, Queen Mary.

[3] At Gloucester House my mother was intrigued by his array of toothbrushes, one for each day of the week. The number of brushes that H.R.H. took away on visits was a useful indication of the length of his absence.—Author.

There followed official presentation at Court, and a ball given by Princess Beatrice at Kensington Palace. Princess Ena was grown up. She was everybody's favourite and her doings were followed as keenly as were those of Princess Elizabeth thirty years later. Pictures of her adorned the covers of girls' magazines and photographs were in much demand. She was now often to be seen with her mother on visits to hospitals, the opening of bazaars and the many other duties undertaken by Princess Beatrice.

Meanwhile, in Spain young King Alfonso was looking around for a bride, a search in which he was urged on eagerly by his people. This knowledge added interest to his forthcoming visit to England, arranged for June 1905.

On his way to London King Alfonso paid a State visit to Paris. There, on 31st May, an attempt was made on his life, a grenade being thrown under the wheels of his carriage. He escaped unhurt. He had extraordinary courage, and took such things lightly. On the journey to Cherbourg, his train was shunted. Putting his head out of the carriage window, he asked laconically of an official, 'Another attempt?'

Officially, the young King's visit to England was a great success, despite the dreadful weather. He made a speech in English at the Guildhall and led his regiment of Lancers past the King at the Royal Review at Aldershot.

Socially, his stay was brilliant, although there were occasions when it must have been rather bewildering. There were mothers and aunts who cherished dreams of Spain for daughters and nieces. Few were as self-effacing as Princess Beatrice.

Asked which of all the lovely Royal young ladies he would like to have beside him, he replied without hesitation, 'The fair one, but I do not know her name.'

The 'fair one' was Princess Ena. He met her, and her mother, at every function staged in his honour, with the exception of the Military Review. He danced with her at Buckingham Palace and paid marked attention to her as they sat together in the box at Covent Garden.

King Alfonso went home, delighted at the success of his visit, while Princess Ena prepared for a family wedding. On 15th June, at St. George's Chapel, Windsor, Princess Margaret of Connaught was married to Prince Gustavus of Sweden. The bridesmaids were Princess Ena, Princess Beatrice of Coburg, eight-year-old Princess Mary,[1] and Princess Patricia of Connaught. Their dresses were of 'St. Patrick's blue', in compliment to Ireland, and white wreaths of marguerites crowned their hair. Here was the new age of Royalty in all its beauty.

Throughout the summer, letters, young people's letters, passed between Madrid and London. One evening in the autumn Princess Beatrice was at Windsor and after dinner told her brother, the King, that she would like to talk to him on an urgent matter after he had finished his card playing. It was nearly midnight when she found him alone in his room. She held a letter in her hand and observed: 'I have heard from Queen Christina and she says that Alfonso is set on marrying Ena.'

'Ena?' queried the King. 'You mean——', mentioning the name of a Princess whose name had been coupled with that of the Spanish King.

'No, Ena,' replied Princess Beatrice. 'It has been Ena all the time.'

Having been assured that Princess Ena was of the same mind and prepared to change her religion, King Edward expressed himself delighted with the idea.

Fortunate indeed that Princess Beatrice had chosen the Empress Eugénie to be her daughter's godmother. Not only had the Empress taken her duties seriously and, in addition, lavished presents upon her godchild, but she had seen much of her. Princess Beatrice paid frequent

[1] The Princess Royal.

The Empress Frederick as a widow (*from the painting by Angeli at Friedrichshof*)

The King and Queen of Spain

Princess Beatrice, 1903

Prince Louis of Battenberg, first Marquess of Milford-Haven

Princess Andrew of Greece with Prince Philip (now H.R.H. the Duke of Edinburgh)

The Battenberg Chapel, Whippingham Church. The picture over the
Rector's desk is 'The Supreme Sacrifice' by Sir John Lavery, R.A.,
the property of Princess Beatrice and hanging in memory of Prince
Maurice. The lectern was presented by Lord Edward Pelham Clinton
in memory of Prince Henry. The frontal screen was embroidered from
the satin of Princess Beatrice's wedding dress

The dining-room at Osborne House. On the left hang the pictures of
Prince Henry (by Angeli) and Princess Beatrice (by G. Sohn), painted
in 1883

visits to Farnborough with her children and there Princess Ena had come to know a number of Spaniards, among them young men who were friends of the King, such as the Duke of Alba—all were relations of the Empress.

For Princess Beatrice, due in part to her long friendship with Empress Eugénie, the channel between Roman Catholicism and the Established Church was not so broad and deep as with most of her contemporaries. And the same tolerance had been inherited by her daughter.

King Edward, who in 1903 had paid a much discussed visit to the Pope, and Queen Alexandra both encouraged the Alfonso-Ena romance. Despite the difference in years the two Kings had much in common, and a mutual feeling of admiration.

In January 1906 Princess Beatrice took her family to Biarritz, staying with Princess Frederica of Hanover and her husband, Baron Paul von Rammingen, at the Villa Mouriscot, two miles outside the town. On the 23rd, King Alfonso's Chamberlain called at the Villa, followed two days later by the King, who had driven the forty miles from San Sebastian in eighty minutes in his 40-h.p. Panhard—fast going indeed for 1906. Thereafter came daily visits, and the young couple often drove together through the countryside in the Panhard phaeton, with Miss Minnie Cochrane, Princess Beatrice's lady-in-waiting, as chaperone.

On the 28th King Alfonso, Princess Beatrice and Princess Ena drove across the Spanish frontier, on their way to San Sebastian to meet Queen Maria Christina. It was not the first time that Princess Beatrice had made this journey. She remembered the 27th of March 1889 when she and Prince Henry had accompanied Queen Victoria on the first visit of a British Sovereign to Spain. On that occasion their hostess had also been Queen Christina. Alfonso was then only three.

Princess Ena of Battenberg accepted the proposal of

marriage made by the King of Spain who, on the 3rd of February, returned to Madrid. On the same day Princess Beatrice telegraphed King Edward, giving news of the engagement and suggesting that her daughter's preparation for entry into the Roman Catholic Church should take place at the Villa Cyrnos, Cap Martin, home of the Empress Eugénie.

King Edward considered that difficulties would be lessened if the instruction were taken elsewhere, quietly in Paris, for example. It would be best, he thought, if the Princess and her daughter did not return to London until after the change in religion had been completed. Mgr. Robert Brindle, Bishop of Nottingham, duly travelled to Versailles to give the preliminary instruction.

As soon as the news of the engagement became known, the ecclesiastical clamour broke out. The King had early warning of the trouble ahead, for in January the Archbishop of Canterbury and the Bishop of London had informed him of the obvious signs of public disapproval. Now the correspondence columns of the newspapers became filled with provocative letters on the subject, the Church Association and the Protestant Alliance called on the King to refuse his consent, and the Bishop of London made a direct appeal to Princess Beatrice not, as he said, as a daughter of Queen Victoria, but as a devout member of the Church of England.

King Edward was determined that the match should take place and gave a series of masterly but evasive replies. He said that, as the Princess's father was a German, then she must be a German, and, as such, the matter had nothing to do with him—blandly overlooking the fact that Prince Henry had become a naturalised Englishman at the time of his marriage.

The marriage plans proceeded. Letters flowed from Madrid to Versailles. The Princesses of Battenberg must have a car. There was not one to be hired, so King Alfonso bought them a small Panhard. He wrote that he was sending them special oranges. Not a crate arrived at the station, but a complete orange tree laden with fruit.

On 5th March the Princesses left Paris. Two days later, at San Sebastian, Princess Ena forsook the Protestant faith and was re-baptized. King Alfonso's mother was her sponsor and the names of Maria Christina were added to her own. On the 9th a simultaneous announcement of the engagement was made in London and Madrid.

Mother and daughter returned to England as King Edward journeyed out to Biarritz. He loved the place, the sound of the breakers, the open views, the golf, and the people one met there. On this occasion he took a number of motor drives into Spain, and these were not unconnected with the forthcoming marriage of his niece. At the Miramar Palace at San Sebastian he lunched with King Alfonso, and afterwards the two had a long conversation, unhindered by the presence of Ministers. The next day King Alfonso drove over to Biarritz, and there were further talks.

Meantime, Sir Edward Grey had studied the religious and constitutional problems connected with the marriage, and forwarded the results to the King. The King replied:

'The King has read Sir Edward Grey's memo of 27th March, relative to the marriage of his niece Princess Victoria Eugénie of Battenberg with the King of Spain. Though the King has given no formal consent in council to her marriage he considers that a Treaty could be concluded as was the case on the marriages of his two nieces, Princess Marie of Edinburgh and Princess Margaret of Connaught.

'The King considers it absolutely necessary that Princess Victoria Eugénie of Battenberg should sign a paper formally renouncing her succession to the English Throne, having become a Roman Catholic.

'Though there will be no public grant asked for on behalf of Princess Victoria Eugénie of Battenberg she will receive a certain sum from her mother Princess Henry of Battenberg, but that, the King presumes, is a private affair. The King having created Princess Victoria Eugénie a Royal Highness (on 4th April) she would have in any further official document to be styled thus.'

On 2nd April King Edward set off for Marseilles to join his Queen, and a few days later King Alfonso sailed in his yacht *Giralda* to meet his fiancée in the Isle of Wight. In the Solent he was met by the barge of the C.-in-C. Portsmouth, on board being Princess Beatrice, Princess Ena, now Her Royal Highness, and her brothers Leopold and Maurice.

King Alfonso stayed at Osborne, and there followed a fortnight of happiness. Princess Ena tried to teach him how to play golf, the greens suffering considerably in the process. Together they planted a tree in memory of their engagement, or rather, they tried to plant it, for the King was so jubilant that when they had finished the trunk was anything but perpendicular. And, in the bark of an age-old Osborne tree, they cut their names deep—Victoria–Alfonso. Queen Victoria would have liked that.

At the beginning of May King Alfonso and the Battenbergs were in London, and on the 4th he began his journey back to Spain. Down the road now labelled A30, so much emptier than it is today, Princess Beatrice, her daughter and her two younger sons drove with the Spanish King as far as Micheldever. There, after lunching with Lady Portal, they parted. The next meeting was to be in Madrid.

On 24th May began the most dramatic episode in the story of Princess Beatrice's life. With Princess Ena and Princes Leopold and Maurice, she began the journey to Spain. Prince Alexander, on leave from his uncle's flagship, H.M.S. *Drake*, was to join them on their way through France.

There was a great send-off for the future Queen of Spain. The previous evening the King had given a farewell party for her at Buckingham Palace, and now there were great cheering crowds all the way from Kensington Palace to Victoria Station. There was a message of congratulations for her from the Lord Mayor of London, and, arm-in-arm with her kindly uncle, King Edward, H.R.H. Princess Ena walked along the platform to her carriage.

Proud, unforgettable moments these for a mother.

King Alfonso travelled to the Spanish frontier to meet the Battenbergs, and there were crowds all the way by the side of the long line to Madrid. Queen Christina was waiting to greet them and, in a carriage drawn by four mules, they drove to the Palace of El Pardo, King Alfonso riding alongside.

The guests began to arrive—the Prince and Princess of Wales, Prince Alexander of Teck and Princess Alice, Prince Henry of Prussia, Princesses Marie of Battenberg[1] and Beatrice of Coburg.

There was much to be seen and done in a short time, and the King had arranged great entertainment. The most novel was a motor rally. The King, in car number 17, had Princess Beatrice of Coburg and Prince Alexander with him, while the two younger Battenbergs, Leopold and Maurice, drove with the captain of the Royal Yacht. The cars were driven to El Pardo, where Princess Beatrice and her daughter were waiting on a balcony to see them arrive.

There was a visit to the theatre, and King Alfonso's description of what was going on, and his translation kept the Princess of Wales and his fiancée in fits of laughter.

On the 29th preparations for the wedding began, and,

[1] Princess Ernst of Erbach-Schonberg.

at the Palace of El Pardo, Princess Ena signed her marriage treaty. She was to be granted 450,000 pesetas a year for the whole of her married life, and 250,000 as a widow.

Princess Beatrice's presents to her daughter included a sample of her exquisite lace; a parure of fine pink pearls and diamonds; a necklet and hair ornaments, including a pendant in the shape of a shell of diamonds; and a satin-wood inlaid jewel case. From King Edward and Queen Alexandra came a parure of diamonds and oblong turquoises. Other presents from England included a bust of herself from forty-five women who knew her personally, and a statuette of a R.N. Cadet at the salute, from the Captain and officers at Osborne.

The Spanish customs were observed. The King gave his bride her crown of jewels and her white wedding dress embroidered in silver, and on the night before the wedding he placed a guard over her.

On the morning of the 31st May King Alfonso came out to El Pardo for Communion. He then returned to Madrid. The Princess's party travelled by car as far as the Ministry of Marine, and there her Procession formed up. It was composed of the bride's brothers, the ladies and gentlemen in waiting, Colonel Lord William Cecil and Lady Cecil, Miss Minnie Cochrane, Miss Bulteel, and, at the rear, in the Mahogany Coach, Princess Beatrice, Queen Christina and Princess Ena. It joined the King's Procession.

Princess Ena's party was late in arriving. King Alfonso had been warned that a bomb might be thrown. He waited, terrified that the attempt had already been made.

In the church of San Jeronimo amid the tapestries, the banks of flowers, and in the perfumed dimness enriched by the coloured sunlight that pierced the stained-glass window, King Alfonso and Princess Ena took their places before the Cardinal-Archbishop of Toledo. Instinctively,

King Alfonso rose and moved across to kiss his mother. Princess Ena was in the arms of Princess Beatrice a few seconds later.

The Princess was wed, the register signed. 'Go in peace', said the Primate of Spain. The procession re-formed, King Alfonso and Queen Victoria Eugenia took their places in the Royal State Coach, at the rear, and they moved off towards the Puerta del Sol, the Calle Mayor, and the Palace.

They little dreamed that they had already missed death by a fraction, not only they, but also probably Princess Beatrice, the future King George V and Queen Mary, and a cousin of the German Emperor. For the gentle-faced, syphilitic maniac, Matteo Morral, who was now waiting for them in the Calle Mayor, a bomb in his hands, had all but succeeded in getting a ticket for the church service as a journalist. Fortunately, that ticket had been claimed at the last moment by an American journalist, who had given it to Morral because he was taken ill. Otherwise, that bomb would have exploded as the Royal couple bowed before the altar, and, in the enclosed space, it is impossible to forecast what casualties there might have been.

The procession reached the Calle Mayor. On a balcony of No. 88 stood Matteo Morral, the flower-covered bomb ready in his hands. There, in the old Spanish high street, a stand had been erected to accommodate ladies and gentlemen of the Spanish Court. It was outside public buildings. The State Coach stopped for a moment, so that the King might acknowledge their special acclaim. He drew the Queen's attention and had just told her that their journey was nearly over, and that now they must be safe. As the coach stopped, Morral dropped his flowered bomb. His aim was short.

The events of this momentous day have been described so many times, in so many different ways, that it may be best to give the impressions of three people who were in the procession—King George V,[1] the Marquess of Carisbrooke,[2] and Miss Minnie Cochrane, lady-in-waiting to Princess Beatrice—and of one spectator, Mrs. George Young, wife of the Second Secretary at the British Embassy, who was giving a party at 96 Calle Mayor, in celebration of the occasion.

Miss Minnie Cochrane said:

'I was riding in a carriage just behind the Royal Wedding Coach with Lord William Cecil when I happened to glance up at the packed balconies. Suddenly I noticed one occupied by one man dressed all in black. At the time I thought it curious that he should have a balcony all to himself, but the thought passed quickly from my mind. Just in front, by some curious dispensation of Providence, the coachman of the Royal carriage halted his horses just for a moment and strangely enough up to this spot the Royal Coach, unlike all the other carriages, had been kept continually on the move. That halt saved a tragedy, for just at that moment the assassin threw his bomb which exploded just in front of the Royal Coach, killing two of the horses. Had not the coachman unconsciously checked his horses, the missile would have landed full on the Royal Coach. . . .'

King George V said:

'Our carriage was just in front of the one in which Queen Christina and Aunt Beatrice were driving and they were just ahead of Alfonso and Ena who were at the end of the procession. Just before our carriage reached the Palace, we heard a loud report and thought it was the first gun of a salute. We soon learned how-

[1] Then Prince of Wales.
[2] Then Prince Alexander of Battenberg.

ever that when about 200 yards from the Palace in a
narrow street, the Calle Mayor, close to the Italian
Embassy, a bomb was thrown from an upper window
at the King and Queen's carriage. It burst between the
wheel horses and the front of the carriage, killing about
20 people and wounding about 50 or 60, mostly officers
and soldiers. Thank God! Alfonso and Ena were not
touched although covered with glass from the broken
windows. The Marquesa Torlosa and her niece were
killed. They were standing on a balcony just below the
window from which the bomb was thrown. The two
wheelers were killed and another horse, the carriage
however went on about 30 yards. Sir M. de Bunsen,
Morgan, Lowther[1] and the four officers of the 16th
Lancers who were in a house close by, rushed out,
stood round the carriage and assisted Ena out of the
carriage, both she and Alfonso showed great courage
and presence of mind. They got into another carriage
at once and drove off to the Palace amid frantic cheering. Am most sorry for poor Aunt Beatrice who feels
the shock very much.

'Of course the bomb was thrown by an anarchist,
supposed to be a Spaniard and of course they let him
escape. I believe the Spanish police and detectives are
about the worst in the world. No precautions whatever
had been taken, they are most happy go lucky people
here. Naturally, on their return, both Alfonso and Ena
broke down, no wonder after such an awful experience.
Eventually we had lunch about 3. I proposed their
healths, not easy after the emotions caused by this
terrible affair. . . .'

The next description of the dramatic moments comes
from a different viewpoint, for Mrs. George Young was
watching the procession from a window. Mrs. Young

[1] Colonel Lowther, Military Attaché.

15

wrote to her mother that same afternoon, whilst every detail was fresh in her mind. The immediate appearance round the Royal Coach of officers of the 16th Lancers, King Alfonso's own regiment, is explained:

96 Calle Mayor,
Madrid,
31 May. 5 o'c.

'I've just got rid of my mantilla, Court train & guests & feel I must write to you as the whole thing happened *just* here . . . I had lunching here the Ambassador [Sir Maurice de Bunsen], the Naval Attaché, the Military Attaché, Colonel Cochrane & Lady A. Cochrane (he is Lieutenant Governor of the Isle of Wight—Princess Beatrice . . . being the Governor) & 4 Officers of the 16th Lancers . . . We got back here by back streets from the Church just in time to see the procession pass, & Sir M. & Lady de Bunsen & the Austrian Ambassadress arrived when it was passing but about 10 minutes before the Royal coach came through. The 2 Ambassadresses, Lady A. Cochrane & I with the de Bunsen children were in the Calle Bailen window of the dining room, & the side window had soldiers & some Royal female guests. The Queen Mother's coach passed amid frantic cheerings & wavings & we all flapped handkerchiefs too & clapped. Then came a gap, & the King's coach came at a foot's pace down the Calle Mayor as the Queen Mother's went round the corner.

'Suddenly we saw a little smoke & something dark dropped from the house next the Italian Embassy opposite, & then a terrific explosion. At the first second, we thought it was the firing of a cannon to greet them as they passed under the triumphal arch; but then we saw the horses bolt & the crowd shrieking & surging & realised the truth. The Austrian Ambassadress (such a nice woman) began to weep & say " *Mein Gott* "; Lady de Bunsen said "Oh Maurice, go & do something". The soldiers & staff gave some deep curses & in a twinkling they were all out of the house & made their way to the Royal carriage, where they surrounded it . . . The Ambassadors & Colonel Cochrane went on to the Palace (Sir Maurice in George's hat, sizes too small & with the wrong cockade), & we waited patiently till the 16th Lancers came in & told us details. The wheeler was killed dead & the front horse too, but the carriage was unhurt except for broken glass. A good many soldiers were killed and wounded, George says the King was just splendid . . . I do thank Heaven that I had—tho' I was very cross about it—invited all these Palace guests & Embassy Staff *here*. Last night I was rather annoyed at the prospect of 4 large 16th Lancers Officers eating & drinking here & gave them a not very gushing invitation to this flat. But today I could have kissed them all for being on the spot.

'The Palace people did not know until the King & Queen arrived themselves, what had happened, as theirs was the last coach, all the others happily waiting in the Palace. The Ambassador kept his head & so did George, & I think did everything they ought. Some of the people wanted the King & Queen to take shelter in the Italian Embassy, but he used such language over this cowardly suggestion that it wasn't pressed. He said "Come on, Ena", & got her into the other coach & laughed & waved & was a trump. There is no doubt he is a very plucky boy. . . .'[1]

Once he had satisfied himself that his bride was unhurt, the King's first question was as to whether his mother and Princess Beatrice were safe.

[1] This letter appeared in *A Victorian Diarist—Later Extracts from the Journals of Mary, Lady Monkswell*, 1895–1909; edited by the Hon. E. C. F. Collier.

In that sudden switch from jubilation and magnificence
to the inferno of terror, suffering and slaughter, when the
sweet smell of early summer gave place to the reek of
dynamite, when the cheering changed to nightmare cries
of human pain mingled with the shrieks of legless horses,
when the stately gait of the marriage procession accelerated
wildly into the stampede of the terrified, when frocks that
had looked so lovely in the sunlight now resembled blood-
stained bandages and houses were spattered red two storeys
high, one light shone clearly—the courage of King Alfonso
of Spain. His bride, too, played her part magnificently,
shielded as she was by her husband and Colonel Lowther
and the officers of the Lancers. Yet she had seen the
horrors, and the severed heads rolling in the roadway.

Those in the forefront of the procession, who had
already reached the Palace, were for some time in ignorance
of what had happened. Prince Alexander had dismounted,
and was waiting by the Palace steps when the bomb went
off. He thought that it was the beginning of a salute.
Then the coach carrying Queen Christina and Princess
Beatrice drew up. Queen Christina was deathly pale, the
Princess fighting to control her tears. Some distance
behind them came the Coach of Respect. As it reached the
steps the King jumped out, shouting the news that a
bomb had been thrown, but that the Queen and he were
unhurt.

The young Queen was too close to the tragedy for the
full effect to be immediately felt. Her one concern was for
the killed and wounded. It has been said that so much was
she in control of herself that, during tea afterwards at the
Palace, she was able to show dismay that her husband
dipped his bread and butter into his cup. '*Mon ami*,' she
exclaimed, '*tu trempes ta tartine dans ton thé!*'

The shock fell squarely upon the shoulders of Princess
Beatrice, as her nephew, the Prince of Wales, noted. The
day had already been sufficiently charged with ordeal.

Add to the emotional strain of the wedding day of her only daughter, the ritual of a religion not her own, a city strange to her, and the age-old splendour of Spanish regality. She knew that an attempt was planned. Her eye was practised in noting the behaviour of crowds, and the precautions taken to control them, and here the control was in marked contrast with that exercised in Britain.

Here was an echo of the day when Maclean had fired at her mother and herself . . . and the echo of Queen Victoria saying, 'Beatrice was so brave. She saw it all.'

And the danger was not over. Morral was still at large. So maniacal was he in his determination to kill the King and Queen that, after he had dropped his bomb, he had raced down to street level and there made an attempt to shoot them. But the chaos was so great, the crowd so thick, that he was foiled.

The shadow of Morral hung over Madrid. There was no doubt in most minds that he would try again. No one knew the danger better than King Alfonso, but he ignored it. His guests must wear their uniforms, regardless of whether it made them conspicuous targets. And, on the day after the wedding, Prince Alexander watched the King drive out alone with his Queen.

Two days later, in a quiet village near Escorial, Morral, the assassin, was arrested. He shot his captor, then turned the gun upon himself.

The wedding festivities went on for a week, saddened by the funerals, which Prince Alexander and the Lancer officers attended, of those who had died in the explosion, and the Royal visits to the wounded in the hospitals. There was a bull fight. A great cheer came up from the arena as Queen Christina and Princess Beatrice entered the Royal box together. Queen Victoria Eugenia waved her handkerchief, and the fights began. Eight bulls were killed.

The occasions when the British Royal Family, in the course of their duties, visited bull fights, were always difficult ones. As King George V[1] said, after his first experience, as a young man: 'I must say that I never saw a more disgusting sight and I never wish to see another one.' In this view he was joined by his German uncle, the Emperor Frederick, who described it as: '. . . a barbaric performance for torturing horse and bull'. Princess Beatrice had been trained by a mother who fought to save stray dogs from being shot and campaigned fiercely for better conditions in slaughter-houses. But her daughter was now the Queen of Spain.

After a reception (replacing the ball which had been planned), and a battle of flowers, the King and Queen left for their honeymoon at La Granja.

Prince Beatrice went with them. She had much to remember by the time that she returned to Kensington Palace, where her mother's statue looks peacefully out across the Gardens and the Park and her father's memory reaches up towards the sky.

[1] At the request of the House of Commons, the Prince and Princess of Wales did not attend on this occasion.

11

War and Peace

PRINCESS BEATRICE reached her fiftieth birthday in 1907. The impression of her mother was indelibly stamped upon her; small wonder, when one considers the seclusion in which she had passed her formative years, that she should have absorbed many of Queen Victoria's beliefs, standards, and ways of living.

Princess Beatrice always had a religious trait in her character and this developed after her husband's death. Carefully she set about the task of beautifying and arranging the Chapel at Whippingham which Queen Victoria had given as a burial place for both of them. Their engagement rings, bearing their names in diamonds, were hung on the stem of the chalice, and the frontal of the altar embroidered on the satin of the Princess's wedding dress. For a time the Princess insisted on always wearing onyx as a token of mourning, but her sons had a horror of these stones and persuaded her to change to pearls.

Prince Henry's anniversaries were as religiously kept as had been those of the Consort. When one such anniversary fell while she was sailing in the Mediterranean on Sir Thomas Lipton's yacht, the Princess insisted, despite the storm that was blowing at the time, on being put ashore at Nice to attend Holy Communion.

Queen Victoria had found peace at Balmoral, where the people understood her wish to be able to drive round without attention being paid, and Princess Beatrice found peace in the Isle of Wight, where the people had the same understanding.

Certain adjustments had inevitably to be made in her

own status and position. At the end of the century she
was the 'Baby' daughter of the Queen, an indispensable
companion and secretary, and the mother of young
children. Only seven years later she was the fifty-year-
old sister of the ageing King; her sons were men; her
daughter was the Queen of Spain; and she was a grandmother.

As the mother of the Spanish Queen, Princess Beatrice
held a unique position in the international public eye,
and one not devoid of worry. No monarch had faced a
more difficult rôle than Queen Ena. It was not limited to
her initiation and the tragedy in the streets of Madrid.
The new Queen, at eighteen, had to grasp a new language
and a new religion, and, in addition, she had to alter the
creed in which she had been brought up—that everything British was right.

All but five of Princess Ena's years had been spent inside
the fortress of Queen Victoria, and its effect showed in
small ways. Queen Ena had cause once to complain to an
official that the Palace stairs were dusty, and the criticism
was made that a Spanish Queen would not even notice
such an insignificant point, but it was one which would
not have been lost on Queen Victoria.

The Queen was beautiful—'*Es una real moya*'—that
was generally agreed, but in her love for dancing, tennis
and golf, she still appeared too English to some who
closely watched her adherence to the stern discipline of
the regal and religious code.

Princess Beatrice made none of the mistakes that
Queen Victoria had made in the case of the marriage of
her eldest daughter. King Alfonso appreciated that, and
so called her the ideal mother-in-law. But during her
first year in Spain, Queen Victoria Eugenia received a
great deal of helpful advice from her mother on the running of charitable organisations, which at that time were
non-existent in that country.

The marriage brought other problems for the British Royal Family. King Alfonso was most pressing that King Edward should pay a State Visit to Spain but, as Sir Charles Hardinge wrote to Lord Knollys in January 1907:

> 'There are, as you will see, considerations which impel us to do all we can to be on friendly terms with Spain, but not to go so far as to risk the life of our King. . . . Our government must be quite firm for some years to come on the subject of a visit by the King to Madrid, as the Spanish police is hopeless, and there appears to be no prospect of any improvement.'

A compromise was found in April when King Edward and Queen Alexandra sailed in the Royal Yacht to Cartagena and met King Alfonso at sea. Queen Ena was unable to meet her uncle and aunt as she was within a few weeks of the birth of her first child.

Princess Beatrice was in Madrid for the confinement and the young Queen had the additional comfort and support of an English doctor, Bryden Glendinning.

On 10th May a son was born—Don Alfonso, Prince of Asturias. The proud father, just twenty-one, carried the naked child on a tray into the presence of his ministers and courtiers, and lifted the veil to show that there was in truth an heir to the Spanish throne. The Pope agreed to be the child's godfather, and Spain went mad with excitement.

Soon it was learned that Don Alfonso suffered from haemophilia, and the news was not well received by the Spanish people. Here lay real tragedy for Princess Beatrice. Both she and the Spanish King's advisers knew full well, at the time of the engagement, of the risk that the young couple were running, but they were so much in love; King Alfonso never feared a risk, and Princess Ena was of good health and high-spirited.

Princess Beatrice was not alone among the daughters

of Queen Victoria to pass on the disease. It had travelled down through Princess Alice and now was to be found in St. Petersburg. It was a human tragedy, flood-lit because it had happened in a palace.

That autumn Princess Beatrice was able to see much of her daughter and son-in-law, for they came to England on a private visit that lasted from the end of October to the beginning of December. A week was spent with the King and Queen at Sandringham and the couple also called on the Empress Eugénie at Farnborough Hill.

Their stay coincided with the State visit of the Emperor and Empress of Germany. Princess Beatrice's eldest nephew had now reached a state which King Edward bluntly described as 'impossible'. When alone with his British relations, he would drink their health with an obvious affection. With his own entourage he would raise his glass to 'Der Tag', indiscreetly ignoring the ears of certain royal servants and their gift for observing without being observed.

The Emperor arrived on the 11th of November and was immediately launched into a programme which King Edward was determined should be memorable. On the 14th there was a shooting party at Virginia Water and the Royal ladies, including the Queens of Spain, Portugal and Norway and the Empress of Germany, joined the Déjeuner de Chasse at the Fishing Temple.[1]

On the 17th Princess Beatrice attended a luncheon at Windsor at which there were present twenty-four men and women of royal rank, a congregation such as seldom, if ever, had been rivalled. So often had she attended great ceremonies as the daughter of Queen Victoria. Now, for the first time, she was there as the mother of a Queen so titled.

[1] A reminiscence of George IV, its wooden balconies overhanging the water. With centre room and roof in Swiss chalet style, the wings, or outer rooms, formed part of the old pagoda.

A second son was born to King Alfonso and Queen Ena in 1908. On this occasion the child, Don Jaime, proved to be a deaf mute. The following year proved more fortunate, for an Infanta was born, strong and healthy, who was named Beatriz after her grandmother.

Princess Beatrice was in Madrid, awaiting the birth of another child to Queen Ena, when the news came of King Edward's last illness. She hurried to London, as did King Alfonso, who stayed with his mother-in-law at Kensington Palace until the funeral was over.

Queen Ena's fourth child was stillborn. This deepened the sadness for Princess Beatrice, for whom the death of King Edward had come as a terrible shock. He had only returned from a holiday at Biarritz on 27th April and yet, a few days later, he was dead.

With the accession of George V the link snapped between Great Britain and Germany. Although only eight years younger than his Aunt Beatrice, King George had been brought up in a very different world. Sandringham was so essentially English. His mother, and for very good reasons, hated Prussia. His father, tied as he was to Germany through close family connections, had referred to the Emperor as: 'a Satan—you cannot imagine what a Satan . . .'.

In a changing world Princess Beatrice aged fast. Her health was not good, and heart trouble forbade her from visiting the Spanish capital, owing to its altitude. There three more children were born to Queen Ena: Maria Christina and Juan in 1911 and 1913, both healthy children, and Gonzalez, another victim of haemophilia, in 1914.

In 1912 the Princess sold Osborne Cottage. The next year she visited Scotland again, spending some time at Abergeldie. Thereafter, she moved into historic Carisbrooke Castle in the Isle of Wight, being most interested in the modernised apartments there. She arranged that the Castle should be taken over by the Ministry of Works.

The Princess, as was her custom, was in the Isle of Wight in July 1914, and it was only on the urgent request of Prince Louis of Battenburg that she agreed to leave. On the morning of the 4th August she telephoned her sister, Princess Christian, to say that she was returning to London immediately. That day there was a family luncheon, at which plans were discussed as to what was to be done in the terrible days ahead. One domestic arrangement decided upon was that Princess Marie Louise should live with her aunt at Kensington Palace.

Princess Beatrice's first concern was for her three sons, now all in the army. Prince Alexander, who had resigned from the Navy in 1908, had been commissioned in the Grenadier Guards in 1911, and his battalion was under orders, as were Prince Leopold and Prince Maurice, both in the 60th Rifles.

It was a strange and awkward position in which the brood of Queen Victoria and Prince Albert found itself in that August of 1914. For fifty years the royal relations had been constant travellers on the Channel boats. Backward and forward they had trooped, between England and Germany, and Germany and England, for the shooting, the sailing, the Season—for marriages, christenings, funerals—for reviews, jubilees, exhibitions—to health resorts, seaside resorts, schools. Now the curtain of war dropped so swiftly that families were separated. The children of the Empress Frederick's daughter, Sophie, Queen of Greece, were on holiday at Eastbourne with their English nurse. King George V arranged that a special boat, escorted by a destroyer, should take the children to Flushing.

The private tragedy lay in the snapping of the family ties, and in the hatred born as cousin fought cousin. Love died swiftly between mothers and sons, sisters and brothers, and hard hit were the families of Queen Victoria's children, Leopold and Helena.

Outstanding among the relatives of the British Royal Family domiciled in Germany who refused to take an active part in the war, was the Grand Duke Ernest of Hesse. 'Ernie', the son of Princess Alice, whom Princess Beatrice had come to know so well in the years after the death of her sister, had married Princess Eleanore of Solms-Hohensolms-Lich in 1905, and, with two young sons, was finding the happiness he had sought for in vain with Princess Victoria Melita. With one sister Tsarina of Russia, and another married to the First Sea Lord, Grand Duke Ernest was open to suspicion in Germany. He ignored it, and devoted his time to the care of the wounded, and rehabilitation of the men whose lives had been shattered.

Hatred for everything German welled up in Britain, and the German name of Battenberg did not escape. The bitter campaign against Prince Louis began.

Part of Princess Beatrice's duties as Governor of the Isle of Wight was the allocation of certain war-time duties. As a result of this she received a letter asking what duties the members of her family were undertaking. She replied, very politely, through an equerry, that she quite understood the query and, though it was unusual for the Royal Family to advertise, she felt that she must say that she had lost her husband on active service, that her three sons had left for the front on 12th August, and that she had no more menfolk to send.

The war was but two months old when Princess Beatrice was told that Prince Maurice had been mentioned in despatches, having shown outstanding gallantry in leading his men into action. A few weeks later he was wounded, and died on 27th October.

The Memorial Service was held at the Chapel Royal, St. James's, on 5th November. The King and Queen,

Queen Alexandra, the Prime Minister, and two Field Mar-
shals, Kitchener and Grenfell, were present. Bravely into
the Chapel came Eugénie, for eighteen years the Empress
of France. This was only the second time in her life that
she had attended an Anglican service, the first having
been when King Edward VII, as Prince of Wales, had
led her into the funeral service for Lord Sydney. Among
those present, Princess Beatrice, Queen Alexandra, the
Empress, Lord Knollys, Miss Charlotte Knollys and Sir
Dighton Probyn were able to look back to the unforgotten
day when the news had come that the Prince Imperial had
died on service in South Africa.

'Lie still, beloved' was played, and Prince Maurice's
epitaph was written:

> 'Those who shared with Maurice of Battenberg the
> perils and glories, the happiness and the miseries of
> life at "the front", will retain memories of his pluck,
> his lovable nature, and his good comradeship. For all
> he had a cheery, kindly word, and all had a kindly
> word for him.'

Lord Kitchener offered to have Prince Maurice's body
brought back to England, but Princess Beatrice said, 'No,
let him lie with his comrades.'

The same months of October brought death to another
descendant of Queen Victoria.[1] The 5th and 16th Lancers
and the 4th Hussars were on the Aisne, revenging themselves after the Mons retreat. They constituted the 3rd
Cavalry Brigade, under Brigadier-General Gough. One
dawn, when the mist hung low over the stubble fields,
scouts brought back news that a company of the crack
Death's Head Hussars was billeted in a monastery nearby.
The brigade advanced under cover of the mist, and sweep-
ing cross-fire caught the enemy unawares.

[1] The story of it was told to me by a soldier who took part in the
action.

A fair-haired German officer ran from the monastery towards the line of tethered horses, and he was hit as his foot reached the stirrup. He lay on the ground until, the action over, the British reached him. He was found to be seriously wounded. He asked the British medical officer how long he had to live and, on being told only an hour or so, gave certain instructions.

This officer was Maximilian of Hesse, grandson of the Empress Frederick, a boy of seven when Princess Beatrice had paid her last visit to her sister at Friedrichshof. He was the son of Princess Margaret, the Empress's youngest daughter, who was 'Benjamina' to her mother as Princess Beatrice had been to Queen Victoria.

Prince Max's last request to the doctor was that a chain, on which hung a locket containing his mother's picture, should be returned to her. The next day the doctor was killed. His widow sent the locket to Queen Mary, who sent it back to Friedrichshof via Margaret of Sweden.

Sergeant Jones, of the 5th Lancers, was also killed in the engagement, and Prince Max was buried beside him. But shortly the soil was turned again, and the royal body spirited away. It lies now in the chapel at Kronberg.

It was of such heartbreaks that World War I was composed for the Royal Family.

In the interval between the death and funeral service of Prince Maurice, the First Sea Lord, Prince Louis of Battenberg, resigned. The burden of criticism, centred on his German ancestry, had proved too heavy for the brilliant sailor who had devoted his life to the British Navy. His resignation could not have come at a worse time for Princess Beatrice. The news of the death of her son was a vivid reminder of that dread day when she had heard of the death of Prince Henry. She had lost her husband in the Ashanti campaign. Now Prince Maurice was dead. Princes Alexander and Leopold were in the British Army. Prince Louis's elder son, George, was serving with the

Fleet and his younger son was a naval cadet. What further proof of patriotism could be given?

It was in 1868 that Princess Alice had arranged that young Louis should come to England and join the Navy. Forty years had gone by since he had sat beside Princess Beatrice at dinner at Osborne, and she had not spoken a word to him all evening because she scented a 'freshness' in his approach. Then the Admiralty had been asked to keep him on foreign stations, well out of her way. Now he was being removed for a very different reason and those who knew best of the capabilities of Prince Louis, notably George V and Winston Churchill, deeply regretted his resignation.

The sad war years dragged on. For Princess Beatrice there was an endless round of Royal duties, bazaars to attend, purses to receive at schools, war savings to boost, hospitals to help and visits to pay to convalescent homes for the wounded. She ran, very efficiently, her own hospital for officers in Hill Street—the Princess Henry of Battenberg Hospital for Officers. A sanatorium that the Princess knew well was that set up by Empress Eugénie for wounded officers at Farnborough Hill, and visited in 1915 by the King, the Queen and the Prince of Wales.

The indomitable Empress, born in 1826, flung defiance at time. She saw the World War as a means of vengeance for Sedan and Metz, and she was determined to see her vengeance complete. Eternally young, she had already been fined for speeding and had had wireless installed in her yacht—which caused certain countries to speculate as to what use it would be put.

At the end of June 1917, *Punch* published a drawing showing King George, armed with a besom, energetically brushing into a heap a collection of crowns marked 'Made in Germany'. 'A good riddance' said the caption. On the 20th of June the King had announced that those among his relations who held German titles should relinquish

Prince Maurice of Battenberg, a posthumous portrait by P. de Laszlo
(*by permission of the Marquess of Carisbrooke*)

Hay Wrightson

The Marquess of Carisbrooke

The Four Generations: H.R.H. Princess Beatrice; H.M. Queen Victoria Eugenia; the Queen's eldest daughter, the Infanta Beatriz; and the Infanta's eldest child, Princess Sandra Torlonia (*by permission of Her Majesty Queen Victoria Eugenia*)

Princess Beatrice in 1927 (*from the painting by P. de Laszlo, by permission of Her Majesty Queen Victoria Eugenia*)

them, and adopt British ones in their place. So into the limbo went Coburg and Schleswig-Holstein, Teck and Battenberg. Queen Mary's two brothers, Adolphus and Alexander, emerged from the spring-cleaning as the Marquess of Cambridge and the Earl of Athlone, with the family name of Cambridge. Prince Louis of Battenberg, the unwanted sailor, became the Marquess of Milford Haven. His family name became Mountbatten, as it did for the children of his brother, Henry.

In the case of Princess Beatrice, the mode of address, Princess Henry of Battenberg, ceased. Her elder son became the Marquess of Carisbrooke and her younger, Lord Leopold Mountbatten.

On 17th July the King held a Council and made a Proclamation 'Declaring that the Name of Windsor is to be borne by His Royal House and Family and Relinquishing the Use of All German Titles and Dignities'. On hearing this, the Kaiser issued a retaliatory order that all future performances in Germany of *The Merry Wives of Windsor* should be given under the title of *The Merry Wives of Saxe-Coburg and Gotha*.

It was a notable month for Princess Beatrice, for two days after the King's Proclamation her son, Alexander, now the Marquess of Carisbrooke, was married to Lady Irene Frances Denison, only daughter of the second Earl of Londesborough. The khaki wedding took place at the Chapel Royal, St. James's, and there were no bridesmaids or formal reception.

As the war drew towards its final phase, the Romanoff family was savagely butchered in circumstances which have often been described. To Princess Beatrice the terrible scene in that cellar in Ekaterinberg had a nightmarish clarity. There, on the night of 16th July 1918, they were shot: 'Nicky', who had run after Prince Philip's mother when she was married at Darmstadt and poured a bag of rice over her head; 'Alicky', who had been allowed

16

to cut short her lessons so that she could be bridesmaid to her aunt, Princess Beatrice; Olga, who had appeared with Queen Victoria and great-aunt Beatrice in the first moving pictures taken of the Royal Family at Balmoral; Tatiana, who had a small dog in her arms; Marie, named after Queen Alexandra's sister; Anastasia, whom hopeful rumour later said had escaped the fusillade; and fourteen-year-old Alexis, blue with cold.

As Princess Beatrice worked diligently on at her task of editing her mother's letters, each page brought reminders of then . . . and now. So few years between, yet so many tragedies.

12

Finale

PRINCE PHILIP[1] blew a trumpet in Kensington Palace. He was told to be quiet, as the noise might upset his great-great-aunt Beatrice, whose apartments were nearby. This was bad luck, as he was only eight.

That trumpet blast might well be taken to mark the fall of the curtain on the old order of Royalty, and its rising on a new. In the nineteen-twenties many of those died who had been familiar characters on the Victorian stage, and there were many new members of the fourth generation after Queen Victoria. For Princess Beatrice there was an important addition to the third generation. On 13th January 1920 the Marchioness of Carisbrooke gave birth to a daughter,[2] and the child's names included that of her grandmother.

This completed the Princess's grandchildren, now numbering seven. Her mother had had thirty-nine. It was fortunate, in many ways, that this rate of expansion did not continue. If each descendant had lived, and followed her example, there would have been over six thousand blood relations by the fourth generation. In the event there was an ample abundance of children arriving on the scene, and mention must be restricted to certain of them.

In 1921, eighteen years after her marriage, and seven years after the birth of the youngest of her four daughters, Princess Andrew of Greece gave birth to a son. This latest addition to the erstwhile Battenberg family was named Philip, and he was born at Mon Repos, Corfu. While still

[1] Now Duke of Edinburgh.   [2] Lady Iris Mountbatten.

a baby he was brought to England in a battleship, his father having been banished from Greece and fortunate to have escaped execution.

In England, grandchildren began to arrive for King George and Queen Mary. In 1922 Princess Mary married the Earl of Harewood, and in the two following years sons were born. In 1923 the Duke of York married Lady Elizabeth Bowes-Lyon and three years later came a daughter who was named Elizabeth.

Friendship and affection blossomed between the Duke of York and Princess Beatrice. This had begun during his visits to his great-grandmother in the 'nineties and flowered during the time that he was at Osborne and was asked to tea with his 'Aunt B' at Osborne Cottage.

On the debit side, Princess Beatrice lost many friends and relations during the early nineteen-twenties. The Empress Eugénie had achieved her ambition, and lived to see Armistice Day. 'It was', she said, 'her first joy since 1870'—but that remark cannot be taken too literally. She died in Madrid on 11th July 1920, whilst on a visit to her great nephew, the Duke of Alba. She was ninety-four. Very distant was the echo of the words she had spoken after hearing of the death of the Prince Imperial—words which were to prove so nearly right: 'I am left alone, the sole remnant of a shipwreck; which proves how fragile and vain are the gardens of this world. . . . I cannot die; and God, in His infinite mercy, will give me a hundred years of life. . . .'

The photograph of the Prince Imperial was still on Prince Beatrice's table.

The Empress was buried beside her husband at Farnborough and the King and Queen of Spain came to London for the ceremony, staying with Princess Beatrice at Kensington Palace.

Empress Eugénie had also lived to see the German Emperor start his exile in Holland, and Doorn more than revenged Wilhelmshöhe, where her husband had walked the gardens under the eye of Prussian officers. At Doorn, in 1921, died the Empress 'Dona', that 'insignificant little Princess' who had dared to criticise the marriage of Queen Victoria's favourite daughter.

In August 1921 Princess Beatrice's brother-in-law, Louis, Marquess of Milford Haven, was promoted to be an Admiral of the Fleet, on the retired list. It was vindication at last, if only partly recompense for the wrong he had endured. The vindication came only just in time, for on 10th September Lord Milford Haven was taken ill, and by the next day he was dead. On the 19th, after the funeral procession to Westminster, where the Marquess of Carisbrooke represented the Queen, a special train took the body to Portsmouth and the destroyer *Ready* carried it to Cowes. There, waiting to receive it, was Princess Beatrice, Governor of the Isle of Wight. The funeral was at the church of her memories, Whippingham.

That night the Marchioness of Milford Haven stayed at Netley Abbey, where she was joined by her daughter, Alice, who had with her her three-month-old son, Philip. It was fitting that Prince Philip's first visit to England should have been for the funeral of the famous sailor in his family.

The following year was a black one for Princess Beatrice, who was on holiday in Sicily in April when the news reached her that her son, Lord Leopold Mountbatten, was to have an emergency operation at Kensington Palace. Lord Leopold appeared to be making a normal recovery, but had a sudden relapse, and died. Whilst his health had in the past given considerable cause for worry, his collapse before either his mother or his sister could reach him came as a great shock. He was only thirty-three when he died.

A few months later Helen, Duchess of Albany, died. Aunt of Queen Wilhelmina of the Netherlands, Helen was the only one of the daughters-in-law who dared to have out differences face to face with Queen Victoria. Princess Beatrice missed her, for they had done much hospital work together.

Princess Beatrice was determined that the high standard that had been achieved in hospitals during the war should be maintained, and took vigorous steps. She also took an active part in the League of Remembrance.

A hospital took her name—the Princess Beatrice Hospital in Old Brompton Road. Originally known as the Kensington, Fulham and Chelsea Jubilee Hospital, standing as it did where three Boroughs met, it had but twelve beds. By the efforts of Lord Carisbrooke, and generous benefactors, the capacity was later increased to eighty.

In 1923 died Helena, Princess Christian—'Lenchen', the tomboy of Queen Victoria's nursery, who was quite up to punching a Prince's nose if he became swelled-headed. Her death left but three of the nine—Louise, Arthur and Beatrice. This trinity was to last until the clouds of Hitler's war were to darken the sky. Alice, 1878 . . . Leopold, 1884 . . . Alfred, 1900 . . . 'Vicky', 1901 . . . 'Bertie', 1910 . . . Helena, 1923. Nearly three-score years and ten were to separate the deaths of the first and last to die of the children of Queen Victoria and Prince Albert.

In 1923 the Earl of Athlone, Queen Mary's brother, was appointed Governor-General of South Africa, and he and Princess Alice invited Princess Beatrice to visit them. She welcomed the opportunity to escape the English winter, and reached the Cape just before Christmas. Princess Beatrice was a close friend of the Athlones; Lord Athlone was her godson. She had seen much of Princess Alice in her childhood days, after the tragic death of Prince Leopold, and, now that the Duchess of Albany was dead, the bond was tightened.

Princess Beatrice received an enthusiastic welcome in the Union and if she had fulfilled all the engagements for

which she was in demand, she might have returned to
London more tired than when she left. The Governor-
General and Princess Alice knew that she needed rest and
sunshine, and saw that she had it. Princess Beatrice loved
to travel, to move around, and she visited the highlands,
although the height was bad for her heart. Much of the
holiday she spent at the Cape, staying with the Archbishop of Capetown. The photographs taken of her during
her stay show her as a bowed old lady, scarcely reaching
to the shoulder of the Earl of Athlone. She wears a white
hat with a mass of flowers on it, and a long, black frock,
embroidered round the hem, not unlike the one her
mother had worn for the Jubilee. Here is marked contrast
with the upright, quietly efficient Princess-cum-secretary-
cum-nurse who had guarded Queen Victoria's approaches
quarter of a century earlier, whom the German Emperor
had referred to as 'the petticoat' who kept him away from
his 'unparalleled grandmamma'.

Rheumatism was now considerably hampering the
movements of Princess Beatrice, and in January 1931 she
slipped on a mat at Kensington Palace and fell heavily.
It was found that she had broken two bones in her left
arm. Bronchial trouble followed and so ill did the Princess
become that the doctors doubted whether she would live
through the night.

A telephone call was put through to Madrid, and Queen
Ena hurried to London. For a month she cared for her
mother, read to her, prayed with her, and gave her the
interest which coaxed her back out of danger.

At the end of February Queen Ena returned to Spain,
together with Lady Carisbrooke, who was recuperating
after an operation. There were prayers in her mother's
room before they left, prayers that the journey back to
the Royal Palace would be safely accomplished. For
Queen Ena had doubts, and fears, as to the reception that
she would receive.

As their train pulled into Madrid station the Queen and her sister-in-law heard the roar of a mighty crowd. They still did not know if that roar was one of acclamation —or revolution. In the event, on that 28th of February 1931, the Queen was given one of the most enthusiastic receptions that had been accorded to her since she had first arrived in Spain.

A wave of optimism and relief swept through the Palace, and in March Alfonso felt that he could safely take a short holiday in London. It was to be his last as King. He returned to Madrid on the 22nd, and at the same time Princess Beatrice travelled to Torquay, to shake off the after effects of her illness.

Easter fell on 5th April and marked the first stage of the local elections in Spain. Twenty-five years before, to the day, Princess Ena had been created a Royal Highness.

The final result of the elections was brought to King Alfonso in his study at midnight on the 12th. This result showed that, while the monarchists had held their majority throughout the country as a whole, there had been a swing towards Republicanism in the big cities. It was here that the revolutionaries wished their fire to burn, and they were quick to fan the flame. Out into the streets of Madrid poured the demonstrators, surging, shouting, towards the Palace. Hooliganism reigned and, as the trams toppled over, the statues fell and shots rang out, the Ministry panicked. The Prime Minister announced that the country had gone Republican—the commander of the Civil Guard said that he could no longer be answerable for the actions of the police. King Alfonso saw that, if he was to stay in Spain, it would only be at the cost of bloodshed. That was a price he would not pay, and he decided to leave.

14th April was Princess Beatrice's seventy-fourth birth-day—a day for celebration. A telegram of greeting came to Torquay from her daughter, with no mention of the momentous events in Madrid.

At five o'clock that afternoon, at the Royal Palace, King Alfonso said goodbye to his Ministers and to his attendants. A few hours later, when the daylight had gone, he walked out on to the terrace for the last time. Three cars were waiting. A few minutes later he began his journey to Cartagena, Marseilles and Paris.

The King, judging that the demonstrations of the revolutionaries were directed against him as Monarch, considered that it would be wiser, and safer, if he left alone, and that Queen Ena, Lady Carisbrooke and the younger members of the Royal Family, travelled the following day by train to Paris via Irun. After the display of loyalty and affection which had greeted the Queen on her return to the capital but a month earlier, it seemed impossible to believe that the crowds would now raise hand or voice against her.

The revolutionaries wanted the Royal Family, all of them, out of Spain as quickly as they could manage it, and before the cry went up again, 'Viva el Rey'. So began a night of terror. A vast human mass, out of control and drunk with slogans, moved against the Palace. The menacing hum became a babel. There were screams for the blood of the Queen, whom so many Spaniards loved. Threats, insults, howls of hate were hurled at the Royal apartments.

Early next morning Queen Ena, her sister-in-law, and her children left the Royal Palace by a back entrance, in much the same manner that the Empress Eugénie had left the Tuileries in 1870. The party were driven to El Escorial, thirty miles away. There Queen Victoria Eugenia of Spain said farewell to her ladies and boarded the train for Paris. At the Hotel Meurice, she was reunited with her husband on the evening of the next day.

The years are still too young to allow of full reward being given to Queen Ena for the part she played in

Spain. A bomb had been part of the fanfare for her wedding day; now, as the curtain dropped, the mob were screaming for her blood. In the interim had come the sadness of sick children, the heartache of divided loyalties, the threat to personal safety, the sweet balm of loving cheers. Only a grandchild of Queen Victoria, trained by Queen Victoria, could have tackled the task that confronted Queen Ena.

Tired and troubled, the Queen and her children moved into a quiet hotel in Fontainbleau. Her mother, convalescing, was mercifully spared the full blow of the tragic fate which had befallen her daughter.

From this time until the end of her life Princess Beatrice was under the care of the doctors, and it was due to their skill that she reached the great age that she did. Always before her was one goal—to complete the scrutiny and editing of her mother's papers. Only when operations on her eyes positively prohibited her from reading did she delegate the task for a while, and Princess Helena Victoria took over. Fitting enough, it was Princess Helena Victoria who had written the Queen's *Journal* during her last illness.

Cataract crept almost unnoticed upon the Princess, and suddenly she found herself nearly blind. She refused to let the handicap alter her plans, and went to Buckingham Palace for Queen Mary's birthday though she could scarce distinguish the cakes upon the plate. An operation gave her back her sight, but she was never able to find a lens which would allow her to read music. She turned for her solace to the radio. It was sad for the Princess who had composed the quick march so often played by the Grenadier Guards.

The letters and diaries upon which Princess Beatrice was now working, had been penned at a time when the grown-up Royalties of the eventful 'thirties were either newly-married or children. Their comings and goings had been faithfully chronicled by Queen Victoria, in hand-writing that grew more and more difficult to read as the century drew to a close.

Princess Beatrice could see them all as if in double vision.

'CIMIEZ, 25th April 1897.—Heard from Georgie that May had given birth to a little girl, both doing well. It is strange that this child should be born on dear Alice's birthday, whilst the last was on the anniversary of her death.'

The little girl was Princess Mary, upon whom the title of Princess Royal was bestowed in 1932.

A letter from the German Emperor to Queen Victoria, dated 31st March 1900:

'MOST BELOVED GRANDMAMA,—How glad am I that I may join to the thanks for your last kind letter the warmest congratulations for the birth of another great-grandson! The Lord's blessing is upon your house, and may it for ever continue to be so! I hope that May and her boy will prosper, and that he may add a new ray of sunshine in the pretty lodge to the sunny little circle in a happy home . . .'

The Prince was named Henry and, as Duke of Glouces-ter, he married Lady Alice Montagu-Douglas-Scott in November 1935.

'BALMORAL, 30th Sept. 1897.—Took leave with much regret of Georgie and May, who are leaving the first thing tomorrow morning. Every time I see them I love and like them more and more and respect them greatly. Thank God! Georgie has got such an excellent, useful, and good wife!'

In May 1935 King George V and Queen Mary cele-brated their Silver Jubilee, and eight months later the King died.

'BALMORAL, 28th Sept. 1896.—Dear little David

with the baby came in at the end of luncheon to say goodbye. David is a most attractive little boy, and so forward and clever. He always tries at luncheon time to pull me up out of my chair, saying, "Get up, Gangan," and then to one of the Indian servants, "Man pull it," which makes us laugh very much.'

Two Kings at her chairside—Edward VIII and George VI.

The 14th of April 1937 was Princess Beatrice's eightieth birthday. It was in 1899 that her mother had reached the same landmark. Then the Princess, the Queen and the Princess of Wales had driven together to the Mausoleum, and in the evening there had been a family dinner,. . . 'Bertie, Alix and Victoria, Ernie and Ducky . . . .'

'Ernie and Ducky' had been the Grand Duke and Duchess of Hesse then, Princess Alice's only surviving son and Princess Victoria Melita of Edinburgh. After their divorce in 1901 both had remarried. The Grand Duke had two sons, George Donatus and Louis. Duke Ernest died in October 1937, and a few days later there was only Prince Louis left in the Hesse family. The widowed Grand Duchess, Prince George, his lovely wife Cecilia,[1] and their three children, were killed in an air crash as they flew to London for the wedding of Prince Louis to the Hon. Margaret Campbell Geddes.

Princess Victoria Melita, the Grand Duchess Cyril, died in 1936 and her sister, Queen Marie of Rumania, in 1938. Both had been bridesmaids to Princess Beatrice.

To mark the Princess's eightieth year, and her record as Governor of the Island since her husband's death forty years before, the people of the Isle of Wight presented her with a chamber organ, to which was attached a fascinating story. Bearing the date '1603' and the Montrose arms, the organ was believed to have been

[1] Prince Philip's sister.

played by Princess Elizabeth, daughter of Charles I. King Charles had escaped to Carisbrooke Castle in November 1647, and it was from there that he was taken by force in December of the next year. Tragic Princess Elizabeth died in 1650, at the age of fifteen.

In the courtyard of the Castle Lady Mottistone made the presentation to Princess Beatrice, who expressed her wish that the organ should remain at Carisbrooke.

The outbreak of war put an end to the visits of the Princess to the Island of which she had been Governor for half her life. She had her first holiday there in the year of the Indian Mutiny.

In December 1939 Princess Louise, Duchess of Argyll, died at Kensington Palace. Only two of Queen Victoria's children now remained, and those her favourite son and her favourite daughter—Arthur and Beatrice. And, in the comparative peace of the countryside, brother and sister saw much of one another.

Friedrichshof, also, had seen many changes since Princess Beatrice had travelled to Germany to see her dying sister. There was Battenberg blood there now, for Prince Philip's youngest sister, Sophie, had married the Empress Frederick's grandson, Christopher.

In February 1941 King Alfonso of Spain died in the Grand Hotel in Rome, and during his last few days Queen Ena scarcely left his side.

It was in that same year that Princess Beatrice came before the public eye for the last time. A book, bearing her name, was published. Entitled *In Napoleonic Days*,[1] it consisted of extracts from the private diary of Augusta, Duchess of Saxe-Coburg-Saalfeld, Queen Victoria's grandmother. The extracts had been selected and translated by Princess Beatrice.

'The King,' she wrote, 'having kindly given me permission to translate for publication some extracts from

[1] See Appendix A.

my great-grandmother's Diary, I hope that this small effort and venture of mine may be of some interest to the public. . . .' The proceeds were to go to war charities.

The Princess was eighty-four when her book was published, the high standard of her translation giving insight into the unheralded work that she had carried out over so many years as the literary executrix of Queen Victoria.

Her work on her mother's papers was over, and it was suggested that she undertake the editing of her great-grandmother's letters so that she could keep her active brain employed and retain her interest in life.

One of the last packets that had been brought from the archives for her scrutiny contained faded and yellow letters written by her father and mother to one another, with revealing information about their intimate marital relations. Princess Beatrice destroyed them and informed King George VI that she had done so.

'I thought that you would,' said the King. 'So I had photostat copies made before you saw them.'

The Duke of Connaught died in January 1942, and Princess Beatrice was alone. She spent the last two years of her life at Brantbridge Park, Balcombe, in Sussex, the home of the Earl of Athlone and Princess Alice. In October 1944 she became very ill. Queen Ena was notified, and reached her mother's side on the 25th. Early next morning the Princess died.

Her funeral was at St. George's Chapel, Windsor, on 3rd November. Queen Elizabeth led Queen Ena to the open vault, and there the two curtsied. Behind, in the choir stalls, stood a slim figure in black, Princess Elizabeth.

Because of the danger of damage from enemy aircraft, the Banners had been taken down in the Chapel. At the order of the King those Banners had been rehung in their appointed places in honour of the passing of Princess Beatrice.

Two months after the war in Europe ended, the Marquess of Carisbrooke asked the King if the time was now suitable for the transference of his mother's body to the Chapel in Whippingham Church[1] which Queen Victoria had given as a burial place for her beloved youngest daughter and Prince Henry.

So it was that a hearse travelled from Windsor to Portsmouth, there to be met by the Princess's eldest son. A Naval Guard of Honour stood at attention on the quay, and everywhere flags were at half-mast.

On that lovely summer's day in 1945, with a naval escort, the earthly remains of H.R.H. Princess Beatrice were taken across the Solent to Whippingham, to lie close to the chalice where hung the engagement rings of her husband and herself.

[1] St. Mildred's lies on a curve in the lane which runs from the outskirts of West Cowes to Whippingham School. Below the road the fields fall sharp to the River Medina, and from it the hundred thousand, and more, tourists who visit Whippingham each summer obtain a splendid view of the countryside of the Isle of Wight.

This quiet lane, along which Queen Victoria used to drive with her family to worship, has now been named 'Beatrice Avenue'. Again, inside the church, designed by her father and built by command of her mother, it is the memory and the presence of Princess Beatrice which predominate.

Her generosity towards, and her love for, the church are everywhere visible. The two windows above the font, 'The Madonna' and 'St. John the Baptist', were her gift, and she and Princess Louise made the carpet which surrounds the font. Above the Rector's desk hangs Sir John Lavery's picture, 'The Supreme Sacrifice', the property of Princess Beatrice, and placed there in memory of Prince Maurice, the first man of the village to die in action in World War I. The Prince's name heads the list on the War Memorial, which was unveiled by his mother.

In a case on the south side of the chancel is a jewel-studded Bible, given to the Princess by 'the maidens of England' on her marriage, and the frontal screen is embroidered from the satin of her wedding dress. The lectern was given by Lord Edward Pelham Clinton, Master of the Queen's Household, in memory of Prince Henry.

The Battenberg Chapel is on the north side of the chancel. On the floor by the marble sarcophagus lies a wreath from the officers and men of the Second Battalion, the Scots Guards, in memory of Prince Henry.

Prince Henry's Banner and Regalia as a Knight of the Garter hang on the wall, and alongside a silk full-Admiral's flag, which was presented to Prince Louis of Battenberg in 1907. Other memories of Prince Henry are the block of wood on which his coffin rested on H.M.S. *Blonde*, and a wood carving which he presented to Queen Victoria.

The windows in the chapel, and the bronze screen, were the gifts of Queen Victoria, and she made the crocheted hassock which lies by the sarcophagus. The cross and candlesticks were provided by Princess Beatrice and her loving work is to be seen in the carpet, stools and prie-dieu.

APPENDIX A

THE PARENTAGE OF QUEEN VICTORIA AND PRINCE ALBERT

EXACTLY one hundred years after the birth of Albert Edward, Prince of Wales, his youngest sister, Beatrice, was to publish, at the remarkable age of eighty-four, a small book called *In Napoleonic Days*. The substance was letters, selected and translated by the Princess, of Queen Victoria's maternal grandmother, covering the years 1806–1821.

Having been appointed literary executrix by Queen Victoria in her will, Princess Beatrice was in a unique position to learn of the happenings of the half century or so before she was born. An experienced translator, she was intensely interested in her subject. The letters help to complete the picture of her ancestors on both the maternal and paternal sides.

In introducing the letters she wrote:

'My great-grandmother, the Duchess Augusta of Saxe-Coburg-Saalfeld, was the daughter of Prince Reusse-Ebersdorf. She was born in 1757 and in 1777 married Franz, Duke of Saxe-Coburg-Saalfeld, by whom she had several children, including Queen Victoria's mother, the Duchess of Kent (Victoire in this diary); Leopold, husband of Princess Charlotte of Wales and afterwards first King of the Belgians; Sophia, Countess Mensdorff-Pouilly; Antoinette, married to Duke Alexander of Württemberg; Juliana, Grand-Duchess Constantine of Russia; Ernest, afterwards reigning Duke of Saxe-Coburg-Gotha and father

of the Prince Consort; and Ferdinand, who married
Maria II da Gloria Queen of Portugal and became King
of Portugal under the title of Ferdinand II. The
Duchess died in 1831. Of her Frederic Shoberl wrote
in 1840: "Gifted with a superior understanding and
adorned with rare accomplishments, this Princess
united all the softness of her own sex with the firmness
of the other. Undaunted by the storms of fate, she never
lost sight for a moment of her destination as a wife and
mother."'

This summary by Princess Beatrice shows clearly
how the young Coburg trees were planted around
Europe.

The Duchess Augusta's husband died in 1806 and she
was left alone to cope with a dukedom, and a family,
hard-pressed for money. The French were in Coburg
and her son, Ernest, was unable to return and claim his
birthright. It was not until the finale of Napoleon that
normal conditions returned to the duchy.

With the end of hostilities the Duchess's sons looked
around them for wives. Already joined to the Imperial
House of Russia through the marriage of Juliana, the
family spread its tentacles when Leopold married
Charlotte of England in 1816. The following year his
brother Ernest, the reigning Duke, married seventeen-
year-old Louise, daughter of Duke Augustus of Saxe-
Gotha-Altenburg. In Princess Beatrice's summary, quoted
above, no mention is made of Duke Ernest's wife—
Prince Albert's mother.

Duke Ernest was sixteen years older than his wife. He
had been through a hard school. She came to him as a girl,
inexperienced, romantic, sentimental, gay, begging for
love and kindness on her way to maturity. The dis-
illusionment of Louise did not take long. The signs were
visible before her second son, Albert, was born in 1819.

17

She knew of the 'pretty ladies' with whom her husband mixed when he was away from home. She fretted at the restrictions and boredom of her ducal home.

Refusing to accept the theory, and the practice, that there was one law for the man and another for the woman, she began flirtations—harmless enough at first. Rumours began, grew wilder as they changed hands, and reached the ears of the Duke. Separation came in 1824, and Louise never saw her husband or sons again. He divorced her two years later. She then married Alexander von Haustein. He was with her in Paris when she died in 1831. She was only thirty. It is said that the happiness that she found in her last years made up for the misery she had previously endured.

Rumours that Prince Albert was not Duke Ernest's son are almost certainly untrue, taking the evidence of his mother's letters and considering the restrictions placed on a girl of nineteen in a ducal home in Germany at that time. Certainly there was little of his father in Albert, the father who was to be later so violently exposed by Pauline Panam. There was also little resemblance, in habits at least, to his brother, whose extravagances were to be a constant source of worry to Queen Victoria. Rather is his character mirrored in the gentleness and sentimentality of his mother, and the strength of character and upright mode of living of his grandmother, Augusta.

As to Queen Victoria's parents, her mother came from that same Coburg home. Her early life was beyond reproach. At seventeen she had married the elderly Prince Ernest Charles of Leiningen, who ruled over the poor and barren territory of Amorbach in Lower Franconia. The Prince died in 1814, leaving 'Victoire' with the Regency, two children, and precious little money. She was therefore pleased to accept the invitation of Edward, Duke of Kent, fourth son of George III, to be his partner in the Royal Marriage Stakes which was being run off in England.

Two years later the Duke died and she was left alone with a great responsibility in a none too friendly land. One of the mistakes she made was to allow her name to be coupled, in an unpleasant way, with that of Sir John Conroy, late of her husband's household. The alliance caused a rift between mother and daughter.

From an inheritancy point of view there was little to fear from either of Victoria's parents. She admired the character of her father, as it was pictured to her, and chose to remember him as a soldier, whom George III had named as the bravest of his sons. She had good reason to know that he had no idea of the value of money—she was paying off his debts until long after her accession. Hard as this proved, it was not the money troubles of her father that upset the Queen—it was the liaison prior to his marriage with her mother.

The Duchess of Kent began the task of rubbing out the name of Julie de St. Laurent from the pages of history. Queen Victoria continued it. So efficient and arduous were they that it is doubtful whether the full story will ever be deciphered.

At first glance it may be difficult to comprehend why, when the other sons of George III had mistresses, changed them at intervals, and even married them, with little attempt at secrecy about their activities, there should have been this veto on the very mention of Edward of Kent's only love. Perhaps one reason was that he had an 'only' love.

The Duke of Kent had passed his fiftieth birthday when he arranged to marry Victoria of Leiningen, whom he hardly knew. In her diary, translated by Princess Beatrice, the Duchess Augusta wrote of the minutes before he arrived to claim his bride: 'We waited with much curiosity, and poor Victoire with a beating heart. She had seen him only once before. . . .'

It would be optimistic, to say the least of it, to suppose that, considering the fashion and the days, there had been no women in his life. But one woman, and to move immediately away from her after twenty-seven years of devotion into a marriage of duty, that was a very different matter. Perhaps the Duchess was unaware of his past when she married him. Maybe it was the ruthless, ambitious Coburg in her which demanded the extinction of a rival, or the fear that the children of the liaison might prove a thorn in the flesh of herself and her daughter.

Certainly in those days after her husband's death, with her jealous in-laws watching her every action, she was in no position to withstand further shocks. Enlisting the help of the Duke of Wellington, she set about the task of wiping out the identity of a lovely French lady. She imbued her daughter with the same idea, and the task was carried on throughout the century. Pictures were destroyed and papers burned. Letters were demanded back, and it is on record that, on an occasion when the demand was met by a refusal, masked men entered a house by night and took the letters away by force.

The Duke of Kent was completely open about his life with Madame Alphonsine Thérèse Bernadine Julie de Montgenet de St. Laurent, Baronne de Fortisson. Convinced, because a gypsy had told him so, that he would have a daughter who would become a great queen, he did not apparently recognise that any action of his might embarrass that daughter in her prophesied rôle. Otherwise, he would not have chosen Creevey as his confidant when, after the death of Princess Charlotte, he wished to make known to the right quarters his terms for marrying for an heir and for the disposal of Madame St. Laurent.

The Duke talked to Creevey on the 11th December 1817 in Brussels where, for reason of economy, Julie and he were living. Creevey wrote of the conversation:

'. . . The Duke begun, to my great surprise, a conversation upon the death of the Princess Charlotte, and upon an observation from me upon the derangement of the succession to the throne by this event, and of the necessity of the unmarried Princes becoming married, if the crown was to be kept in their family; and having in addition asked him, I believe, what he thought the Regent would do on the subject of a divorce, and whether he thought the Duke of Clarence would marry, the Duke of Kent, to the best of my recollection, and I would almost say word for word, spoke to me as follows.

'"My opinion is the Regent will not attempt a divorce. I know persons in the Cabinet who will never consent to such a measure. Then, was he to attempt it, his conduct would be exposed to such recrimination as to make him unpopular, beyond all measure, throughout the country. No: he never will attempt it. Besides, the crime of adultery on her part must be proved in an English court of justice, and if found guilty she must be executed for high treason. No: the Regent will never try for a divorce.

'"As for the Duke of York, at his time of life and that of the Duchess, all issue, of course, is out of the question. The Duke of Clarence, I have no doubt, will marry if he can; but the terms he asks from the Ministers are such as they can never comply with. Besides a settlement such as is proper for a Prince who marries expressly for a succession to the Throne, the Duke of Clarence demands the payment of all his debts, which are very great, and a handsome provision for each of his ten natural children. These are terms that no Ministers can accede to. Should the Duke of Clarence not marry, the next prince in succession is myself; and altho' I trust I shall be at all times ready to obey any call my country may make upon me, God only knows the sacrifice it will be to make, whenever I shall think it my duty to become a married man. It is now seven and twenty years that Madame St. Laurent and I have lived together: we are of the same age, and have been in all climates, and in all difficulties together; and you may well imagine, Mr. Creevey, the pang it will occasion me to part with her. I put it to your own feeling—in the event of any separation between you and Mrs. Creevey. . . . As for Madame St. Laurent herself, I protest I don't know what is to become of her if a marriage is to be forced upon me; her feelings are already so agitated upon the subject. You saw, no doubt, that unfortunate paragraph in the *Morning Chronicle*, which appeared within a day or two after the Princess Charlotte's death; and in which my marrying was alluded to. Upon receiving the paper containing that article at the same time with my private letters, I did as is my constant practice, I threw the newspaper across the table to Madame Saint Laurent, and began to open and read my letters. I had not done so but a very short time, when my attention was called to an extraordinary noise and a strong convulsive movement in Madame St. Laurent's throat. For a short time I entertained serious apprehensions for her safety; and when, upon her recovery, I enquired into the occasion of this attack, she pointed to the article in the *Morning Chronicle* relating to my marriage.

'"From that day to this I am compelled to be in the practice of daily dissimulation with Madame St. Laurent, to keep this subject from her thoughts. . . ."'

Record of the conversation reached the Duke of Wellington at the moment when a doctor was sounding his bladder with one hand and a finger of the other, trying to ascertain whether there was a stone within. The Iron Duke's sudden outburst of laughter shook the doctor considerably.

Tactless as this conversation might have been, it

establishes that Julie was approximately fifty at the time; that she and Edward had been together since either 1790 or 1791; and that their partnership had been unbroken, and a happy one.

In January 1790 Prince Edward was at Geneva, completing his education under a stern Governor, Baron Wangenheim. Rebelling against the treatment meted out to him by the Baron, including the interception of letters, Edward returned to London without leave. The King was furious and, although he had not seen his son for several years, posted him to Gibraltar, with orders to sail within a fortnight. Edward was on the Rock from February 1790 to May 1791. From there, as Colonel of the Seventh Fusiliers, he sailed direct to Canada. He was in Quebec and the West Indies for the ensuing three years. From 1794 to 1798 he was in Halifax, as Commander-in-Chief of the troops in Nova Scotia and New Brunswick.

When the first meeting of Edward and Julie took place remains obscure. It may have been in Geneva, and one reason for the trouble between the Prince and Baron Wangenheim, and the anger of George III. It may have been in Quebec, where Julie had close friends in the de Salaberrys, her name often appearing in the published correspondence of the family. Certainly Edward and Julie were together in July 1792, when they acted as godfather and godmother at the baptism of the de Salaberrys' youngest son.

No confirmation of the marriage of Edward and Julie can be traced. She was a Roman Catholic, and it seems likely that they were married in the eyes of God, particularly as they were godparents to the same child. Legally, the marriage would have had no force in England.

Julie's surname was Montgenet. The addition, 'de St. Laurent', is suspect. As Mrs. Clarke wrote in a pamphlet at the time of the inquiry into the conduct of the Duke of

York, it was in her power to make interesting remarks about 'the discovery of the St. Lawrence'.

There are many discrepancies in the statements of those who claim that they are descendants of the Duke of Kent and Madame de St. Laurent. This is fully understandable, as they are largely dependent on the spoken word passed down from parent to child. Only the better authenticated are mentioned.

The eldest son was born in Canada, but was left behind in Quebec, in the care of *un serviteur*, when the Duke moved to Halifax. The child was known as Robert Wood.

Other children were given the surname of Green. A son, William Goodall Green, was born in Quebec in 1792. In 1815 he married Margaret Gray, daughter of John Gray, of Perthshire. They had a son, Commissary-General William George Green, of Selwyn Castle, Graham's Town, Cape Colony. In the next generation were a number of sons, including Frederick, an explorer and elephant hunter; Arthur, who became Deputy of Barbados; and Edward Lister, who became Sheriff of Auckland, New Zealand, and died in 1887. A daughter was also born in Quebec.

On the Duke of Kent's marriage in 1818, Julie went into a convent in Paris for a while. Thereafter she lived at the Montgenet home in Paris, at 116 Rue de Grenelle.

A family version of the events of the ensuing years is that Madame St. Laurent returned to England and made her home at Bognor. On the death of the Duke she wrote to her son, William Goodall Green, telling him to return to England to look after his interests, and also collect moneys due to him under a loan which she had arranged to be made to the Duke by the banking family of Esdaile. He duly presented himself at Kensington Palace and asked for certain documents, including, it is said, the marriage certificate. Although these documents were handed over, the reception which he received from the Duchess of Kent was such that he vowed he would have no more dealings with her.

On his return to Canada masked and armed men entered his house, threatened him, extorted an oath that he would never press the subject of his parentage and forced him to sign a paper to this effect, and took away all his private papers relevant to his father and mother.

Julie de St. Laurent died in 1835, two years before the Duke's daughter became Queen of England—and the gypsy prophecy was fulfilled.

However faint, and broken, is the trail back to the days when Edward and Julie loved in Quebec, the woman who caused it to be so, the Duchess of Kent, cannot be blamed too harshly for the steps that she took. A stranger in England, she adopted the German approach. She was in no financial position to pay off loans incurred by her husband before she met him. She naturally wished her daughter to regard the memory of her father with love and respect. And, as she would not let the Princess meet the Fitzclarences, whom she referred to as 'bastards', it is difficult to see how she could have introduced the Greens.

APPENDIX B

SANDRO OF BULGARIA

THE romance of Prince Alexander (Sandro) Battenberg and Princess Victoria of Prussia was one of
the most controversial, and certainly one of the
most sad, among royal romances of the nineteenth
century.

During the five storm-laden years of its duration, their
engagement introduced the name of Princess Beatrice into
power politics; involved Prince Henry in the strange and
unenviable task of smuggling letters out of Germany
under the noses of the secret police; brought into duel
the iron wills of Queen Victoria and Bismarck; led to bad
feeling between Germany, Britain and Russia; widened
the rift between the Crown Princess Frederick, and her
eldest son and her Prussian relations; gave to British
Ambassadors in Europe endless worries and fears; and
caused Princess Beatrice's brother-in-law to change his
name in consideration for her position as daughter of the
Queen.

As for the Prince and Princess who fell in love, Sandro
finally married an opera singer and died at thirty-seven.
The last milestone in Princess Victoria's life was her
marriage to an adventurer, quickly followed by dis-
illusionment and tragic death. As Daisy, Princess of Pless,
wrote, Bismarck ruined the lives of three of her friends—
Empress Frederick, Empress Eugénie and Princess
Victoria of Prussia.

Politically, the career of Prince Alexander of Battenberg was of secondary importance to Princess Beatrice.
From the personal and human standpoint, it was one of

the most important problems of her early married life. The two young people, with whose futures Germany and Russia were juggling, were both close to her. Prince Henry was very attached to his brother and his anxiety and worry for him was shared in the normal husband-wife relationship by Princess Beatrice.

Princess Victoria was a favourite niece, pretty, fair-haired, with romantic notions which had caused consternation in the British Fleet when she visited Malta. There was only nine years between them in age, and Princess Beatrice seemed to her more like an elder sister than an aunt. So Princess Beatrice was faced with the very human problem—would these two young people, with whom she was so close, be happy together, even if they were able to overcome the opposition to their marriage? To the Princess was added the bitter knowledge that it was her marriage that formed one of the stumbling blocks in the romance, and that in Prussia her husband's family was not considered good enough to marry the sister of Prince William.

To turn to Prince Alexander's political career. The Treaty of Berlin of 1878 had set up the new state of Bulgaria. While this autonomous principality came under the suzerainty of the Sultan of Turkey, Russia regarded it as tied to her through reasons of creed and race. In 1879 the Tsar, backed by Bismarck and the Grand Duke of Hesse, proposed that Sandro Battenberg should be the ruler of the new state, and the young Prince travelled to Sofia to take up his duties.

He soon showed that he was not content to be a mere tool of Russia. He assumed the virtual powers of dictatorship and took up the cry of 'Bulgaria for the Bulgarians'. He added further territory to the new state, and in 1885 defeated, brilliantly, an invasion by Serbian forces. But he had tried the Tsar too far, and in August 1886 he was kidnapped in his Palace and taken to Russia. He was allowed to return a fortnight later, but his prestige had gone, and he retired from the Bulgarian scene, to live quietly at Darmstadt.

Bismarck, scheming in Berlin, saw many dangers, real and imaginary, in the drama that was being played out in Bulgaria. He saw that interference in any way might lead to estrangement between Germany and Russia. He saw, or thought he saw, the hand of England shuffling the cards in the Balkans, and Queen Victoria pressing the cause of her favourite Battenbergs. Yet it was Bismarck who had urged Sandro to be Prince of Bulgaria.

When in 1879, Sandro, then only twenty-two and an officer in the Prussian army, had been told of his nomination as the ruler of Bulgaria, he had visited Bismarck and told the 'great man' that he did not wish to accept the offer and that he thought someone of more mature years would be better suited. Bismarck had shut the door of the room and told the Prince that he would not let him out until he agreed to take it. Sandro had then asked what would happen if he failed, as his whole career would be ruined. Bismarck's reply had been: 'You will at all events take away a pleasant recollection with you.'

That year the new Prince of Bulgaria visited Queen Victoria at Balmoral, and Princess Beatrice met her future brother-in-law for the first time. The Queen was much taken with the young man, and wrote to Lord Salisbury that any help or encouragement given to him would be well bestowed.

It was in 1883, when relations between Bulgaria and Russia were already strained, that Sandro went to Berlin on an official visit and met Princess Victoria. The Princess, second daughter and fifth child of Crown Princess Frederick, was then seventeen. Known in the family as 'Vicky' or 'Moretta', she was a favourite of her mother and her grandmother, Queen Victoria. She fell deeply and immediately in love with the tall and handsome

Battenberg who ruled Bulgaria, and he returned the feeling, sending her 'beautiful gifts of jewellery.'

Their days of happiness lasted only until the time came to seek approval to their engagement. The request brought violent opposition from the Emperor, the Empress and Prince William. The Crown Prince was doubtful about it, his position made most awkward by the fact that his wife and his mother-in-law, Queen Victoria, were strongly in favour of the match.

At the wedding of Prince Louis of Battenberg to Princess Victoria of Hesse at Darmstadt in the summer of 1884, when Princess Beatrice met Prince Henry, the Empress arrived with the determination to break up the romance, and matters became so tense that it was thought that Sandro would leave Darmstadt.

The friendship that sprang up there between Princess Beatrice and Prince Henry brought a new complication and danger, and in September the Queen wrote to Sir Howard Elphinstone, who was in Berlin:

'. . . *he* should *know* that Princess Victoria of Prussia is very much attached to the Prince of Bulgaria and vice versa; the Crown Princess favours the project and the Crown Prince is now not disinclined to it, but the Emperor and Empress are violently against it, and they are very unkind, and the Empress especially won't look at or speak to the poor girl, and her brothers and sisters are also most unkind. Sir Howard should therefore take care *not* to join in the Empress's views, but rather put in a friendly word as he can say he knows the Queen is strongly in favour of it, having a high opinion of the Prince of Bulgaria and of his elder brother Prince Louis of Battenberg who is universally liked in England.'

The announcement at the end of the year of the engagement of Princess Beatrice to Prince Henry brought matters to a head. The Crown Princess became involved in a furious row with her eldest son, which ended in Prince William leaving Potsdam. Thereafter the Crown Princess, determined that the marriage should take place, went underground. She planned and worked in secret, taking extraordinary precautions that her son, her parents-in-law and her arch-enemy, Bismarck, should not know what she was about.

On his own statement, Bismarck did not as yet know of the engagement of Sandro of Bulgaria to Princess Victoria. Yet it would appear that he was well aware of it, though it suited his book to allow the Crown Princess to believe that he did not.

The internal espionage system in Germany was most efficient and little escaped Prince Bismarck's net. Neither letters nor telegrams were safe from interfering eyes. The words of confidential conversation were somehow learned in Berlin and several members of the British Royal Family had unpleasant shocks when they discovered how much was known about their movements. The Crown Princess was fully aware of this. Without under-estimating her man, she set about the task of out-witting Bismarck. Resolutely determined that her daughter should marry the Prince of her choice, to lull suspicion she purposely let it be thought that the matter was 'over and done with'. It was her intention to keep the engagement in suspended animation until the old Emperor died, and, as he was eighty-eight years old, she did not think that she would have to wait long.

Throughout 1885 the Crown Princess was writing constantly to Sandro. She lived in dread that one of her letters to Sofia would be intercepted by Bismarck's spies. Sometimes she wrote at intervals of a few days; then weeks would pass without a letter. The first link in the secret chain between Potsdam and Bulgaria was Sir Howard Elphinstone. Sir Howard and his wife were close friends of the Crown Prince and Princess, so that first link was safe and sure. Thereafter the letters followed many routes to Sofia, some taking months and a number of carriers before they reached their destination.

One link in the chain, used on a number of occasions, was Prince Henry. At the end of January 1885, after the Crown Princess's quarrel with her son as a result of the engagement of Princess Beatrice, Sir Howard received the first of the communications for onward passage to Sofia. She wrote to him:

'. . . You know the *Post* is not to be *trusted*, and it must go SAFE. Could it not go as a letter from you to the English minister at Sofia or is it not *safe*. I wonder whether they watch what letters you write at your hotel? Please direct the letter to Prince Henry of Battenberg. . . .'

She added a postscript: 'You must ask Pce. Henry of B. merely to *let* YOU *know* by *Post* that he has received your *letter* as I shall be in terrible anxiety.'

It was not until the autumn of 1885, when the Queen, Princess Beatrice and Prince Henry were at Balmoral, that Bismarck showed his hand. Affairs in Bulgaria had reached a crisis, Prince Alexander's fight for independence making him very popular with the people but very unpopular with the Russians, and the Queen was in constant touch with Lord Salisbury as to how matters were shaping there. Bismarck chose this moment to announce that the news of the engagement of Sandro and Princess Victoria had only just come to his ears, and that he had been hoping for a Portuguese marriage for the Princess.

There was another reason which forced him out into the open at this moment. He knew that the Queen was planning to visit Berlin with Princess Beatrice and Prince Henry, and that was a visit which he decidedly did not relish.

Three years later he was to write of his actions when he heard of the engagement:

'As soon as I heard of it I made representations to the Emperor, verbally and in writing. He allowed himself to be convinced by the reasons I adduced, and refused to give his consent, although he said the Princess loved him. Of course, he is a handsome man, with a fine presence; but I believe her nature is such that she would accept any other suitor, provided he were manly. Moreover, that is entirely beside the question. We must look at the political objections and dangers. The old Queen is fond of matchmaking, like all old women, and she may have selected Prince Alexander for her grand-daughter, because he is a brother of her son-in-law, the husband of her favourite daughter, Beatrice. But obviously her main objects are political—a permanent estrangement between ourselves and Russia—and if she were to come here for the Princess's birthday, there would be the greatest danger that she would get her way. In family matters she is not accustomed to contradiction, and would immediately bring the parson with her in her travelling bag and the bridegroom in her trunk and the marriage would come off at once!'

Yet the Emperor had known of the engagement for two years and had already refused his consent. Prince William had already told the Tsar in St. Petersburg that Germany would not allow the marriage to take place. It may well have been convenient for Bismarck to pretend that he was in ignorance, and also to know of the contents of the letters which passed from Berlin to Sofia. But here-after he was in the open and it became a duel between himself, seconded by Prince William, and Queen Victoria, seconded by the Crown Princess Frederick.

It was in the marriage of Princess Beatrice to Prince Henry that Bismarck saw a very real danger to the engagement of Sandro to Princess Victoria. He knew full well how close were the relations between the Queen and her youngest daughter, of the trust which she imposed in her, and of how Princess Beatrice and her husband were rarely away from the Queen's side. Another Battenberg brother was serving in the British Navy and married to the Queen's granddaughter from Hesse. If a third brother were to marry the daughter of the Crown Princess, a lady with whom he was at dagger's drawn, then there might well be the making of a powerful influence hostile to his aims.

Bismarck cared not a fig for love or romance, but the emotional strain was beginning to tell on the young Prince of Bulgaria. His task was difficult enough without the additional burden of interference with his private affairs. In April 1886 he wrote to his brother in England:

'. . . If only I knew Princess V were to be allowed to be Princess of this country, then everything would be all right. Everything I would do to improve my country, to safeguard my position in this country, would be for her, that would give me immense strength, courage and endurance. But is it possible that Bismarck would agree to this in view of the hatred that Emperor Alexander bears me?'

Three months later the Prince was kidnapped in his Palace and taken away down the Danube. Although he was returned after a few weeks, his power was broken, his prestige gone, and, tired and disillusioned, he went back to his home near Darmstadt. In 1879 Bismarck had forecast that, even if he was a failure, at least he would have a pleasant recollection to take away with him. In the event, he had not even that. Only tiredness of being hated and thwarted at every turn, and a bitterness that even his love was not allowed.

The Crown Princess dearly loved a fight and not for

18

one moment did she relax her efforts to ensure her daughter's happiness. When she learned in 1887 that the old Emperor had no more than six months to live, she thought that victory was in her grasp. But Princess Beatrice did not entirely share her sister's vehement enthusiasm for the marriage. Unlike the Crown Princess, she was a person who liked to consider a problem from all its angles before making a decision and, if she gave advice, that advice was carefully worded.

Both Princess Beatrice and Prince Henry had kept in very close touch with affairs in Bulgaria and the progress of the romance with Princess Victoria, but the news of the kidnapping of Sandro came as a great shock to them. Prince Henry, with his brother Louis, went out to Heilenberg to see the deposed ruler and Louis wrote back to the Queen that Sandro was much shaken, wanted for a while to retire from the limelight, and that wild horses would not drag him back to Bulgaria.

Princess Beatrice was soon able to judge for herself the effect that the experiences of recent months had had on her brother-in-law. In December he came to Windsor. He was immediately taken up to Princess Beatrice's room, where she was waiting for him. When the Queen joined her daughter for tea that afternoon she found Sandro closeted with sister-in-law and brother.

Both the Queen and Princess Beatrice found him a very changed man. Of breakfast next morning the Queen wrote:

'He said he had slept well, almost for the first time, as he has been constantly in the habit of waking, still seeing those faces and hearing those words and cries of the dreadful 21st of August. He spoke of the bad feeling having been spread pretty widely in the Army by the Russians, who bribed and seduced the young and very ignorant men. When he returned there he had been in great danger. They tried to upset the train, and he was to have been murdered in the Cathedral. It was intensely interesting to hear him speak of his terrible experiences, but his poor face looked so sad while doing so.'

Listening to the details of the tragic story, noting the haunted look in his eyes, Princess Beatrice began to doubt the wisdom of his marrying her young niece Victoria, and whether he now bore much resemblance to the dashing young ruler with whom the seventeen-year-old girl had fallen so deeply in love in Berlin three years before.

There were rumours, too, running round Europe, regarding that August night in Sofia when Sandro was kidnapped, and these rumours may well have come to the ears of Princess Beatrice. It was said that the sister of one of the conspirators was spending the night with him, and was found in the bedroom when the kidnappers forced their entry.

The Battenbergs were most attractive, as she had found. For one of them to be a ruler, forbidden the company of a wife, was to expose him to many temptations. Had Sandro's responsibilities and experiences so altered his outlook and approach to life that now his chances of finding happiness with a girl, still under the strict discipline of the Prussian Royal family, were diminished? That was the question for which an aunt and a sister-in-law had to find the answer.

Then fate dealt a trump to Bismarck. Another suitor came along for the hand of Princess Victoria. No suitor could have been less welcome to the Crown Princess, and none could have complicated matters more than they already were. Bismarck's own son, Herbert, fell in love with the Princess and suggested to his father that he should marry her.

In 1881 Bismarck, so that he could learn even more of what was happening in England than he already knew, had

attached his son to the German Embassy in London. The
Crown Princess had sent a warning to Windsor:

> 'He is unfortunately very narrow-minded and of a
> violent, vindictive character. He has great influence over
> his father and when anyone is in the father's black book
> the son fans the flame and persecutes the unfortunate
> individual whoever he or she may be. . . .'

Whether Herbert's love was real or part of a scheme is
in doubt, but in either case the idea both amused and
pleased Bismarck. It had the opposite effect on the Crown
Princess, who redoubled her efforts to bring the romance
of her daughter to fruition. As for Princess Beatrice, it
confirmed her in the opinion that a marriage, begun under
such a handicap and with such poisonous influences at
work, would be neither desirable nor achieve a happy
result.

To Sandro the suggestion came both as a challenge and
bugle call to waken him from his weariness and sense of
defeat. Since his expulsion from Bulgaria it had been
noticed that the old fire had gone out of him, and that
this covered his ardour and determination to gain the
hand of Princess Victoria. But the proposition of Herbert
he considered to be an insult, and he was determined not
to be further humiliated by being cut out and relegated
to the position of discarded suitor.

When the old Emperor died in March 1888 and his
very ill son Frederick took over the reins, it seemed at
last that Sandro and Victoria would be able to bring their
five-year-old engagement to its rightful close by marriage.
The new Emperor had altered his opinion and agreed to
allow his wife's dearest wish. But time was their enemy,
for cancer was fast stealing away the days of the Emperor,
and there remained the Bismarcks and William, now
Crown Prince, with whom to cope.

There now broke out in Europe a row which reached

such dimensions that the British Ambassador in Berlin sent word to London advising against the Queen paying a visit to Germany to see her dying son-in-law, in case there should be a demonstration against her in the streets. The German press howled its threats and Bismarck even threatened to resign. All over the now insignificant question of whether Sandro, the deposed and powerless Prince of Bulgaria, should be allowed to marry the second daughter of the Emperor.

The objection was said to be the danger of offending Russia. Yet the Russians did not care any more—they had finished with Sandro and found a more pliable substitute. Russia was only an excuse. The real reason behind the flare-up was that the Bismarcks and the Crown Prince were not going to tolerate the Empress and Queen Victoria having their way—to take advantage of the Emperor Frederick's few days of power, for the doctors had told them that he would not last out the summer. It was Queen Victoria versus the Chancellor—the battle of the wills. Or so people thought.

The final act, the interview between Queen Victoria and Bismarck, has often been quoted as one of the few occasions when the Queen met her match, and that she had to bow to the will of the iron man of Germany. In the event it was the Queen who triumphed, who settled the affair her own way, and who turned hisses into cheers.

In those tangled weeks of March and April 1888, of all those involved very few knew the real truth and could foresee an answer both politic and tactful. Of the few Queen Victoria was one and Princess Beatrice another.

The Emperor was too ill to be told. The Empress Victoria,[1] dead set on the marriage, was being led along a false trail by Bismarck. Princess Victoria was kept in ignorance so that her feelings should not be hurt. The

[1] The designation, 'Empress Frederick', was not conferred upon her until after her son's accession.

Bismarcks were raving and ranting against a danger which did not exist. The misguided Crown Prince was causing his parents much unnecessary trouble. Members of the Household, politicians and diplomats were only half in the picture and therefore a prey to guess-work and rumour.

The truth was that Sandro had fallen in love with an opera singer and no longer wished to marry Princess Victoria.

The row began when, a few days after the death of old Emperor William on 9th March, the Emperor Frederick personally gave to Princess Victoria his consent to her marrying Sandro. 'I believe,' she wrote, 'that he planned to bring about the marriage then and there, knowing that he had but a short time to live.'

The Empress at once sent the good news to her mother. Guardedly the Queen replied:

> 'I can understand how, with the painful uncertainty which dear Fritz's health causes you, you would wish to settle and arrange everything that is of importance, but do not too suddenly alter things and above all do not carry out anything which is in direct opposition to the poor departed Emperor's wishes. I mean for instance the projected marriage of Moretta with Sandro. Above all do not even contemplate such a step without the perfect acquiescence of William. You must reckon with him, as he is Crown Prince, and it would never do to contract a marriage which he would not agree to. It would simply bring misery on your daughter and Sandro, besides placing her in an impossible and humiliating position. . . .'

The Emperor decided to call Sandro to Berlin and bestow on him a suitable honour and reinstate him in a military appointment, thus preparing the way for his marriage to Princess Victoria. Somewhat reluctantly Sandro prepared to answer the summons. He had already

met and fallen in love with Fraülein Loisinger, a singer at
the Darmstadt and Dresden court theatres. In addition
he did not relish the idea of entering the ring with
Bismarck again or, as the husband of the Princess, occupying what he considered would be a secondary and difficult
rôle.

In the meantime Bismarck had sought an interview with
the Emperor, in the course of which he raised violent
objections to any honour or military appointment being
given to the deposed ruler of Bulgaria. So determined was
the attack of the Chancellor that the Emperor had to give
ground. He instructed Bismarck to draw up, and submit
to him, a full report on the matter, and also to discuss it
with the Empress. A telegram was sent to Sandro telling
him to postpone his visit to Berlin. Two days later Sandro
received the following written message from the Crown
Prince: 'If you marry my sister I shall consider you the
enemy of my family and my country.'

On 22nd March the Queen, Princess Beatrice and
Prince Henry left Windsor to spend a month's holiday in
Florence. It was the Queen's intention that they should
return via Berlin, so that she might see her dying son-in-
law.

On 3rd April Bismarck submitted his report to the
Emperor. It was strongly worded. He said that, in
deference to the feelings of Russia, no favours should be
given to Prince Alexander. He considered that the proposed marriage with Princess Victoria was nothing but a
British scheme to harm the relationship of Germany and
Russia, and that Queen Victoria was the power behind
the scheme. He added that, if his objections were not
supported, he would retire from the Chancellorship.

On the 5th Bismarck, as he had been bidden, visited
the Empress. Neither knew of Sandro's love for the opera
singer. At the interview he proved once again what a
master of diplomacy he was, and succeeded in outwitting

the Empress. He did not reject the marriage out of hand, but made vague promises for the future. He left the Empress well satisfied with the conversation.

On the same day Bismarck let loose in the German press a virulent campaign against Queen Victoria and the proposed marriage, threatening his resignation if it took place. He repeated the accusation that he had already made to the Emperor that the marriage was but a British intrigue designed to set Germany and Russia at logger-heads. Yet so clever had Bismarck been with the Empress, that the same night she telegraphed her mother: 'Please be in no anxiety. Crisis of Chancellor is an invention; we have never been on better terms and the understanding is perfect. Your visit must on no account be given up.'

While this message was on its way Bismarck was talking with the British Ambassador, Sir Edward Malet. In most forceful terms he spoke of the importance he attached to the cancellation of the marriage plans, and repeated his retirement threat. On the 8th Lord Salisbury telegraphed to the Queen in Florence:

'I have received several private telegrams from Sir E. Malet showing that Prince Bismarck is in one of his raging moods about the proposed marriage.

'He shows temper against Your Majesty and as at such times he is quite unscrupulous he will probably try to give currency to statements which are designed to make Your Majesty personally responsible for any evil results of his own passion. He has a vast corrupt influence over the press and can give enormous circulation to rumours. I would humbly advise Your Majesty to avoid any action which could operate with the controversy which is going on. The newspapers say that Your Majesty is going to Potsdam or Berlin. I would humbly submit that this visit at this time would expose You to great misconstruction and possibly to some disrespectful demonstration. German Chancellor is reported by his son to be in a state of intense exasperation. . . .'

This not only perturbed the Queen, it made her very angry. She told Lord Salisbury that she had had nothing to do with the plans for the marriage, but, on the contrary, had warned the Empress against making such a move at the present time. She added that she would certainly not give up her idea of going to see her sick son-in-law.

On the 9th the Queen had letters from Sandro, expressing indignation at all the fuss that was being made over 'young Vicky' and himself, and from the Empress Victoria, who told her mother not to take any notice of the reports in the newspapers.

On the 10th Princess Beatrice, with the help of Sir Henry Ponsonby, wrote to Sandro. It was a tactful and balanced letter, over the composition of which she was unable to call on the aid of Prince Henry, as he was on a visit to Malta. Princess Beatrice advised Sandro to tell Crown Prince William that he could not discuss the question of his marriage with anyone, even his brother, while the matter was in the hands of the Emperor and the Empress. She 'also advised him that he, Sandro, cannot give up Princess Victoria himself but if (as she, Princess Beatrice, hopes) he does do so to avoid unhappiness to both—the breaking off should be done by his father, old Prince Alexander of Hesse.'

Meantime Herbert Bismarck had seen Sir Edward Malet, and, maybe to further his own chances, had tried to persuade the Ambassador to use his influence with the Empress to stop the marriage. His efforts to prevent the Queen going to Berlin were passed on by Sir Edward to London. But Lord Salisbury would have none of the suggestion. The Queen had decided to go, and that was that.

It was now time that Sir Edward Malet was put in the picture, and Sir Henry Ponsonby wrote to him: 'The Queen is opposed to the marriage and so are Prince and Princess Henry of Battenberg, but it is not desirable to make it public or repeat it to the Empress Victoria.'

The news was kept from the Emperor who, in making his will, left this instruction to the Crown Prince regarding the marriage: 'I charge you as a filial duty with the accomplishment of this my desire, which your sister Victoria for so many years has cherished in her heart.'

It was also kept from Princess Victoria. The 12th of April was her birthday and on it she received a letter from Sandro. If she had been able to read between the lines she would have seen that all was over. But she read only what her heart wanted to know, remembering Sandro's words to her when last they had met: 'Those whom God hath joined let no man put asunder.' The day was made bright for her as her father asked her to lunch alone with him in his room, and gave her a diamond necklace.

Such then was the muddled and dangerous state of affairs as the Queen, Princess Beatrice and Prince Henry prepared to leave Florence and journey to Berlin, straight, as Ponsonby said, into the hornet's nest. Even the great Private Secretary was shaken. 'So many conversations go on about this marriage affair that one gets bothered.'

The curtain went up at first light on 24th April, as the train bearing Queen Victoria, Princess Beatrice, Prince Henry and their retinue neared the end of its journey through Germany. Princess Beatrice dressed, and sat by the carriage window, looking out. They were passing close to the outskirts of Berlin, in whose streets the Prime Minister had sent warning a hostile demonstration might be staged. The sky was grey, and in the flat fields soldiers were drilling.

On the platform of the small station at Charlottenberg the Empress and her children were waiting. William, the

Crown Prince, and Princess Victoria were there. The
Empress was first into the carriage to greet her mother
and sister. She looked careworn and thin. Then William
led his grandmother to a four-horse barouche. He handed
her in. His mother followed. Then his aunt Beatrice, for
it was part of routine that she should be by her mother's
side at moments such as this. The barouche drove off to
the Palace, the approach to which was lined by men of
Prince Henry's former regiment, the *Gardes du Corps*.

Even before breakfasting the Queen went to the bedside of Emperor Frederick. She knew that he was dying.
He raised his hands in delight at seeing her, and gave her
some flowers.

That afternoon, with Princess Beatrice again at her
side, the Queen drove through the streets of Berlin. There
was no demonstration. They paid a visit to the old Empress
Augusta, paralysed and shaking, a pathetic figure in her
deep mourning.

Behind the scenes things were moving; Bismarck asked
for an interview with the Queen. This was arranged for
twelve o'clock on the morning of the next day.

The Chancellor was anything but at his ease when he
arrived at Charlottenburg Palace, and showed unmistakable signs of nerves. He was received by Major Bigge,
and of him he asked a number of questions regarding the
procedure of meeting the Queen, whether she would be
seated or standing, etc. To add to the strain he was kept
waiting for a while.

Sir Henry Ponsonby then conducted the Chancellor to
the Empress. He also noted the nervous tension. Conversation was confined to the decoration and contents of
the rooms through which the two passed.

The Empress took over and led the man who had been
the poisoned thorn in her life to the presence of her
mother. The door closed. The words spoken behind it
were lost for ever on the April air.

Both the Queen and Bismarck later wrote of what had passed between them. The Queen was tactful, vague, non-committal, with attention on minor and unimportant detail. They shook hands. She asked him to sit down. He said that he remembered seeing her in Paris when she visited Emperor Napoleon and Empress Eugénie. He spoke of the strength of German arms. She asked him to be kind to 'Vicky'. She spoke of William's lack of experience. And, the *pièce de résistance*, she said she would like to meet Princess Bismarck.[1] She also said that they talked of 'other personal affairs'. She made no mention of the Sandro-Victoria marriage.

Bismarck, on the other hand, did. In rather facetious sentences, in which the Queen is referred to as 'Grandmamma', he wrote that the Queen declared that the Berlin attitude to the marriage was the correct one. In other words, that the marriage was off. But he did say that the Queen 'behaved quite sensibly', and gave her credit for bringing about a reconciliation, temporarily at least, between William and his mother.

Time shows more clearly what happened behind that closed door. Bismarck entered, intent on pitting his strength against that of Queen Victoria. Although the German Emperor had said that his daughter could marry Sandro, he, Bismarck, had decided that she should not, and to prove his power he was going to make Queen Victoria change her mind. He broached the question, only to be disarmed by the Queen saying that she agreed with him completely. Both she and Princess Beatrice had been agreed about that for some time. Sandro did not want to marry Princess Victoria. He was in love with an opera singer. Of course the Chancellor would understand that this news had to be kept secret. There were the feelings of

[1] The Queen, with Princess Beatrice, received Princess Bismarck that afternoon. She found her 'an elderly, masculine and not very *sympathique* lady'.

the dying Emperor to consider. The Empress was already hard enough pressed without this new burden. It would be difficult for the Princess Victoria if it were baldly announced that a singer was preferred to herself. Of course, she knew that the Chancellor would keep the secret to himself.

On his return from the interview Bismarck pressed a switch, and everything was altered. By the time the Queen, the Empress and Princess Beatrice and her husband drove that afternoon to the British Embassy the miracle had happened. 'Almost the whole way we passed through double lines of carriages, and when we got into the town there were great crowds, who were most enthusiastic, cheering and throwing flowers into the carriage. . . .'

The dinner at Charlottenburg that evening was one which Princess Beatrice was long to remember. Prince Bismarck sat opposite to the Queen. It had been a trying programme for an old lady of seventy, but she looked well and happy. Rarely had the Chancellor been more amiable. The two had a secret, and an understanding. When the dessert was served he espied a bonbon bearing on it a photograph of the Empress Victoria. The Chancellor selected it and, unbuttoning his coat, placed it next to his heart. But, talking together after dinner, the Queen could not resist taking a dig at the Chancellor. She told him of the enthusiastic reception she had received in Berlin that afternoon. With a straight face Bismarck replied that it was quite spontaneous. She shook hands with him before he left. She had won. But she was very tired by the time Princess Beatrice helped her back to her bed-room.

Back in London Lord Salisbury expressed himself as somewhat mystified as to why, after all the threats of a hostile reception, the Queen's visit had turned out to be such a great success.

Another person who enjoyed the Queen's visit to Charlottenburg was Princess Victoria. She wrote:

'One event cheered these dark days, and that was the visit of Queen Victoria and her daughter, my Aunt Beatrice, with Prince Henry of Battenberg. . . . The Queen seemed extremely interested in the Prince (Bismarck) and very much enjoyed talking with him. . . . For my poor mother this visit brought a great deal of comfort. At a time of such deep sorrow it meant much to her to see her mother and sister once again. To me dear grandmamma was very kind. I often sat with her, and she would sometimes be pleased to discuss my future with me.'

The Empress and her daughter still did not know of the opera singer, and the Queen and Princess Beatrice were gradually preparing them for the shock. In May the Queen wrote to the Empress on the subject; 'Have you ever thought or wondered what Sandro's own feelings would be. . . .'

On the 14th of June the Emperor Frederick died and, with the succession of his son, all possibility of the marriage ended. The new Emperor, disregarding the instruction left to him in his father's will, told Prince Alexander that the engagement must be considered over, 'in consequence of the profound conviction previously held by my late deceased grandfather and father'.

Thus was Sandro released, and on 6th February 1889 he married Fraülein Loisinger. The Queen, understanding so much, commented: 'Perhaps they loved one another.' But nevertheless, when the Queen and Princess Beatrice read in the newspapers that the marriage had taken place and that Sandro had changed his name to Count Hartenau, it came as a shock. Then Prince Henry received a letter from his brother explaining matters, saying that, as he had little money and no occupation, he was determined to live a happy life. The Queen read it, and sent a note to Lord Salisbury, putting the case that Sandro had acted correctly in the matter.

A few weeks later the Queen received a most touching letter from Sandro, saying how much it meant to him that she had pardoned him. He explained that it was in consideration for Princess Beatrice that he had changed his name to Count Hartenau. He wrote: 'My Gracious Aunt. You were always so good to me and the most beautiful memories of my life are of your graciousness and kindness. . . .'

The Queen and Princess Beatrice met Sandro again, in Rome, in the spring of 1891. He was thinner and looked sad. In November 1893 he became ill. Princess Beatrice kept in touch with Countess Hartenau. As she travelled south from Balmoral a telegram was handed to her at Aberdeen telling her that Sandro was dead. He was buried in the cathedral at Sofia, Prince Henry attending the funeral.

As for Princess Victoria, she married in 1890 the Prince of Schaumburg-Lippe, a kind and gentle man who died in 1916. But she never forgot Sandro. In 1929 she married again. There was opposition, wise opposition. But Princess Victoria said: 'I have pleased others all my life; now I shall please myself.'

Before many months had passed her second husband left her, and she was alone again. Her youngest sister, Margaret, did all that she could to help her. But Princess Victoria was tired. She went alone for a walk in the rain, caught a chill, and soon afterwards was dead.

BIBLIOGRAPHY

For permission to quote copyright material the author is indebted to the publishers of the titles marked by an asterisk. These and other historical sources or material are listed below.

1. *A Queen at Home*, by Vera Watson (W. H. Allen, 1952)
2. *The Life of William Ewart Gladstone*, 2 volumes, by John Morley (Edward Lloyd Ltd., 1908)
3. *H.R.H. The Duke of Connaught and Strathearn*, by Major-General Sir George Aston (Harrap, 1929)
4. *My Memoirs*, by Princess Victoria of Prussia (Eveleigh Nash and Grayson, 1929)
5. *Encyclopaedia Britannica*
*6. *Letters of the Empress Frederick*, edited by Sir Frederick Ponsonby (Macmillan, 1929)
7. *Sidelights on Queen Victoria*, by Sir Frederick Ponsonby (Macmillan, 1930)
8. *Lord Goschen and his Friends*, edited by Percy Colson (Hutchinson, 1946)
9. *Victoria the Widow and her Son*, by Hector Bolitho (D. Appleton-Century Co., 1934)
10. *Queen Victoria's Relations*, by Meriel Buchanan (Cassell, 1954)
11. *Queen Victoria's John Brown*, by E. E. P. Tisdall (Stanley Paul, 1938)
*12. *Henry Ponsonby*, by Arthur Ponsonby (Macmillan, 1942)
13. *My Memories of Six Reigns*, by H.H. Princess Marie Louise (Evans, 1956)
14. *The Life Story of H.R.H. The Duke of Cambridge*, by Ethel M. Duff (Stanley Paul, 1938)
15. *The Life Story of H.R.H. Princess Louise, Duchess of Argyll*, by David Duff (Stanley Paul, 1940)
16. *Daughters of Queen Victoria*, by E. F. Benson (Cassell, 1939)
17. *King Alfonso*, by Robert Sencourt (Faber & Faber, 1942)

18. *Queen Victoria: The Story of a Noble Life* (Standard Library Co., 1901)

19. *The Queen's Resolve*, by Charles Bullock (Home Words Publishing Office, 1887)

20. *Victoria: Her Life and Reign*, by Alfred E. Knight (S. W. Partridge, 1897)

21. *Queen Victoria*, by Sidney Lee (Smith, Elder & Co., 1902)

22. *More Leaves from the Journal of a Life in the Highlands*, by Queen Victoria (Smith Elder & Co., 1884)

23. *1914*, by Field Marshal Viscount French of Ypres (Constable, 1919)

24. *V.R.I.: Her Life and Empire*, by The Duke of Argyll (Eyre & Spottiswoode, 1902)

*25. *The Letters of Queen Victoria*, Three Series (John Murray, 1907-1932)

26. *Osborne House* (Ministry of Works, 1955)

27. *Queen Victoria*, by Lytton Strachey (Chatto & Windus, 1921)

28. *Punch* (1886-1914)

29. *'Fritz' of Prussia*, by Lucy Taylor (Nelson, 1891)

30. *The Windsor Tapestry*, by Compton Mackenzie (Rich & Cowan, 1938)

31. *The Last Empress of the French*, by Philip W. Sergeant (Werner Laurie, 1908)

32. *Behind the Throne*, by Paul H. Emden (Hodder & Stoughton, 1934)

33. *A Royal Correspondence*, edited by John Stephenson (Macmillan, 1938)

34. *In My Tower*, 2 Volumes, by Walburga, Lady Paget (Hutchinson, 1924)

35. *Dizzy*, by Hesketh Pearson (Methuen, 1951)

36. *King Edward VIII*, by Hector Bolitho (Eyre & Spottiswoode, 1937)

37. *The Life and Times of H.R.H. Princess Beatrice*, by M. E. Sara (Stanley Paul, 1945)

*38. *A Blessed Girl*, by Lady Emily Lutyens (Rupert Hart-Davis, 1953)

*39. *In Napoleonic Days*, by H.R.H. The Princess Beatrice (John Murray, 1941)

19

40. *A Birthday Book*, by H.R.H. The Princess Beatrice (Smith, Elder & Co., 1881)

41. *The Adventures of Count George Albert of Erbach*, translated from the German of Emil Kraus by H.R.H. The Princess Beatrice (John Murray, 1898)

42. *Memoirs of the Aga Khan* (Cassell, 1954)

43. *The Gay Victorians*, by Ralph Nevill (E. Nash & Grayson, 1930)

44. *Victorian Sidelights*, by A. M. W. Stirling (Ernest Benn, 1954)

45. *A Page from the Past*, by the Earl of Desart and Lady Sybil Lubbock (Jonathan Cape, 1936)

46. *Happy and Glorious*, by Laurence Housman (Jonathan Cape, 1945)

47. *George, Duke of Cambridge*, 2 Volumes, edited by Edgar Sheppard (Longmans, Green, 1907)

48. *The Empress Eugenie and her Son*, by Edward Legge (Grant Richards, Ltd., 1916)

49. *Gladstone to his Wife*, edited by A. Tilney Bassett (Methuen, 1936)

*50. *A Victorian Diarist, Later Extracts from the Journals of Mary, Lady Monkswell, 1895-1909*, edited by the Hon. E. C. F. Collier (John Murray, 1946)

51. *Victoria's Heir*, by George Dangerfield (Constable, 1942)

52. *From my Private Diary*, by Daisy Princess of Pless (John Murray, 1931)

53. *King Edward VII*, 5 Volumes, by Edgar Sanderson and Lewis Melville (Gresham Publishing Co., 1910)

54. *The Mother of Queen Victoria*, by D. R. Stuart (Macmillan, 1942)

55. *King Edward and his Times*, by André Maurois (Cassell, 1933)

56. *King Edward VII*, by E. F. Benson (Longmans Green, 1933)

*57. *King George V*, by Sir George Arthur (Jonathan Cape, 1929)

58. *Concerning Queen Victoria and her Son*, by Sir George Arthur (Robert Hale, 1943)

*59. *The Queen Thanks Sir Howard*, by Mary Howard McClintock (John Murray, 1945)

60. *Prince Consort*, by Frank B. Chancellor (Philip Allan, 1931)

61. *Victoria, Queen and Ruler*, by Emily Crawford (Simpkin, Marshall, 1903)

62. *Recollections of Three Reigns*, by Sir Frederick Ponsonby (Eyre & Spottiswoode, 1951)

63. *A Great Lady's Friendships, Letters to Mary, Marchioness of Salisbury, Countess of Derby*, 1862-1890, with introductions by the Lady Burghclere (Macmillan, 1933)

64. *Monarchy in the Twentieth Century*, by Sir Charles Petrie, Bt. (Andrew Dakers, 1952)

65. *The Coburgs*, by Edmund B. D'Auvergne (Stanley Paul, 1911)

66. *Correspondence of Sarah Spencer Lady Lyttelton 1787-1870*, Edited by the Hon. Mrs. Hugh Wyndham (John Murray, 1912)

67. *Letters of the Prince Consort 1831-1861*, selected and edited by Dr. Kurt Jagow and translated by E. T. S. Dugdale (John Murray, 1938)

68. *A Biographer's Notebook*, by Hector Bolitho (Longmans Green, 1950)

69. *The Reminiscences of Lady Dorothy Nevill*, by Ralph Nevill (Edward Arnold, 1906)

70. *Florence Nightingale*, by Cecil Woodham-Smith (Constable, 1950)

71. *Five Roads to Royal Exile*, by the Hon. Mrs. Francis Lascelles (Mellifont Press, 1938)

72. *The Personal Papers of Lord Rendell* (Ernest Benn, 1931)

73. *George VI*, by J. T. Gorman (W. & G. Foyle, 1937)

74. *The Patriot King*, by Grace E. Thompson (Hutchinson, 1932)

75. *Edward VIII, Duke of Windsor*, by Basil Maine (Hutchinson, 1957)

76. *Kings, Commoners and Me*, by Gertrude Massey (Blackie, 1934)

77. *The Greville Memoirs*, Volume 3, by Charles C. F. Greville (Longmans Green, 1885)

*78. *The English Empress*, by Egon Caesar Conte Corti (Cassell, 1957)

79. *King Edward VII*, 2 Volumes, by Sir Sidney Lee (Macmillan, 1927)

80. *Mrs. Brookfield and her Circle*, by Charles and Frances Brookfield (Sir I. Pitman & Sons, 1905)

81. *The Daily Express*

82. *Alice Grand Duchess of Hesse*, by Princess Christian (John Murray, 1885)

83. *Scenes and Memories*, by Walburga, Lady Paget (Smith, Elder & Co., 1912)

84. *The Creevey Papers*, edited by Sir Herbert Maxwell, Bt. (John Murray, 1923)

85. *The Life of His Royal Highness Edward, Duke of Kent: Illustrated by his Correspondence with the de Salaberry Family*, by Dr. W. J. Anderson (Hunter, Rose & Co., Ottawa & Toronto, 1870)

86. *The Life of His Royal Highness the Prince Consort*, 5 Volumes, by Theodore Martin (1875-1880)

87. *Edward VII and his Circle*, by Virginia Cowles (Hamish Hamilton, 1956)

88. *Embassies of Other Days*, 2 Volumes, by Walburga, Lady Paget (Hutchinson, 1923)

89. *Lord Randolph Churchill*, by Winston S. Churchill (Macmillan, 1906)

90. *Ceremonial to be observed at the Wedding of Princess Helena Augusta Victoria* (1866)

91. *Further Letters of Queen Victoria*, edited by Hector Bolitho (Thornton Butterworth, 1938)

92. *The Private Life of Queen Alexandra*, by Hans Roger Madol (Hutchinson, 1940)

93. *The Times*

94. *Queen Victoria as I Knew Her*, by Sir Theodore Martin (Wm. Blackwood & Sons, 1908)

95. *Letters of Lady Augusta Stanley*, edited by the Dean of Windsor and Hector Bolitho (Gerald Howe, 1927)

96. *The Annual Register*

97. *The Western Morning News*

98. *The Private Life of the Queen*, by one of Her Majesty's Servants (C. Arthur Pearson, Ltd., 1897)

99. *The Last Love of an Emperor*, edited by La Comtesse de Montrigand (Heinemann, 1926)

100. *The Graphic*

101. *Edward of Kent*, by David Duff (Stanley Paul, 1938)

102. *The Daily Telegraph*

103. *Chinese Gordon*, by Archibald Forbes (George Routledge & Sons, 1885)

104. *Manifest Destiny*, by Brian Connell (Cassell, 1953)

105. *Queen Victoria*, by Mona Wilson (Thomas Nelson, 1933)

106. *Queen Mary*, by Kathleen Woodward (Hutchinson, 1927)

107. *All Sorts of People*, by Gladys Storey (Methuen, 1929)

108. *Uncensored Recollections*, Anon. (J. B. Lippincott, 1924)

109. *The Life and Tragedy of Alexandra Feodorovna, Empress of Russia*, by Baroness Sophie Buxhoeveden (Longmans, 1928)

110. *Prince Louis of Battenberg*, by Mark Kerr (Longmans Green, 1934)

111. *The Book of the Duffs*, by Alistair and Henrietta Tayler (William Brown, 1914)

112. *The Leisure Hour* (1888)

113. *Whippingham to Westminster*, by Lord Ernle (John Murray, 1938)

114. *King George V*, by John Gore (John Murray, 1941)

115. *Queen Victoria*, by Richard R. Holmes (Boussod, Valadon, 1897)

116. *A Sermon Preached on the Sunday after the Funeral of Prince Henry of Battenberg*, by H. J. Meres (1896)

117. *The Private Lives of William III and his Consort*, by Henry W. Fischer (Heinemann, 1904)

118. *Life at Balmoral*

119. *Illustrated Bits*

120. *Royal Riviera*, by Charles Graves (Heinemann, 1957)

121. *Royal Romances of Today*, by Kellogg Durland (T. Werner Laurie, 1912)

*122. *The Queen of Spain*, by Evelyn Graham (Hutchinson, 1929)

123. *The Spanish Royal Wedding*, by A. F. Calvert (Privately printed, Taunton, 1906)

124. *Royal Chef*, by Gabriel Tschumi (William Kimber, 1954)

125. *The Cronberg Archives*

126. *King Edward VII and his Court*, by Sir Lionel Cust (John Murray, 1930)

127. *The Royal House of Greece*, by Air Vice Marshal Arthur S. Gould Lee (Ward Lock, 1948)

128. *Private Information*

129. *The Life of the Empress Eugenie*, by Robert Sencourt (Benn, 1931)

130. *Milestones to the Silver Jubilee*, by H. C. Dent (Halcyon Book Co., 1935)

131. *My Own Story*, by Louisa of Tuscany (Eveleigh Nash, 1911)

132. *The House of Teck*, by Louis Felberman (John Long, 1911)

133. *Bodas Reales (Marriage of Alphonso XIII of Spain to Princess Victoria)*, by P. Zancada (Madrid, 1906)

134. *The Public Record Office*

135. *Grossherzog Ernst Ludwig*, by Dr. Max Wauer (Berlag, Darmstadt, 1938)

136. *Leaves from the Journal of our Life in the Highlands*, by Queen Victoria (Smith, Elder & Co., 1869)

137. *H.R.H. Princess Mary Adelaide of Teck*, by C. Kinloch Cooke (John Murray, 1900)

138. *King George V—His Life and Reign*, by Harold Nicolson (Constable, 1952)

139. *Church of St. Mildred, Whippingham*, by R. W. Trelease (1958)

140. *The Book of the King's Jubilee*, edited by Sir Philip Gibbs (Hutchinson, 1935)

141. *Life of Her Majesty Queen Victoria*, by G. Barnett Smith (George Routledge, 1897)

Sources Consulted

The numbers below are set out in order of first reference to the authorities cited in the preceding Bibliography.

Prologue
49, 66, 12

Chapter One
78, 25, 95, 54, 18, 61, 26, 15, 80, 60, 49, 59, 87, 24, 91

Chapter Two
25, 21, 70, 22, 89, 95, 37, 18, 24, 9, 4, 49, 59, 61, 90, 12, 82, 15, 67, 94, 96

Chapter Three
59, 25, 21, 51, 53, 4, 24, 9, 88, 138, 22, 12, 15, 99, 48, 3, 1, 45, 37, 61

Chapter Four
22, 91, 21, 102, 109, 44, 10, 59, 104, 14, 78, 47, 25, 61, 12, 128, 37, 4

Chapter Five
78, 108, 21, 61, 111, 1, 134, 109, 94, 34, 37, 47, 24, 25, 98, 62, 20

Chapter Six
21, 119, 25, 61, 20, 122, 15, 92, 51, 88, 41, 37, 118, 98, 90, 43

Chapter Seven
117, 25, 12, 62, 21, 107, 15, 61, 38, 113, 116, 121, 26, 24, 115

Chapter Eight
13, 25, 120, 20, 57, 62, 102, 98, 28, 124, 21, 78, 125, 6, 10, 42, 50, 76, 24

Chapter Nine
53, 13, 3, 55, 62, 37, 21, 79, 55, 114, 24, 25, 15, 16, 30, 36, 73, 125

Chapter Ten
121, 122, 128, 127, 10, 110, 53, 14, 102, 15, 71, 3, 17, 79, 92, 25, 56, 57, 37, 123, 50, 128, 33, 78

Chapter Eleven
   128, 48, 98, 17, 79, 37, 71, 62, 10, 23, 4, 110, 114, 28
Finale
   10, 25, 39, 104, 127, 128, 130, 135, 72, 75, 114, 129, 110, 37,
   13, 57, 71, 93, 102
Appendix A
   39, 84
Appendix B
   4, 25, 59, 6, 78, 117, 21, 12, 52, 56, 16, 27, 29, 71, 110, 125,
   128, 131

Index

INDIVIDUAL INDEX

BEATRICE, H.R.H. Princess:

An early reminiscence of Gladstone at Balmoral, 9; 1857—birth and christening, 20, 21; love for her father, 24; her early upbringing and anecdotes, 25–29; holidays, 31, 49; first photographs, 35; 1858–9—becomes aunt, 29; affection for Duchess of Kent, 25, 34; 1861—taken to see her dying father, 38; Queen Victoria turns to her in her grief, 39; 1862— visits, 41–2; at wedding of Princess Alice, 41–2; meets Princess Alexandra at Laeken, 42; engagement of Prince of Wales, 43; 1863—at wedding of Prince of Wales, 44–5; the Queen leans on her, 46; her nurses, teachers, and schoolroom curriculum, 48–9; aptitude for music, 49–50; life at Osborne, 53; 1865—at Coburg, 55; 1866—at opening of Parliament, 57; at wedding of Princess Helena, 58; 1868—visit to Switzerland, 63; 1869 —holiday at Invertrossachs, 68; 1870 —engagement of Princess Louise, 68; visits Empress Eugénie at Chislehurst, 70; at wedding of Princess Louise, 70; 1871—assistance to her mother during Queen's illness, 71; at Sandringham during illness of Prince of Wales, 72; 1872—drives with Queen to St. Paul's, 73; 1873— at Windsor for visit of Shah of Persia, 75; engagement of Duke of Edinburgh, 76; 1874—her nieces and nephews, 77; troubled by reporters in Scotland, 79; friendship with Disraeli, 80; 1875—on Royal Yacht when in collision, 80–1; rumours of her engagement, 82; visit to Inveraray, 82; her name coupled with Prince Imperial of France, 83; Prince Imperial volunteers for Zulu campaign, 87; she receives news of his death, 87; at his funeral, 88; her 21st birthday, 89; engagement of Duke of Connaught, 90; death of Princess Alice, 91; the Queen's wish for her to be step-mother to Grand-Duke's

BEATRICE, H.R.H. Princess:
—(continued).
children, 92; 1878—at wedding of Duke of Connaught, 93; 1881—publication of her Birthday Book, 94; death of Disraeli, 94; assassination attempt at Windsor, 95; first visit to Riviera, 95; marriage of Duke of Albany and victory at Tel-el-Kebir, 96; the Princess and John Brown, 98; his death, 97–9; 1883—takes cure for rheumatism at Aix-les-Bains, 101; 1884—grief at deaths of Duke of Albany and General Gordon, 102–3; first meeting with Battenberg family, 103; to Darmstadt, for wedding of Princess Victoria of Hesse to Prince Louis of Battenberg, 108–11; meets Prince Henry, 108; the Queen's silent opposition to her engagement to Prince Henry, 113; engagement announced, 115; 1885—opposition to marriage in Europe, 117; preparations for the wedding, 122; the wedding at Whippingham, 126; honeymoon, and early married life, 128, 129; 1886—the Colonial and Indian Exhibition, 136; visit to Liverpool, 136; upset at kidnapping of Prince of Bulgaria, 137; birth of Prince Alexander, 142; 1887—visit to Cannes and Monastery of Grande Chartreuse, 144–5; her part in Jubilee, 145; birth of Princess Ena, 148; 1888 —visit to Italy, and to Berlin to see dying Emperor Frederick, 149; 1889 —first visit to Spain, 151; birth of Prince Leopold, 151; visit to Wales, 152; 1890—visits to Cannes and Darmstadt, 152–3; 1891—birth of Prince Maurice, 153; life with her children, 154–5; 1892—at funeral of Duke of Clarence, 160; her keenness for theatricals, 163; 1893–at wedding of Duke and Duchess of York, 166; 1894—and of Princess Victoria Melita to Grand Duke Ernest of Hesse, 167; the floods at Windsor, 167; visits Kronberg and Hesse with Prince